A Billiards and Snooker Compendium

Gary Clarke

Published by Gary Clarke
Publishing partner: Paragon Publishing, Rothersthorpe
First published 2008
© Gary Clarke 2008

The rights of Gary Clarke to be identified as the author of this work have been asserted by the company in accordance with the Copyright, Designs and Patents Act of 1988.
All rights reserved; no part of this publication may be reproduced, stored in a retrieval system, or transmitted in any form or by any means, electronic, mechanical, photocopying, recording or otherwise without the prior written consent of the publisher or a licence permitting copying in the UK issued by the Copyright Licensing Agency Ltd, 90 Tottenham Court Road, London W1P 9HE.

Condition of Sale
This book is sold subject to the condition that it shall not, by way of trade or otherwise, be lent, resold, hired out or otherwise circulated in any form of binding or cover other than that in which it is published and without a similar condition including this condition being imposed on the subsequent purchaser.

ISBN 978-1-899820-46-7

Book design, layout and production management by Into Print
www.intoprint.net
Printed and bound in UK and USA by Lightning Source

I would like to thank the following publishers for their kind permission to use Copyright material: Reflections of a Bygone Age for permission to use the covers from 'Billiards and Snooker : A Postcard Album' (1996) by Roger Lee; E. A. Clare & Son Ltd. (trading as 'Thurston') for permission to use the covers of 'A Short History of Billiards and Snooker' (1981) by Norman Clare, and 'Billiards and Snooker Bygones' (1996) also by Norman Clare; Mainstream Publishing for permission to use the cover from 'Masters of the Baize : Cue Legends, Bad Boys and Forgotten Men in Search of Snooker's Ultimate Prize' (2005) by Luke Williams and Paul Gadsby; The Octopus Publishing Group Ltd. for permission to use the cover of 'Cliff Thorburn's Snooker Skills' (1987) by Cliff Thorburn and Peter Arnold (editor); Bloomsbury Publishing for permission to use the covers of 'Snooker Masterclass' (1996) by Stephen Hendry, and 'The Embassy Book of World Snooker' (1993) by Clive Everton; Random House for permission to use the covers of 'The Golden Rules of Snooker' (1985) by Ian Heath, and 'The Breaks Came My Way' (1976) by Joe Davis; and finally, David & Charles for permission to use the cover of 'Snooker : the Dictionary' (1987) by John Haselden.

For Mum, Dad and Kevin

In loving memory of Thomas William Clarke

~ DISCLAIMER ~

Whilst the values listed in this book have been carefully and extensively researched this work is intended as a guide only and the author cannot be held responsible for the price paid/realised by buyers/sellers. All prices of books in print were correct at time of going to press.

~ CONTENTS ~

Acknowledgements 6-7

Notes on the Entries 8-9

Abbreviations 10

Billiards & Snooker Books – An Overview 11-14

Autobiography & Biography 15-30

History & Development 31-40

Trick Shots, Humorous & Cartoons 41-53

Snooker – Instructional 54-80

Billiards & Snooker – Instructional 81-94

Billiards 95-169

Miscellaneous 170-208

Reference Books 209-222

Handbooks & Rule Books 223-249

Appendix 250-254

Index of Authors, Editors & Compilers 255-261

Index of Titles 262-272

References 273-275

~ ACKNOWLEDGEMENTS ~

I wish to thank the following people and organisations for their help and guidance in the writing of this book and without whom it would never have been possible to complete it.

Firstly, the staff of the British Library reading rooms in St. Pancras, London for their tireless efforts and courteous and efficient service.

Suffolk Libraries and all their staff play an invaluable role in helping to provide a first class service and I am indebted to the excellent inter-library loans service they operate.

Thanks must also go to the staff of Cambridge University library for their help and assistance.

I am very much indebted to The Bibliographical Society who very generously provided me with a Minor Grant to enable me to carry out this research. Details of the Bibliographical Society and the invaluable work they do can be found on their website at www.bibsoc.org.uk.

The following have provided information regarding print runs of specific books and have enabled me to gauge how popular modern snooker books are - namely, Jim Crawley of Sutton Publishing; Andy Searle of The Parrs Wood Press; and Tiffany Stansfield of Hutchinson.

I am indebted to the BBC Information Centre for information regarding various TV programmes.

Particular thanks to Peter Clare, Managing Director of E. A. Clare & Son Ltd. (trading as 'Thurston') for providing bibliographical data for 'The Noble Game of Billiards' [1987].

I am indebted to Keith Potter and Peter Cook for responding to my appeal for billiards and snooker books in the Ipswich 'Evening Star' newspaper.

Thanks also to J. Michael Young for providing information on certain books from his vast collection. Please see the Cue Sports Memorabilia link on Roger Lee's excellent web site www.billiardsandsnookerarchive.co.uk for further details.

Special thanks to my good friend Richard Evans for writing the entry for the Welsh language publication 'Dewch i Chwarae Snwcer' (Come to Play Snooker).

I certainly could not have completed the book without the invaluable assistance and superb hospitality of Jack Ben-Nathan who very generously made his personal collection of books available to me and for bringing to my attention books I was not aware of. The book would have been a poor work indeed without his advice and guidance.

Particular thanks to Roger Lee for allowing me to scan the covers of a selection of books from his superb collection.

Particular regards go to Mark Webb of Into Print for advising me on the book and guiding me through the whole publishing process.

Finally, special thanks must go to my brother, Kevin Clarke, for proof reading the manuscript, offering advice and constructive criticism and for his overall encouragement of the whole project. I must also thank my parents for their patience and tremendous support during the time it took to write the book.

~ Notes On The Entries ~

The entries that form this work are of English billiards and snooker books published in the United Kingdom and Ireland only. The only exceptions to this are the Eddie Charlton books that were originally published in Australia but subsequently published in the UK; the 1976 Australian edition of Walter Lindrum's book 'Billiards', that was originally published in the UK in 1930; plus 'Horace Lindrum's Snooker, Billiards and Pool' that was also originally published in Australia and subsequently published in the UK.

The book has been divided up into the broad categories of 'Autobiography & Biography', 'History & Development', 'Trick Shots, Humorous & Cartoons', 'Snooker – Instructional', 'Billiards & Snooker – Instructional', 'Billiards', 'Miscellaneous', 'Reference Books' and 'Handbooks & Rule Books'. A 'Miscellaneous' category is never fully satisfactory but some books are so varied in their content that they would not sit easily in any other category. Some books, e.g. 'Guinness Book of Snooker', could have quite easily fitted into two categories (in this case 'History & Development' and 'Miscellaneous'). When this scenario has occurred I have placed the book in the category that the majority of text is devoted to. I hope in doing so I have not upset too many readers and hope that readers will agree that the recording of the bibliographic data and book descriptions, ultimately, is more important than the category the book has been placed in.

Within each section the books are listed chronologically. Where two or more books have the same publication date, the books have been listed alphabetically by title. If two books have the same publication date and title they are listed by order of author surname. When listing titles alphabetically, I have ignored such title words as 'and', and 'the'.

Title - each entry has as its starting point the title of the work taken from the ***title page*** of the book and ***not*** the front cover. Some works have extraordinarily long titles and in these instances I have truncated the title to its first portion.

Author - the next line of each entry notes the author, editor, collaborator or compiler of a work. Where two or more authors have been responsible for the work then all names have been listed.

Date, publisher and place of publication - any date of publication found within square brackets, for example [1924], signifies that there is no publication date given on the title page and this date is therefore an estimate or has been gauged from elsewhere (either within the book or from another source).

ISBN - in the more modern entries the next line of bibliographic data lists the ISBN (International Standard Book Number) where the book has been assigned such a number. Some earlier books use an SBN (Standard Book Number). Please see footnote 22 for details of a website explaining the new 13 digit ISBN, introduced on 1st January 2007.

Hardback / paperback - I have used the terms 'hardback' and 'paperback' throughout although 'paperback' is not a very satisfactory term for early books. Strictly speaking early 'paperback' books very often had card covers, wrappers or thin cloth. These terms are interchangeable throughout the book descriptions. Any description with the words 'boards' or 'bound in cloth' means that, essentially, the book is a hardback.

Page numbers - the number of pages stated in each entry is the *numbered* pages of a book only. Any entry that has the number of pages in square brackets, e.g. [32]pp, signifies that the book has no printed page numbers. The entries also include any preliminary pages in the book that are numbered in Roman numerals.

Illustrated, plates, portraits and book size - the term 'illustrated' refers to drawings or diagrams contained in books, normally table diagrams illustrating instructional points. I have taken that any formal photograph of a person posing specifically for the camera to be a portrait and any general photograph, e.g. of the Crucible Theatre or match in progress, to be a plate. The measurements of the books have been given as height x width and are rounded up to the nearest centimetre.

Notes - the notes line of each entry is a miscellaneous section where illustrators, photographers, contributors to Forewords and Introductions, edition details, Indexes and Appendices etc. are noted. This line also contains information on any Series the book may be part of.

Descriptive section - the next section of each entry is the detailed description of the book. Here I have tried to achieve some kind of balance between listing and discussing the contents, physically describing the book and dustjacket, and including details specifically to interest collectors such as print runs, scarcity, and auction prices realised etc. Descriptions are based on the *1ˢᵗ edition* of a book unless otherwise stated.

Value - finally, on the last line of each entry the estimated value of the *1ˢᵗ edition* is recorded unless otherwise stated. If a book is still in print I have listed the current price. However, the majority are out of print so I have listed the price of books, with dustjackets if applicable, from collected sources such as Abebooks, Amazon, secondhand bookshops, auction records, eBay and 'Book and Magazine Collector'. This task has been especially unenviable as prices can be so volatile and many books have simply not appeared for sale whilst I was researching the book.

~ ABBREVIATIONS ~

Abe = abebooks

B. A. & C. C. = Billiards Association & Control Council

B. & S. C. C. = Billiards & Snooker Control Council

BBC = British Broadcasting Corporation

col. = colour

collab. = collaborator

comp. = compiler

Corp. = corporate

Ed. = editor

facsim/s. = facsimile/s

hb = hardback

ill. = illustrator/illustrated

I. B. & S. F. = The International Billiards & Snooker Federation

n.d. = no date

pb = paperback

photog. = photographer

port/s = portrait/s

pseud. = pseudonym

W. P. B. S. A = The World Professional Billiards & Snooker Association

~ Billiards & Snooker Books – An Overview ~

The origins of the games of both billiards and snooker are shrouded in some mystery, especially those of billiards, and it is doubtful now whether a definitive origin will ever be established. Thankfully, the history of publishing and literature concerning both sports is a little clearer.

There had been numerous mentions of billiards in the literature of antiquity but more recently there were references to the game in Shakespeare's 'Anthony and Cleopatra' and by Edward Spencer in 1591. Cotton, in his 'Compleat Gamester' of 1674, describes billiards more precisely but it was not until almost 100 years later, in 1772, that the first books dedicated solely to the subject were published. The earliest volume I have been able to personally see is 'A Treatise on Billiards, with Instructions and Rules' by John Dew published by J. F. & C. Rivington and others in 1779. When this book was last sold at auction in 1997 it fetched £900 and according to 'The Amateur Billiard Player' of November 1997 only 2 copies of this book exist (the other being the copy held by the British Library).

Early in the 19th century other books began to appear specifically concerned with billiards including 'Game of Billiards' by 'An Amateur', E. White's 'A Practical Treatise on the Game of Billiards', 'The Noble Game of Billiards' by Mingaud, and Edwin Kentfield's 'The Game of Billiards Scientifically Explained'. As Bob Ledger correctly points out in his 1989 article, 'Billiards and Snooker Books', few of these early titles offer any instructional value to today's player but they certainly command high prices when coming onto the market. For example, a first edition of E. White's book published in 1807 fetched £575 on eBay in August 2006; and a 3rd edition of Mingaud's work realised an impressive £820, against a rather low estimate of £200-£300, at the Dominic Winter sale of July 2007.

There were almost 40 instructional billiards books published during the 19th century and getting on towards 100 if new editions and reprints are included. The earliest of these books are difficult to obtain and, as mentioned above, command high prices. However, some titles appear to be relatively common and can be purchased for more modest sums. For example, a copy of the first edition of 'A Handbook of Billiards, with the Theory of the Side-Stroke' etc. (1862) by George Pardon usually sells for around £150-£180. Later editions of this and other books, as would be expected, fetch lower prices; and a very good copy of the 3rd edition of Mardon's 'Billiards : Game, 500 Up' published in 1858 realised £180 when sold on eBay in January 2007, whereas the first edition of 1844 would probably fetch at least £900.

The number of books published on billiards grew as the popularity of the game increased and there were at least 38 books issued on the subject between 1900 and the start of the First World War. John Roberts Junior and his brother, Charles, published 8 books between them during this period and they are normally priced quite modestly by dealers. For example, a 1905 edition of John Roberts Junior's 'The Game of Billiards and How to Play It' in very good condition normally sells for £25-£35. The first edition of 'Billiards for Everybody' by Charles Roberts is a little more expensive and commands prices of £40-£50. However, another of Charles Roberts' books from this era, 'The Complete Billiard Player' (1911) is a lot more expensive and usually changes hands for £150-£180 depending on condition.

An early mention of the game of snooker in a billiards book occurred in the 1889 publication 'The Art of Practical Billiards for Amateurs' (which usually sells for £60-£75 in very good condition) where the author, A. W. Drayson, states "the game, which is not as yet generally known, or much played, is an amusing extension of the game of pyramids". A couple of the earliest books dedicated principally to snooker are Willie Smith's 1924 book 'How to Play Snooker and Other Pool Games' and especially 'Snooker : How to Improve Your Play' by The 'Bos'un'. This latter book, according to Ledger, was written by two players by the names of Osworth and Beeson. In 1989 Ledger valued a very good copy of this book at £15-£20 and since then prices have stalled somewhat as the book normally sells for around the same price today.

Instructional billiards books continued to be published after the First World War and around 40 new books were published during the 1920s and 1930s, by such publishers as C. Arthur Pearson, Mills & Boon, W. Foulsham & Co., and Methuen. Prices of books issued during this period vary considerably; a very good copy of Tom Newman's 1923 book 'How to Play Billiards' normally realising £40-£50, whereas his 'Advanced Billiards' of the following year commands £80-£100. While W. G. Clifford's 1927 paperback, 'Billiard Table Games', is quite common and sells for £10-£15 in very good condition, a copy of 'Roberts' Billiards Guide and Rules of Games', published by his brother Charles Roberts, would set the collector back more than £100 in very good condition. Acknowledged as the greatest billiards player ever by the overwhelming majority of commentators, Walter Lindrum's 1930 offering, 'Billiards', published by Methuen, perhaps surprisingly only commands £30-£40; but this relatively modest price may be accounted for by the late publication date and, I imagine due to Lindrum's immense standing in the game, a large print run.

The last book of any length wholly devoted to billiards published in the UK and Ireland must surely be Victor Anton's 'The 100-Break Target' published in 1947. This book is a difficult book to find and, as Ledger notes, Anton's amateur status has almost certainly contributed to the scarcity of the title. It would probably fetch between £100 - £150 if it came up for sale today.

One author warrants special mention in connection with billiards literature and that is Riso Levi, a native of Manchester whose books on the subject total close to 4,000 pages between them. As Ledger correctly points out, Levi's books are highly prized by the collector especially those with the scarce dustjackets. They also command high prices; one dealer on Abe, perhaps rather optimistically, offering 'Billiards in the 20th Century' in very good condition, signed by the author and complete with the white dustjacket for £450. To give an example of how prices have risen for Levi's books, Ledger valued the 3-volume set of 'Billiards : the Strokes of the Game' at £100-£150 in 1989 whereas today the collector would have to pay at least £180 to secure all three volumes. Such is Levi's importance to the literature of billiards that one of his titles, 'Billiards in the 20th Century' (see entry 6.106), has recently come back into print.

From the 1930s onwards there was a distinct shift in books concentrating on billiards to those focussing chiefly on snooker as the popularity of snooker itself increased. However, a number of books aided this transition by including details of both games. Early examples include W. G. Clifford's 'Billiard Table Games' of 1927, 'Billiards and Snooker' (1928) by Arthur Peall, 'Billiards and Snooker for Amateurs' (1937) by Horace Lindrum, and B. Scriven's 'Billiards and Snooker' of 1938. These books are not particularly expensive and all should be available for £10-£25 in very good condition complete with the dustjackets if applicable.

From 1927 onwards 'Mr Snooker' himself, Joe Davis, began writing on billiards and snooker and his books are usually more collectable and more valuable than other authors. One reason for this, in addition to Davis' standing in the game, is that a large proportion of copies coming up for sale have the all important dustjackets intact. Most of Davis' books were published by Country Life which was an imprint of George Newnes. As Ledger notes, one of the most valuable of Davis' books is 'Sykes' Miniature Billiards', a paperback that was published by Sykes of Yorkshire and was included with a small table. This scarce book rarely surfaces for sale but copies available on Abe in recent times have all been advertised for £50+ and none have stayed on sale for long! However, possibly due to the large numbers of copies that appear for sale on eBay, Davis' books have not risen in value quite as much as might have been expected. Ledger valued a very good copy of 'Improve Your Snooker' (1936) complete with dustjacket at £15-£20 and copies now sell for around £20-£30. Similarly, 'How I Play Snooker' of 1949, complete with the dustjacket and in very good condition, commands £20-£30 in today's market and Ledger valued this book at £10-£12 in 1989.

Any fan of snooker, or historian of the game, will know that the game went into a severe decline during the 1950s and 1960s and as a result of this the number of books published fell dramatically. For example, the reader will note in the text of this book that only two instructional snooker books were issued in the 1960s – 'Tackle Snooker This Way' (1965) by John Pulman and Joe Davis' 1967 offering 'Complete Snooker for the Amateur'. Ledger felt that books published in this period would be highly sought after simply because at the time they would not have seemed collectable. However, this isn't necessarily reflected in today's prices as a copy of the Pulman book mentioned above can still be bought for £10-£15 in very good condition complete with the jacket.

After 1970 billiards is largely dropped as a subject from books in any meaningful way, the content predominantly focussing on snooker. The enormous success of the TV programme 'Pot Black' from 1969 onwards helped restore snooker's popularity and heralded the start of a boom that peaked in the 1980s. Because of the popularity of snooker and subsequent increase in books published during this period (there were well over 100 books in all categories published during the 1980s) there are very few collectable snooker books issued after 1970. Indeed, the majority of books published in the 1980s can be picked up for less than £10. A couple of notable exceptions are 'The Breaks Came My Way', the autobiography of Joe Davis published in 1976 and 'Billiards and Snooker : a Trade History' compiled by J. R. Mitchell in 1981. The latter book is dealt with in the text of this book but Joe Davis' biography is becoming increasingly harder to find and usually sells for £15-£20 in very good condition with the jacket. There also appear to be a few anomalies with certain snooker books, where copies do not appear for sale regularly but do not realise high prices when they do surface. Several instances of this have been highlighted in the main body of text and one example includes 'The Golden Rules of Snooker' by Ian Heath.

Rule books are notoriously difficult to track down and are even harder to value, and I confess that the 'Handbooks & Rule Books' section of this work is the part where prices may fluctuate most from my estimates. Indeed, I have seen 1930s rule books sell for an astonishing 99p on eBay! A quick search on Abe normally only reveals a handful of copies for sale at any one time and they are normally priced around the £20 mark. However, recent prices achieved include £55 for a 1907 billiards rule book on eBay, £33 for a 1931 mixed rule book, and £51 for a 1936 mixed rule book. A general rule of thumb would be that earlier copies sell for higher sums and that billiards rule books are the most sought after, followed by mixed rule books and then snooker rule books. In addition, hardback copies would be expected to sell for more than paperback copies.

The 21st century has seen the publishing world focus almost exclusively on snooker biographies and autobiographies and it would appear that general snooker books may well have lost their appeal. Autobiographies and biographies published since the turn of the century include offerings from Ronnie O'Sullivan, Willie Thorne, the late John Spencer, and three of Alex Higgins. All of these books are highly readable and entertaining and are fine additions to any billiards and snooker collection.

A collection of billiards and snooker books would be highly prized by any sports collector and someone owning every 1st edition billiards book listed in section 6 of this work alone would have a collection worth an absolute minimum of £22,000! With their sense of nostalgia and a bygone age, recording of sporting and social history, wonderful decorative designs and colourful dustjackets, billiards books especially are still highly sought after by collectors and will almost certainly continue to be so in the future.

~ AUTOBIOGRAPHY & BIOGRAPHY ~

1.0   **The Reminiscences of a Professional Billiard Player**

William Mitchell / F. M. Hotine (Ed.)
1902   Anthony Treherne & Co., London
Paperback   134pp, 19 x 13cm

This book says of Mitchell that he has been a professional billiard player for something like 30 years and that if he had taken a bit more care of himself he might have run John Roberts close for the top honours in the sport. The book details matches Mitchell played in places such as Sheffield, Scarborough and Huddersfield chiefly during the 1870s and 1880s[1]. One tale describes details of a match Mitchell played at the Cherry Tree Hotel in Huddersfield around 1872 against a man called Kilkenny whom Mitchell's backers thought he would beat easily. However, after telling Mitchell to go easy on his opponent the plan backfired because Mitchell made the game too close a contest and eventually lost. Needless to say his backers were none too pleased about losing their money. An interesting quote contained in the book is Mitchell's opinion of John Roberts Senior of whom he says – "It was in the winter of 1866 that I first met old John Roberts, father of the present best player, and perhaps an even greater player than his son". This book has thin green card covers and like all early player autobiographies is understandably scarce.

Value   £600 - £800

1.1   **The World's Billiard Celebrities : Portrayed by Word and Camera**

S. A. Mussabini ('Ivor')
[1903]   The Cricket Press, London
Paperback   [68]pp, ill., plates, ports., 13 x 9cm

This small paperback book features short portraits of leading players of the late 19th and early 20th centuries such as Edwin Kentfield, Charles Dawson, W. J. Peall and others. Included are some humorous rhymes and verses such as – "I'm Willie Holt, A Lancashire colt, Who won two games, Then 'shot my bolt', In the B.A. Tournament"! The book is bound in pale green, thin card wrappers and has red writing and an illustration on the cover. The book is incredibly scarce and it is doubtful whether there are more than a handful in existence.

Value   £300 - £500

---

[1]   For further details of Mitchell's life and playing career see Watson & Kemp's "Snooker's Crucible" (see entry 2.11) particularly the chapter entitled "A Class Divide".

1.2   **Roberts' Billiard Life**

John Roberts Senior / Charles Roberts
[1908]   Henry J. Drane, London
Hardback   125pp, plates, ports., 19 x 13cm

In the Preface to this publication it states that part one of this volume includes some of the best work of the publication 'Roberts on Billiards' edited by Buck (see entry 6.20). The second part goes behind the scenes of billiard life and commentaries are noted for some of the remarkable games and incidents in Roberts' career, especially those at the never-to-be-forgotten 'Egyptian Hall'[2] the aristocratic home of billiards. This is a thoroughly engrossing read and has some unusual chapters, not least the one called 'The First Lady Billiard Champion 1896-1906' describing the career of Grace Fairweather "the pioneer of professional ladies' billiards".

Value   £280 - £320

1.3   **The Life and Times of John Roberts**

Charles Roberts ('Vivid')
1927   The Newspaper World Press, London
Paperback   75pp, ports., 19 x 13cm
Notes   Includes Appendix – a reprint of an article that appeared in
                the 'Billiard Player' in December 1925 called 'Those Indian
                Days : John Roberts' Palmiest Years Recalled'

'The Life and Times of John Roberts' has stiff card covers, predominantly green in colour, with a photograph of a majestic looking Roberts to the right hand side. The frontispiece features a formal photo of Roberts and there are plenty of b & w photos throughout the book.

Charles Roberts' study of his brother's life provides a fascinating insight into the world of late 19th century and early 20th century billiards and as such is highly prized by historians of the game. There are no chapter headings in the book but each piece of text has its own heading and each separate piece rarely runs for more than a page. Tales of Roberts' time in India, S. Africa and Australia are all relayed and he says, rather ruefully, of a solid gold and diamond encrusted chalk case that was given to him by the Maharajah of Patiala "it is a magnificent specimen ... and is good to look at ... but it is a failure as a chalk case, because the diamonds cut one's pockets all to pieces".

Value   £240 - £260

---

[2]   A famous billiard hall that was located in Piccadilly, London.

1.4   **Cannons and Big Guns**

Tom Reece / H. Kingsley Long (Ed.)
[1928]   Hutchinson & Co., London
Hardback   256pp, ill., plates, ports., 20 x 13cm

Tom Reece, whose first love was swimming, only ventured into a billiard hall because he had to pass through one on his way to the swimming pool. This was quite an inauspicious start for a man who went on to compile a break of 499,135 at Burroughes & Watts, Soho Square, in 1907. 'Cannons and Big Guns' is a biography of Tom Reece compiled by Long from stories that Reece had related to him "on a score of different occasions" and the result is an entertaining series of stories and anecdotes of Reece's time playing billiards around the globe. One amusing tale recalls the time Reece played an exhibition in Cape Town and couldn't persuade a taxi driver to drive him to the docks after dark. Reece decided to walk and once inside the dock gates realised a gang of desperadoes were lurking in the shadows. Instantly fearing for his safety, Reece ran to the dock-side and jumped into the water and then swam to the ship he was staying on. Once on board he was told that the docks were so dangerous at night that he was lucky not to have been murdered! The final section of the book is called 'Twenty-Five Hints for Amateur Players' and is a series of illustrated articles that Reece had previously contributed to 'The Sporting Life'.

Value   £100 - £200

1.5   **The Breaks Came My Way**

Joe Davis
1976   W. H. Allen, London
ISBN   0491016867
Hardback   xv, 240pp, ill., plates., ports., facsims., 23 x 14cm
Notes   Foreword by Harold Lewis; includes tables of 'Records'

Bound in burgundy cloth, 'Mr Snooker's' autobiography covers 240 pages and provides a fascinating insight into the 20th century history of billiards and snooker. Some of the photos in the book are real eye openers, especially the one showing a 13 year old Davis on an advertising card stating that he is "Open to Play Exhibition Games in Hotel Clubs and Public Billiard Halls". There is also a facsimile reprint of a cartoon celebrating Davis' 52nd birthday and 500th snooker century. This was drawn by Roy Ullyett who went on to publish 'Cue for a Laugh' in 1984 (see entry 3.7). 'The Breaks Came My Way' rather fittingly ends with a chapter dedicated to the TV programme 'Pot Black'. If Davis was the man who helped snooker gain in popularity from the late 1930s, then 'Pot Black' launched it into the stratosphere in the late 1970s and 1980s. Davis' opinion that "the good snooker player today requires three essential skills : the ability to pot, a knowledge of the strategy of the game and complete control of the cue ball" still holds true today.

Very good copies of this book complete with the jacket are becoming increasingly hard to find and it is one of the most expensive modern autobiographies for the collector to acquire; a 1st edition selling on eBay in June 2007 for £26.

Value £15 - £25

1.6 Talking Snooker

Fred Davis
1979   A & C Black, London
ISBN   0713619910
Hardback   106pp, ill., plates, ports., 21 x 14cm
Notes   Reprinted 1980; includes table of 'Championships Records'; includes Index

1983   A & C Black, London
ISBN   0713624094
Hardback   123pp, ill., plates, ports., 21 x 13cm
Notes   2nd edition; includes table of 'Championships Records'; includes Index

Be careful if you remove the dustjacket from the 1st edition of this book – it has exceptionally bright yellow boards! 'Talking Snooker' is split into two sections, the first dealing with Davis' life in snooker and covering only 41 pages. The brevity of this section is summed up by Davis only according the death of his brother, Joe, a single paragraph. The second part of the book is entitled 'How to Improve Your Snooker', and as the book's title suggests, adopts a more conversational tone on improving your play. The 2nd edition (which has a different photo on the cover and no jacket) is slightly longer than the 1st simply because the chapter entitled 'Modern Snooker' has been added to and the 2nd edition carries more photos. 'Talking Snooker' is nowhere near as valuable as Joe Davis' biography and collectors should have no trouble picking up a very good 1st edition complete with the dustjacket, the book appearing regularly on eBay and Abe.

Value £5 - £10

1.7 "Hurricane" Higgins' Snooker Scrapbook

Alex Higgins / Angela Patmore
1981   Souvenir Press, London
ISBN   0285624865
Hardback   128pp, plates, ports., 24 x 19cm
Notes   Reprinted May 1981

1981   Souvenir Press, London
ISBN   0285624857
Paperback   128pp, plates, ports., 24 x 18cm

This was the first Higgins autobiography to be published and it is doubtful whether any other player has had more written about him (there have been four further books published on Higgins' flamboyant and rollercoaster life since). Higgins tells his own story over the 128 pages and, in addition, there are sections called 'Other Players Talking' where top professionals express their opinions on Higgins, his lifestyle and his own inimitable way of playing. For example, Ray Reardon says of Higgins "he's worn out two bodies already" and Tony Meo says "he plays to the crowd most of the time. He can't help it, it's the only way he knows how to play"; a style of playing that Higgins himself admitted cost him many matches. There are dozens of fantastic b & w photos throughout and the book has green boards and a green and white pictorial dustjacket that collectors should insist on being present.

Value £5 - £10

1.8 Steve Davis Snooker Champion : His Own Story as told to Brian Radford

Steve Davis / Brian Radford
1981   Arthur Barker, London
ISBN   0213168170
Hardback   xii, 137pp, plates, ports., 24 x 16cm
Notes   Introduction by Barry Hearn; includes Appendices

1983   Pan Books, London
ISBN   0330268643
Paperback   170pp, plates, ports., 18 x 11cm
Notes   As above

Steve Davis lost no time in cashing in on his 1981 World Championship triumph, penning this book and following it up with 1982's 'Frame & Fortune'. This is the expected autobiographical trawl through early years, breakthrough and success and it is nice to see Davis acknowledging the importance of Joe Davis' instructional books as the bedrock of his success. Davis says of constantly practicing "some lads of my age might have found the hours of practice tediously repetitive, but I lapped up every minute of it". As Davis is a true giant of the game this book is a crucial part of any snooker collection and very good copies, with the jacket, can be picked up quite easily. The book has bright red boards and the jacket is red, white and green with a colour picture of Davis on the cover and a b & w one on the rear.

Value £5 - £10

1.9 Ray Reardon

Ray Reardon / Peter Buxton
1982   David & Charles, Newton Abbot
ISBN   0715382624

Hardback	159pp, plates, ports., 23 x 15cm
Notes	Includes Appendix of 'Career Highlights'

David & Charles had previously published two books by Reardon - 'Classic Snooker' and 'Ray Reardon's 50 Best Trick Shots' - before this autobiography appeared in 1982. This is a highly readable and thoroughly entertaining book recounting the career of one of snooker's most beguiling players. Interestingly, interspersed throughout the text are short quotes from literary figures such as Aristotle, Samuel Johnson, Goethe, Mark Twain and Shakespeare. These quotes serve to highlight the subject matter in the text so when chapter nine begins with Samuel Johnson's quote "every man wants to appear considerable in his native place", Reardon then goes on to talk about his immense pride in being elected South Wales Sportsman of the Year in 1974. The book has green boards and a green and white jacket with a formal portrait of Reardon on the front.

Value £5 - £10

1.10 Steve Davis : Frame and Fortune : as told to Brian Radford

Steve Davis / Brian Radford	
1982	Arthur Barker, London
ISBN	0213168405
Hardback	146pp, ill., plates, ports., 24 x 17cm
Notes	Includes Appendix of Steve Davis' 1981–2 season

A second Davis autobiography published by Arthur Barker, the dustjacket of this book depicts Davis with all the trappings of success. Perched on his gleaming white Porsche with personalised number plate and resplendent in dinner suit, this image could sum up the 1980s for some people. This book is standard fare, recounting as it does tournaments, exhibition matches and tales from the snooker circuit. Chapter twelve is slightly different and features a 23 page account of Davis' historic 147 break at the Lada Classic in 1982. The break was the first televised 147 and it is retold here with the aid of line drawings.

Value £5 - £10

1.11 Between Frames : Ted Lowe talking to Frank Butler

Ted Lowe / Frank Butler	
1984	A & C Black, London
ISBN	0713624469
Hardback	161pp, plates, ports., 26 x 20cm
Notes	Includes Index of Personalities

The venerable former commentator, 'whispering' Ted Lowe, recounts his life in snooker over the first half of this book, whilst the second half focuses on 'The

Champions' – short profiles of Joe Davis, Horace Lindrum, Reardon, Pulman, Spencer et al. Lowe was the former manager of Leicester Square Hall (formerly Thurston's) and says when the hall closed in 1955 "the closing of the hall was not the end of snooker, but it was a terrible blow to the professional side of the game which almost died as a spectator sport over the next fifteen years". Lowe has been involved with snooker for most of his life and this book is an absorbing description of snooker's changing fortunes through the years, although somewhat let down by the final chapter, 'Trouble in Paradise', where Lowe does rather preach on the supposed greed prevalent in the modern game. The dustjacket features a line drawing of Lowe but, unfortunately, like so many white jackets it is prone to discolouration.

Value   £5 - £10

1.12   **Frame By Frame Dennis Taylor : My Own Story**

Dennis Taylor
1985   Queen Anne Press, London
ISBN   0356121798
Hardback   160pp, ill., plates, ports., 23 x 15cm

1986   Futura Publications, London
ISBN   0708831486
Paperback   172pp, ill., plates, ports., 18 x 11cm

1988   Chivers Press, Bath
ISBN   0745106528
Hardback   211pp, 23 x 14cm
Notes   Large Print edition; a Lythway book

It would be fair to say that Dennis Taylor was an ordinary snooker player who was involved in the most extraordinary frame of snooker ever played. His victory on the final black to defeat Steve Davis 18–17 in the 1985 World Championship final was a truly dramatic encounter watched by a TV audience of 18.2m. This book recounts Taylor's early years, his subsequent move to Lancashire, and emergence on the professional circuit. The book ends with a dramatic re-telling of his black ball triumph. The 1st edition was published by Queen Anne Press, who published several snooker books, and it was then reissued in paperback by Futura in 1986. The Large Print edition published by Chivers Press contains text only and, unusually, all three editions have different covers. The serious collector will no doubt wish to own all three editions, the 1st edition probably being the most common and the Chivers edition rarely coming up for sale.

Value   £4 - £8

1.13 Alex Through the Looking Glass

Alex Higgins / Tony Francis
1986   Pelham Books, London
ISBN   0720716721
Hardback   iv, 172pp, plates, ports., 24 x 16cm
Notes   Includes Index

1987   Sphere Books, London
ISBN   0722148496
Paperback   178pp, plates, ports., 18 x 11cm
Notes   As above

Pelham published a number of snooker books (including autobiographies of Terry Griffiths and Stephen Hendry) but none as entertaining as this 1986 effort from Tony Francis. Higgins' wild lifestyle of drink, women, domestic strife, fights and scrapes with authority are all retold here in lurid detail. For example, Higgins says of a ruckus he had with Graham Miles "he took a swing at me and sent me tumbling into the crowd. He missed but I'd overbalanced. I got my revenge in the dressing room. They had to send a couple of bouncers to pull us apart". And Higgins' ex wife, Lynn, says of his cavalier attitude towards money "he would squander money stupidly. I had to force him to put his winnings away in the Building Society". Any book on Higgins is of interest to the collector and this book currently represents good value for money, has a great dustjacket and can be picked up easily enough.

Value   £4 - £8

1.14 Higgins, Taylor and Me

Jim Meadowcroft / John Hennessey
1986   Arthur Barker, London
ISBN   0213169339
Hardback   175pp, plates, ports., 23 x 15cm
Notes   Foreword by Dennis Taylor; Dave Muscroft (photog.)

Jim Meadowcroft took part in his first World Championship in 1973 but never really fulfilled the early promise he had shown. But as Dennis Taylor says in the Foreword, to come up against Ray Reardon at the World Championship in 1973 and 1974, Terry Griffiths in 1979, and Alex Higgins in 1982 surely indicates that Meadowcroft never really had the rub of the green as a pro (all his opponents went on to win the title in those years). In this autobiography Meadowcroft recounts his friendship with Taylor and Higgins, starting from the days when they would all practice at the Benarth club in Blackburn, before moving onto the Elite club at Accrington in February 1970. The usual run-through of anecdotes follows by the player who turned commentator in 1982. Even though he gets no mention in the title, there is also a chapter on John Spencer a third of the way through the book.

The book includes 16 pages of photos, is bound in red cloth and collector's should make sure they look for copies with the colourful dustjacket.

Value £5 - £10

1.15 Playing for Keeps

Cliff Thorburn / Clive Everton
1987 Partridge Press, Haywards Heath
ISBN 1852250119
Hardback 142pp, ports., 26 x 18cm

Cliff Thorburn's autobiography was arranged and pieced together by Clive Everton using nearly 30 hours of taped conversation between the two men. Thorburn's comments have been supplemented by Everton, and these passages, plus the use of 'Snooker Scene' match reports, are clearly set out in the book in a different typeface. This offering represents a journey through Thorburn's difficult childhood, his time as a hustler in the pool rooms of Canada and America, and his emergence and success on the professional circuit. There is a rather poignant photo spread across pages 136–137 showing Alex Higgins, Eugene Hughes, Dennis Taylor, Bill Werbeniuk, Kirk Stevens and Thorburn before the final of the snooker version of the 1986 World Cup. Of the six players pictured only Taylor is still involved with the game in any high profile capacity, Werbeniuk is dead, and three of the four others have all had problems in their personal lives. The book has pale yellow boards and a picture of a smiling Thorburn in formal attire on the jacket and, I imagine due to a small print run, is one of the more expensive autobiographies for the collector to acquire.

Value £15 - £20

1.16 Griff : the Autobiography of Terry Griffiths

Terry Griffiths / Julian Worthington
1989 Pelham Books, London
ISBN 0720718864
Hardback vi, 202pp, plates, ports., 24 x 16cm

The genial Terry Griffiths published his autobiography in 1989, ten years after his sole World Championship triumph. Griffiths was in many ways a reluctant hero and snooker player and says in the final pages of the book that he often hankered after a normal life and an everyday job. This book is readily available from secondhand bookshops and features a smiling Griffiths pictured on the colourful dustjacket. The book has an unusual combination of grey boards with turquoise lettering to the spine.

Value £4 - £8

1.17   **Remember My Name : the Authorised Biography of Stephen Hendry**

Stephen Hendry / John Docherty
1990   Pelham Books, London
ISBN   0720718848
Hardback   143pp, plates (some col.), ports. (some col.), 25 x 18cm

A biography of Stephen Hendry doesn't offer the same intrigue and excitement as one concerned with, say, Alex Higgins. Nevertheless, because of Hendry's immense stature in the game this book is a must-have for collectors. This effort hit the bookshelves in 1990 after Hendry had won his first World Championship title. Published by well-know snooker publisher, Pelham, I'm sure Hendry cringes at the awful photo on the cover – a formal portrait of him, complete with acne and wearing a dreadfully dated, stonewashed denim jacket. Large parts of the book consist of Hendry's manager, Ian Doyle, speaking and he states rather prophetically that "Stephen has the ability and the tenacity required to become possibly the greatest player to grace a snooker table". Written by John Docherty, a sports writer with the Scottish Daily Record, whilst this book is an adequate study an updated account of Hendry's career is long overdue.

Value   £3 - £5

1.18   **Right On Cue : an Autobiography**

John Parrott
1991   Robson Books, London
ISBN   0860517780
Hardback   192pp, plates, ports., 24 x 16cm

This book has brown coloured boards with large gilt lettering to the spine and a dustjacket featuring Parrott playing a rest shot. With chapter titles such as 'Growing Up', 'Leaving School', and 'Television Debut' the content is self-explanatory. Parrott's 1991 World Championship victory is relived in all its glory, as is the day Parrott paraded the trophy at Liverpool's Anfield football ground. One of the more interesting sections for the reader is entitled 'Friends, Rivals and Others'.

Value   £5 - £10

1.19   **Behind the White Ball : my Autobiography**

Jimmy White / Rosemary Kingsland
1998   Hutchinson, London
ISBN   0091801265
Hardback   230pp, plates, ports., 24 x 16cm

1999   Arrow Books, London

ISBN	0099271842
Paperback	292pp, plates, ports., 18 x 11cm

The b & w photo on the dustjacket of this book sums up the irrepressible Jimmy White's cool, mercurial persona – against a pitch black background he is clad in leather jacket and open necked shirt, casually lighting a cigarette with a Bacardi lighter! Packed full of picaresque tales detailing the life and times of a lovable snooker rogue (White's former manager Harvey Lisberg says of White "I always think of you being like the Rolling Stones. [Steve] Davis is more like the Beatles"), this is certainly one of the more engrossing autobiographies for the collector to acquire. The book regularly appears on eBay and will not prove too difficult to find in secondhand bookshops, Amazon or Abe, especially as the 1st edition print run was a staggering 20,000 copies.

Value £4 - £8 (hb)
in print £7.99 (pb)

1.20 Eye of the Hurricane : the Alex Higgins Story

John Hennessey
2000	Mainstream Publishing, Edinburgh & London
ISBN	1840183853
Hardback	224pp, plates (some col.), ports. (some col.), 25 x 17cm
2001	Mainstream Publishing, Edinburgh & London
ISBN	184018440X
Paperback	256pp, 20 x 13cm

In 'Eye of the Hurricane' John Hennessey, the Daily Express journalist, takes the reader through the life of "the only true genius the game has ever had". Although there have been several biographies written about Higgins, the story is so thrilling it never seems jaded by re-telling. The strength of this book is the access Hennessey has to Higgins, other players and tournament officials which results in a portrait of Higgins from many different angles. Unfortunately, the 12 pages of photos in the 1st edition are set against some ugly backgrounds but the photos do not appear in the paperback edition.

Value £4 - £8 (hb)
in print £7.99 (pb)

1.21 The Hurricane : the Turbulent Life and Times of Alex Higgins

Bill Borrows
2002	Atlantic Books, London
ISBN	1903809916
Hardback	xv, 368pp, ill., plates, ports., 24 x 16cm

Notes	The reverse of the title page states there was a trade paperback edition with an ISBN of 184354069X; includes Notes and Index
2003	Atlantic Books, London
ISBN	1843540118
Paperback	xvi, 367pp, ill., plates, ports., 18 x 11cm
Notes	Revised edition; includes Notes and Index

This bumper 368 page volume has a wonderfully evocative b & w picture of Higgins on the cover, jet black boards and the title in huge silver lettering on the spine. Borrows was one of the founders of lads' mag Loaded and has also edited Maxim, and the 'Hurricane' is just the kind of character that Loaded readers eulogized in its heyday. This book has been exhaustively researched from numerous sources (listed in the 15 pages of Notes), is very well written and includes a substantial Index, allowing the reader to select subject areas to dip in and out of at will. Borrows ends the book on a somewhat poignant note, asking Higgins if he has enjoyed his life. After a pause Higgins replies "I haven't really had much to do with my life. All I've done is take part in it".

Value in print £16.99 (hb)
in print £6.99 (pb)

1.22 Ronnie : the Autobiography of Ronnie O'Sullivan

Ronnie O'Sullivan / Simon Hattenstone	
2003	Orion Books, London
ISBN	0752855824
Hardback	216pp, plates, ports., 24 x 17cm
Notes	Includes Index
2004	Orion Books, London
ISBN	0752858807
Paperback	v, 298pp, plates, ports., 20 x 13cm
Notes	Revised and updated edition; includes Epilogue written since the 1st edition; includes Index

The dustjacket of 'Ronnie' has a photo of an enigmatic O'Sullivan smoking a cigarette against a black background and is slightly reminiscent of the cover of Jimmy White's autobiography, 'Behind the White Ball' (see entry 1.19). This volume is every bit as entertaining as White's book, with the Guardian journalist Simon Hattenstone re-telling the scrapes that O'Sullivan has very often got into. O'Sullivan doesn't shy away from the difficult periods in his life and talks candidly about his father (who was sentenced to life imprisonment in 1992 for murder), his battle with drugs and depression, and his spell in the Priory.

Value £3 - £5 (hb)
in print £7.99 (pb)

1.23   Double or Quits

Willie Thorne / Derek Marsden
2004   bigbluetube, Liverpool
ISBN   0954584112
Hardback   143pp, plates, ports., 24 x 16cm
Notes   Foreword by Gary Lineker

Willie Thorne talks about his problems openly in this frank autobiography – gambling, bankruptcy, marital breakdown, depression and attempted suicide are just a few of the painful subjects covered. Younger snooker fans will associate Thorne with his TV work rather than his playing days, but this book is a reminder that Thorne was a very useful player at his peak, although as Thorne himself admits he struggled with the mental side of the sport. The story does become a touch depressing towards the end and it is with welcome relief that the final chapters discuss the modern game and Thorne's opinions of today's players. The publisher, bigbluetube, was founded in 2000 and deals primarily in sports memorabilia. 'Double or Quits' follows the recent trend for snooker books to have black, rather than green, boards and dark dustjackets.

Value   in print £12.99

1.24   Out of the Blue Into the Black : the autobiography of John Spencer

John Spencer
2005   The Parrs Wood Press, Manchester
ISBN   190315863X
Hardback   206pp, plates (some col.), ports. (some col.), 22 x 16cm
Notes   Foreword by Ted Lowe; includes Appendix containing information on Myasthenia Gravis and the Myasthenia Gravis Association[3]

John Spencer was introduced to the game of snooker at the age of 13 when he sat on a garden wall watching his brother and a friend play snooker through the window. Much happened in his life since that day including winning the World Championship three times (surprisingly, only 6 pages are devoted to this feat), marital breakdown and depression. The latter was brought on by Spencer being diagnosed with Myasthenia Gravis on May 9th 1985 (described by Spencer as "the worst day of my life"). Because of the frankness with which the author deals with his troubles the latter part of the book makes difficult reading, particularly the chapter entitled 'Into the Black'. However, Spencer comes across as a warm and genuine character and there are some amusing anecdotes sprinkled throughout. One remarkable statistic included reveals that Spencer's highest tournament

---

[3]   See www.mgauk.org for further information.

earnings was the mere £9,000 he received as a quarter finalist in the 1987 British Open. The book is bound in black cloth and has a grey dustjacket with a b & w photo of Spencer on the cover and had a 1st edition print run of 2,000 copies.

Value in print £17.99

1.25 From the Eye of the Hurricane : My Story

Alex Higgins / [Sean Boru]
2007   Headline Publishing, London
ISBN   9780755316595
Hardback   xi, 307pp, plates, ports., 24 x 16cm
Notes   Includes 'Career Record'; career statistics compiled by David Hendon; includes Index

2007   Headline Publishing, London
ISBN   9780755316618
Paperback   xi, 307pp, plates, ports., 20 x 13cm
Notes   Includes 'Career Record'; career statistics compiled by David Hendon; includes Index

In the Note to the 'Career Record' on page 298 of this book it states that "Higgins is still on the ranking list as a W.P.B.S.A. member despite not having played in a ranking tournament since 1997". Extraordinary then, that ten years later Higgins should have yet another book published and that there is still so much interest surrounding the man and his life. This is Higgins' own story and he comments on the myths and legends that have grown up around him and is best read alongside other biographies of Higgins, especially Bill Borrows' 'The Hurricane' (see entry 1.21). For example, on page 105 of Borrows' book he claims only a threat from Higgins to return home from Trinidad caused the sponsors to transfer him from low-rent accommodation to the Holiday Inn. However, in Higgins' book on page 151 he blandly states "we stayed at the Holiday Inn and we loved it". Regarding the infamous 'shooting' spat with Dennis Taylor, Borrows quotes Taylor as stating Higgins said "the next time you're in Northern Ireland I'll have you shot". Whereas, on page 254 of 'From the Eye of the Hurricane' Higgins says that he really said "look, you, if I had a gun in my hands, I'd blow your brains out" and that "at no point did I say that the next time Taylor was in Northern Ireland I would have someone else shoot him".

The book is bound in grey cloth with gilt lettering to the spine and has a black, white and gold dustjacket and fantastic colour photographic endpapers.

Value in print £18.99

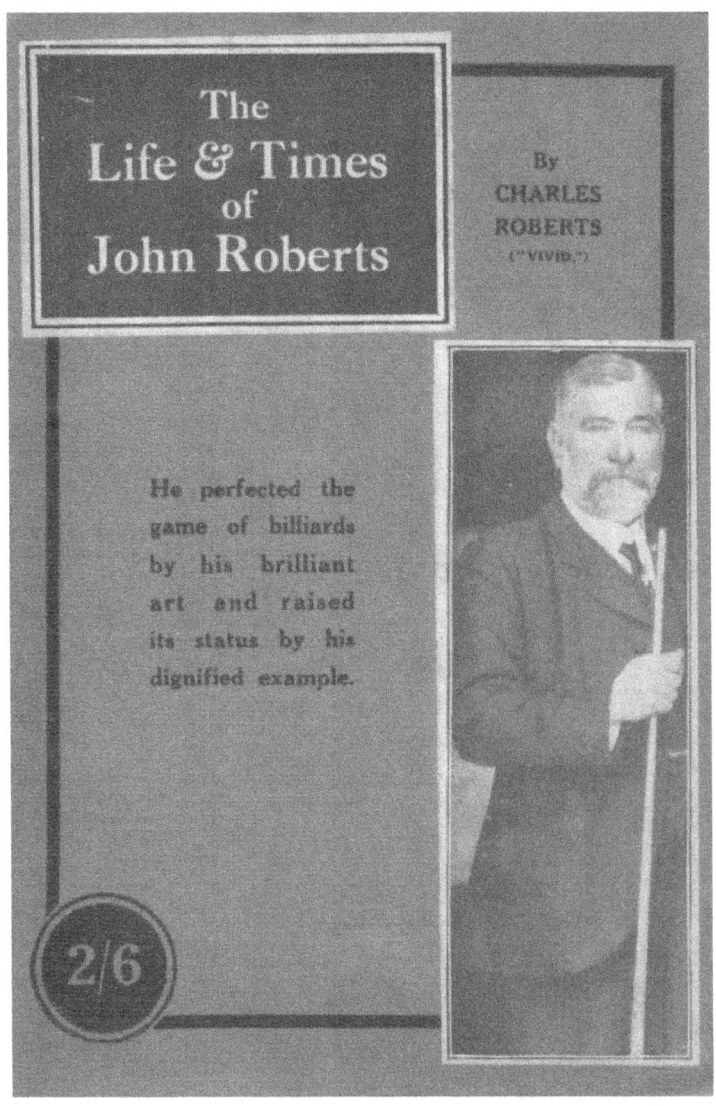

'The Life and Times of John Roberts' is one of only a handful of player biographies published before the Second World War. It is valued at around the £250 mark in very good condition. See entry 1.3.

Joe Davis' autobiography normally sells for £15-£25 in very good condition complete with the dustjacket. The back of the jacket carriers an inspired cartoon drawn in 1942 by Tom Webster, with the caption "Joe Davis. The sultan of snooker and the emperor of pot"! See entry 1.5.

~ HISTORY & DEVELOPMENT ~

2.0   Billiards through the Centuries

W. G. Clifford
[1933]   Printing-Craft, London
Hardback   37pp, 25 x 19cm
Notes   Includes Erratum

This book has a lovely decorative title page but unfortunately no date of publication but the British Library has catalogued it as a 1933 publication. The boards are dark green with a rectangular pattern on the front with the title and author in gilt and the endpapers are predominantly light green with a white 'vein' pattern running through them. As the title suggests this is largely an historical account of the sport encompassing origins, development of rubber cushions and cloth. There is a lot of mention of 'Janus' cloth which, conveniently, is advertised at the rear of the book manufactured by F. Reddaway & Co. of Manchester and London. A copy of Clifford's work, with pages distressed by damp but generally very good, sold for £77 on eBay in February 2007; and a further copy, described as good to very good with the spine slightly loose, realised £56.50 on eBay in December 2007.

Value   **£60 - £80**

2.1   Billiards for all Time

Riso Levi
1935   Riso Levi, Wilmslow
Hardback   xii, 244pp, ill., 22 x 14cm

Levi was in his 70th year when he wrote this book and it would be fair to say that he made a major contribution to the literature of billiards. This is another vast and detailed offering and contains some interesting chapters, not least the Preface where Levi records some verbal sparring he engaged in with the rather truculent Walter Lindrum. This article originally appeared in many newspapers, although collectors wishing to track it down should note that some changed the title from its original 'My Two Hours Battle With Lindrum'. Another fine chapter is 'Newman's Strange Suggestion' where Levi pours scorn on Tom Newman's suggestion that the table should be decreased in size to 10ft x 5ft. There are further press articles reprinted in the book and all make for fascinating reading and prove what a passionate man Levi was when it came to his beloved billiards. The book also includes a few snooker chapters. Originally costing 7/6, it is bound in dark green cloth with a table in gilt at the foot of the cover and title and author in gilt at the top.

Value   **£50 - £80**

2.2 The Earlier History of Billiard Tables and Accessories as seen from the Sales Journals of John Thurston 1818 – 1843

Sidney Gillett / Thurston & Co. (Corp.)
[1940] Thurston & Co., London
Paperback 26pp, ill., plates, 1 port , 19 x 13cm

As the title indicates, this small paperback pamphlet-type book takes data from the sales journals of John Thurston and summarises the development of tables, cushions, cues, chalk, balls, pocket openings and lighting. In addition, there is a brief section describing the various games played on a billiard table. No date of publication is given but on page 26 Gillett talks of Thurston's Leicester Square premises being blitzed in the war so it must have been published after October 1940. Sid Gillett was a former director of Thurston's who later became managing director of their South Africa operations. The book is printed on glossy, light yellow paper and is bound with decorative card wrappers.

Value £50 - £100

2.3 The Noble Game of Billiards

Thurstons (Corp.)
[195?] Thurstons, London
Paperback 25pp, ill., plates, 19 x 26cm

[1966] Thurstons, London
Paperback 25pp, ill., plates, 19 x 25cm

Thurston & Co.
[1987] Thurston & Co., London
ISBN None given
Paperback 25pp, ill., plates, ports., facsims., 19 x 25cm

This is not a reprint of Mingaud's 'Noble Game of Billiards' but a reproduction of certain articles that appeared in 'The Times' of January 14th, 18th, 24th, 29th, and February 4th and 8th, 1908. The book begins with the rise of the game ("the origin of the game is obscure in the extreme") and then moves onto specific details regarding Thurston's ("in 1826 he revolutionized his method of construction by the introduction of the solid slate bed") and then discusses the making of a billiard table and accessories. This book is a suitable companion to Norman Clare's 'Billiards and Snooker Bygones' (see entry 2.9) and ends with a chronology of the significant advances in billiard table and accessory manufacture.

Value in print (1987 ed.) £2.50

2.4   **About Billiard Cushions**

Thurston & Co. (Corp.)
[1951]   Thurston & Co., London
Paperback   [4]pp, ill., 21 x 14cm
Notes   Cover title is 'A word about . . . Billiard Cushions'

This slim pamphlet briefly details the history and development of billiard cushions from the days of 'stuffed' cushions built up with layers of list or felt; through to the development of 'Stanfast' cushions manufactured by Thurston's. The publication is essentially an advertising vehicle for Thurston but warrants inclusion in the 'History and Development' section for its discussion of the development of billiard cushions.

Value   **£30 - £50**

2.5   **The Story of Billiards and Snooker**

Clive Everton
1979   Cassell & Co., London
ISBN   0304303739
Hardback   192pp, ill., ports., 22 x 15cm
Notes   Includes 34 pages of Tables detailing selected tournament
                  results from 1870–1978; includes Index

The blurb on the dustjacket of this book says it is "a mixture of history and anecdote, facts and personalities", and today's foremost authority, Clive Everton, weaves the story of both games over fourteen chapters. The book begins with an investigation of the origins of billiards and ends with the 1978 World Championship final between Ray Reardon and Perrie Mans. As one would expect from Everton, the book is packed with fine detail and covers all the major shifts in the two games. This is an essential book for any serious collector and, although not expensive, is becoming increasingly difficult to find especially in very good condition complete with the colourful red and green dustjacket.

Value   **£8 - £10**

2.6   **Billiards and Snooker : a Trade History**

J.R. Mitchell (Comp.)
[1981]   British Sports & Allied Industries Federation, UK
ISBN   0950742201
Paperback   97pp, ill., plates, 24 x 18cm
Notes   Includes contributions from John K. Bennett and
                  C. G. Kenyon

33

This poorly written but highly sought after book is unique in snooker literature in that it details the manufacturers of billiards and snooker accessories, drawing heavily on the earlier work of Sidney Gillett (see entries 2.2, 7.32, 7.33 and 7.35). Early tables, the making of billiard cloth, cues, tips and chalk ("No sales of billiard chalk are recorded before 1819"), are detailed in Part 1; whilst Part 2 covers company histories and concentrates on such famous names as Burroughes & Watts, E. J. Riley, E. A. Clare & Son, and so forth. The final part is a miscellaneous section covering, amongst other topics, match and exhibition halls, care of the billiard table and care of the cue. There are some beautiful b & w plates in the book showing antique billiard tables, and accessories such as 'maces' and cue stands. Many of these plates are reprinted from antique line drawings. There are also plenty of contemporary adverts and the unusual cover features fine detail from the carvings of the legs of a billiard table[4]. The collector will be lucky to get this book for less than £30 and copies often sell for £40+ on eBay; one copy selling for an impressive £51 in November 2006.

Value £30 - £40

2.7 **Guinness Book of Snooker**

Clive Everton / Anne Marshall (Ed.)
1981   Guinness Superlatives, Enfield
ISBN   0851122302
Hardback   162pp, plates (some col.), ports. (some col.), 27 x 20cm
Notes   Bert Hackett (ill.); includes Index

Clive Everton / Josie Holtom (Ed.)
1982   Guinness Superlatives, Enfield
ISBN   0851122566
Paperback   177pp, ill., plates (some col.), ports. (some col.), 26 x 19cm
Notes   Revised edition; as above

This book is predominantly a history of billiards and snooker but also has player biographies and match statistics to complete an overall picture of both games. Any publication by Clive Everton is worth owning simply because of his encyclopaedic knowledge and his stature as the sport's major chronicler. This offering draws on his previous publication of 1979, 'The Story of Billiards and Snooker' (see entry 2.5), but is much more accessible and contains many more photos. The chapter entitled 'Round the World', where Everton discusses billiards and snooker in various countries is particularly interesting. The book is bound in red cloth with gilt lettering to the spine and can often be picked up on eBay for cheaper than the valuation given below.

Value £4 - £8

---

[4] Specifically, an Orme & Sons table of special design made in the 1870s.

2.8   **A Short History of Billiards and Snooker**

        Norman Clare
        [1981]   [Thurston & Co.], London
        Paperback   16pp, ill., plates (mostly col.), 1 port., facsims., 23 x 12cm

Norman Clare's study is a history of billiards and snooker equipment plus the rules, rather than a history of the game, although the first few pages detail the origin of billiards. Included in the slim volume are some splendid colour photos of antique cues, tables and billiard balls. This book should be viewed as a companion to Clare's 'Billiards and Snooker Bygones' (see entry below) and 'The Noble Game of Billiards' (see entry 2.3) published by Thurston & Co. in 1987. This is another of those relatively modern publications that does not appear for sale very often and will take some patience in tracking down.

Value   £5 - £10

2.9   **Billiards and Snooker Bygones**

        Norman Clare
        1985   Shire Publications, Princes Risborough
        ISBN   0852637306
        Paperback   31pp, ill., plates, ports., facsims, 21 x 15cm
        Notes   Shire Album number 136

        1996   Shire Publications, Princes Risborough
        ISBN   0852637306
        Paperback   31pp, ill., plates, ports., facsims., 21 x 15cm
        Notes   Reprint with amendments; as above

Written by Norman Clare, the former Chairman of the snooker table manufacturing group, E. A. Clare & Son Ltd., this slim volume details the history and development of early billiard tables, cues (or 'maces'), billiard balls, table lighting, score boards etc. The book is illustrated with many fascinating b & w photos that will appeal to all historians of billiards and snooker. The book is part of the Shire Album Series, featuring books on subjects as diverse as Toby jugs, rocking horses, walking sticks and teddy bears.

Value   in print (1996 ed.) £3.50

2.10   **The History of Snooker and Billiards**

        Clive Everton
        1986   Partridge Press, Haywards Heath
        ISBN   1852250135

Hardback	192pp, ill., plates, ports., 26 x 22cm
Notes	Includes 20 pages of Tables giving tournament results from 1870–1985; includes Index

Clive Everton's previous 'history' was published by Cassell in 1979 and was called 'The Story of Billiards and Snooker'. By the time this effort was published in 1986 snooker had become so popular that snooker, rather than billiards, was the lead word in the title. This book is rather large and is bound in green cloth and has a predominantly green dustjacket. Parts of the book are reprinted from Everton's 1979 'Story' and others have been updated, while new sections (e.g. 'The Steve Davis Era') have been added and there are far more illustrations and portraits in this book compared to the previous effort. This book is also a must-have for the collector, although it is much easier to find than 'The Story of Billiards & Snooker'.

Value £5 - £10

2.11 Snooker's Crucible : How Sheffield became the Snooker Capital of the World

Jeremy Watson / Geoff Kemp	
1988	Sheffield City Libraries, Sheffield
ISBN	0863210791
Paperback	117pp, ill. (some col.), plates (some col.), ports. (some col.), facsims., 30 x 21cm
Notes	Foreword by Fred Davis

This is another of those relatively recent snooker books that can be difficult to acquire and may take a bit of hunting down. It is essentially a trawl through the story of billiards and snooker in the Sheffield area, culminating in the story of Mike Watterson's decision to bring the World Championship to Sheffield's Crucible Theatre in 1977. A chapter is also dedicated to the Crucible champions between 1977–1987. The authors, both local journalists, have written a fine book, the pages dealing with the early billiards scene being especially absorbing.

Value £5 - £10

2.12 The Embassy Book of World Snooker

Clive Everton	
1993	Bloomsbury Publishing, London
ISBN	0747516103
Hardback	192pp, ill. (some col.), plates (mostly col.), ports. (mostly col.), 26 x 20cm
1993	Ted Smart (Published for 'The Book People Ltd.'), [London]

ISBN	None given
Hardback	192pp, ill. (some col.), plates (mostly col.), ports. (mostly col.), 26 x 20cm

The fourth publication from Clive Everton regarding history and development, this compact book draws on his 1986 book, 'The History of Snooker & Billiards' (see entry 2.10), especially in the early chapters. After the beginnings of the game have been explored there follows an account of each season from '75-'76 to '92-'93. There is a 10 page reference section at the rear including 4 pages of colour caricatures drawn by artist and illustrator Geoff Tristram who was featured on BBC TV drawing caricatures of the top 16 players during the 2006 World Championships. The Bloomsbury edition has plain black boards and the Ted Smart edition has laminated pictorial boards and both have the same colourful dustjacket, the former having 'Bloomsbury' written at the bottom in silver. Most dealers price this book at £10-£12 but in truth copies often sell for a quarter of that sum on eBay.

Value £8 - £12

2.13   On Snooker : the Game and the Characters Who Play It

Mordecai Richler	
2001	Yellow Jersey Press, London
ISBN	0224061496
Hardback	194pp, 18 x 11cm
Notes	Part of Yellow Jersey's 'On' series; includes Bibliography and Index

2002	Yellow Jersey Press, London
ISBN	022406150X
Paperback	194pp, 17 x 11cm
Notes	As above

The majority of snooker and billiards books understandably focus on the colours red and green and, with its bright red boards and predominantly green dustjacket, the 1st edition of this book is no exception. The book forms part of the 'On' series that includes such titles as 'On Beckham', 'On Penalties', 'On Bullfighting' and 'On Golf'. Richler was born in Montreal in 1931 and has written several novels for both adults and children. 'On Snooker' is part autobiography and part snooker journal, and is filled with anecdotes and stories from Richler's time on the snooker circuit.

Value in print £10

'Billiards and Snooker : a Trade History' is a highly collectable work that usually commands £30-£40 when appearing for sale. The ornamental cover shows details of fine carving from an Orme & Sons table of the 1870s. See entry 2.6.

'A Short History of Billiards and Snooker' is a slim paperback volume that may take some tracking down. When it does appear it normally sells for £5-£10. See entry 2.8.

'Billiards and Snooker Bygones' is currently in print and traces the history and development of billiard tables, cues and accessories. See entry 2.9.

'The Embassy Book of World Snooker' provides snooker fans with a thorough history of the sport and can be picked up for around £5-£8. See entry 2.12.

~ TRICK SHOTS, HUMOROUS & CARTOONS ~

3.0   Fun on the Billiard Table : Being a Collection of Amusing Tricks and Games for Amateurs, with Photographs

'Stancliffe'
1899   C. Arthur Pearson, London
Hardback   x, 114pp, ill., plates, 18 x 13cm

1900   C. Arthur Pearson, London
Hardback   x, 114pp, ill., plates, 19 x 13cm

[1901]   C. Arthur Pearson, London
Hardback   x, 114pp, ill., plates, 19 x 13cm
Notes   2nd edition

1910   C. Arthur Pearson, London
Hardback   viii, 114pp, ill., plates, 19 x 13cm
Notes   3rd impression

1916   C. Arthur Pearson, London
Paperback   x, 114pp, ill., plates, 19 x 13cm
Notes   4th edition; title is '**Fun on the Cottage Billiard Table**'

[1919]   C. Arthur Pearson, London
Hardback   x, 114pp, ill., plates, 19 x 13cm
Notes   4th impression

This book is essentially a trick shots publication and features 75 shots, games, spoofs and tricks all fully illustrated with rather rudimentary b & w photographs. Some of the shots have amusing names, such as 'Squeeze Shot', 'Round the Woodwork' and 'The War Game', and these all help to hold the reader's attention. The book itself is bound in bright red cloth and has the title in attractive black typography on the cover. A copy of the 1900 edition, in very good condition, sold for £49 on eBay in February 2007; and later editions have achieved prices somewhat lower than that.

Value   **£40 - £60**

3.1   **Billiards in Mufti**

F. L. Billington Greig
[1919]   The Billiard House, Glasgow
Paperback   108pp, 20 x 13cm

Originally retailing at 2/- this book is a light-hearted series of articles and verses that had previously appeared in 'Punch' and 'The Billiard Monthly'. There are some wonderful comic verses and ballads in this book, including 'A Tragedy in 250 Up'! Plus there is also a skit on the Sherlock Holmes stories – 'The Mystery of the 3 Grey Pellets'. However, the finest thing about the book is the great pictorial cover in white, purple and green. Underneath a drawing of an old maid at the billiard table reads the caption "Inman appeared at the table in the character of "Mrs Gummidge" and talked about his troubles while he played". Frederick Lewis Greig (1875/6-1961) was well placed to write a book on billiards as he was a manager for a billiard table manufacturer[5]. He married the suffragette and political theorist Teresa Mary Billington[6] (1877-1964) and their names were united in a nuptial concord which guaranteed equal rights in marriage. 'Billiards in Mufti' is a very rare book and does not appear for sale very often at all and when it does the fragile cover is often the worse for wear and has lost its brightness.

Value £200 - £300

3.2 Tricks on the Billiards Table

Newman Mond
[1954] W. Foulsham & Co., London
Paperback xiii, 50pp, ill., 1 plate, 18 x 12cm
Notes One of Foulsham's 'Popular Manuals' (no. 8)

'Tricks on the Billiards Table' has pale orange card covers and the title in black at the top and a green and white dustjacket. There is no date of publication on the title page and the book itself offers no clues so I have stuck with the British Library estimate of 1954. The author took no part in competitive billiards and snooker, yet he could easily put on a 2-hour act and entertained audiences in the UK as well as Egypt, India, Burma and Singapore (Mond was attached to the RAF as a Liaison Officer and visited these places as part of his duties). Mond also helped to design a series of cigarette cards "some years before the war"[7]. There are 50 trick shots described in the book, each accompanied by a small diagram. Very few copies of this book come up for sale but a very good copy, without the green and white dustjacket, sold for £17 on eBay in April 2006.

Value £15 - £20

---

5 According to J.R.Mitchell (see entry 2.6) the company Greig worked for was Burroughes & Watts.
6 Mitchell says that Mrs Billington Greig worked hard to bring women into the game in the 1930s and organised "Women's Billiard Circles".
7 A set of 50 cards issued by Ogden's in 1934 entitled 'Trick Billiards'.

3.3 Eddie Charlton's Trick Shots

Eddie Charlton
1977   Macmillan, Australia & London
ISBN   0333229746
Hardback   80pp, col. ill., col. plates, 1 col. port., 25 x 19cm

This book screams snooker - having green cloth boards, green endpapers and a green title page. Over the course of the book Charlton takes the reader through 70 trick shots, all of which are lavishly illustrated with colour photos. The book was subsequently incorporated into 'The Complete Book of Snooker' first published in the UK in 1987 (see entry 4.21).

Value   £4 - £8

3.4 The Bad Players Guide to Status Snooker

Unknown author
[198?]   Degan Publishing Group, [Hampshire]
ISBN   None given
Paperback   28pp, ill., 21 x 15cm
Notes   Includes Glossary

This slim book originally sold for a mere 35p and has colourful card covers; the front carrying an illustration in red, green, black and white of a rather aged player, 'The Traditionalist', shown ripping the cloth of the table. This amusing book is chiefly concerned with how aspiring amateurs can achieve some 'status' in the game and attempts this by identifying certain snooker 'types' the amateur can aspire to. These include 'Flash Harry' – "nearly always slim"; 'The Shark' – "he can be found lurking generally . . . in the seedier establishment"; and 'The Traditionalist' – "a type to suit more refined tastes". The Glossary includes some snooker slang such as 'Toby Jug' - a mug (or beginner) and 'Iron Duke' – fluke.

Value   £5 - £10

3.5 Ray Reardon's 50 Best Trick Shots

Ray Reardon
1980   David & Charles, Newton Abbot
ISBN   0715379933
Hardback   [96]pp, ill. (mostly col.), 22 x 14cm
Notes   2nd impression 1988

This hardback book was issued without a dustjacket, the laminated boards are predominantly yellow and there is a photo of Reardon on the cover. The book is divided into 'Party Tricks', 'Snooker Trick Shots', 'Stunts and Bottle Shots', 'Billiards

43

Trick Shots', and 'An Extra Touch'. The text is accompanied by b & w diagrams plus full-page (mostly colour) table illustrations.

Value £3 - £5

3.6   **Bedside Snooker**

Ray Reardon / Michael Leitch (Ed.)
1983   Century Publishing Co., London
ISBN   0712601309
Hardback   88pp, col. ill., ill. endpapers, 26 x 20cm
Notes   Colin Whittock (ill.)

1983   Book Club Associates, London
ISBN   None given
Hardback   88pp, col. ill., ill. endpapers, 26 x 20cm
Notes   As above

1984   Fontana / Collins, London
ISBN   000636845X
Paperback   88pp, ill., ill. endpapers, 20 x 16cm
Notes   As above

This is a book of humorous tales and anecdotes from one of snooker's true characters, Ray Reardon, with the text illustrated throughout with colour cartoons by Colin Whittock. The 1st edition is a hardback with laminated pictorial boards and the 1984 edition is a reprint, albeit in a smaller paperback format, that originally cost £2.95. There was also a hardback edition published by Book Club Associates in 1983 in arrangement with Century Publishing that was issued without an ISBN. All editions can be found easily and cheaply and often appear in charity shops and on eBay.

Value £2 - £4

3.7   **Cue for a Laugh**

Roy Ullyett
1984   David & Charles, Newton Abbot
ISBN   0715386700
Paperback   78pp, ill., 24 x 16cm

Roy Ullyett drew cartoons for the Daily Express for over 30 years and by the time 'Cue for a Laugh' was published in 1984 he had illustrated more than 20 books. The book is divided into sections named 'At Home', 'Clubs and Pubs', 'The Pros', 'Women' and 'Stately Homes'. Each page contains a b & w cartoon, most of which are wittily and acutely observed and display Ullyett's sharp sense of humour. This is one of the more expensive humorous books but copies still appear for sale quite regularly and copies can usually be picked up for less than £10.

Value   £4 - £8

3.8   The Duffer's Guide to Snooker

Mike Gordon
1985   Columbus Books, London
ISBN   0862872340
Paperback   80pp, ill., 14 x 21cm
Notes   Reprinted 1985, 1986 and 1987; Introduction by
                           Dennis Taylor

This 80 page paperback book was published in 1985 at the height of snooker's popularity and was one sport in a series that also featured rugby, golf, fishing and cricket. 'The Duffer's Guide' is a humorous look at the game, the real appeal of the book lying in the brilliant b & w cartoons that appear on every page which take a satirical swipe at the sport.

Value   £2 - £4

3.9   The Golden Rules of Snooker

Ian Heath
1985   Corgi Books, London
ISBN   0552125997
Paperback   48pp, ill., 16 x 11cm

Ian Heath wrote several 'Golden Rules' books, covering football, golf, fishing, sailing etc. A pocket-sized paperback of only 48 pages, this charming little book illustrates in humorous b & w cartoons some of the rules of snooker and some of the etiquette to be observed when playing the game. Although not a valuable book it can be difficult to find and it rarely appears on Amazon or eBay, the best place to find it seemingly being Abe where it pops up periodically.

Value   £2 - £4

3.10   Natural Break

Dennis Taylor
1985   Queen Anne Press, London
ISBN   0356121801
Hardback   127pp, ill., plates, 23 x 19cm
Notes   Reprinted 1986; Foreword by Steve Davis; Graham
                           Thompson (ill.); David Muscroft (photog.)

1986	Queen Anne Press, London
ISBN	0356125661
Paperback	127pp, ill., plates, 22 x 19cm
Notes	Reprint; as above

'Natural Break' is similar in look and feel to 'The Book of Snooker Disasters & Bizarre Records' (see entry below), but features anecdotes exclusively from Dennis Taylor. As a former World Champion, now turned commentator, Taylor has a wide range of tales to choose from and the best are relayed over the 127 pages. The book features some amusing cartoons and a few photos of Taylor's fellow professionals. [description based on 1986 paperback edition].

Value £3 - £5

3.11 The Book of Snooker Disasters and Bizarre Records

Chris Rhys (Comp.)
1986	Stanley Paul & Co., London
ISBN	0091660009
Hardback	119pp, ill., plates, ports., facsims, 26 x 19cm
Notes	Introduction by Steve Davis; Joe Wright (ill.)

Chris Rhys (Comp.) / Michael Leitch (Ed.)
1989	Lennard Publishing, Oxford
ISBN	1852910682
Paperback	119pp, ill., plates, ports., 25 x 18cm
Notes	As above

Other sports, including rugby, cricket and golf, featured in this series but not all were originally published by Stanley Paul. As the title suggests, bizarre stories, humorous anecdotes and amusing situations form the subject matter for this light-hearted volume. The book is often found on the shelves of charity shops and its main interest lies in the fascinating older photographs and facsimilies of antique drawings and illustrations that appear throughout.

Value £3 - £5

3.12 John Virgo's Snooker Sideshow

John Virgo / Edward Horton (Ed.)
1987	Willow Books, London
ISBN	000218270X
Hardback	96pp, ill., 26 x 20cm
Notes	John Ireland (ill.)

1987	Book Club Associates, [London]

ISBN	None given
Hardback	96pp, ill., 26 x 20cm
Notes	This edition published by arrangement with William Collins & Sons; John Ireland (ill.)

John Virgo's book is illustrated by the satirical cartoonist, John Ireland, and with the aid of his cartoons Virgo takes a humorous look at the snooker world and the characters who populate it. Chapter titles include 'Making People Laugh', 'Starting Out', 'Holiday Camps', 'The Snooker Life', 'The Racing Game' and 'My Fellow Pros'. This last chapter is particularly charming and Virgo's affection for flair players such as Jimmy White and Alex Higgins shines through – "but if you're looking for an outright genius for snooker, Alex is your man". The book has laminated pictorial boards and the collector should have no problem finding a very good copy.

Value   **£3 - £5**

3.13   Snooker : the Dictionary

John Haselden	
[1987]	David & Charles, Newton Abbot
ISBN	071539066X
Paperback	78pp, ill., 1 port., 20 x 20cm
Notes	Cover title is 'The Snooker Dictionary'; John Headford (ill.)

There is no date of publication in this paperback book but the British Library has catalogued it as 1987. A light-hearted examination of the game in A-Z fashion, the book features vibrant b & w cartoons, some of which are rather risqué. Another of those publications that, whilst not valuable, is sometimes tricky to find.

Value   **£3 - £5**

3.14   Snooker Rules OK

Geoff Hales	
1987	A & C Black, London
ISBN	0713656247
Paperback	72pp, ill., 21 x 14cm
Notes	Bryan Flaherty (ill.); includes Index

The blurb on the back cover of this book states that it has "the answers for all those questions that puzzle snooker enthusiasts". In essence, this book is a humorous look at the rules of snooker (as the title makes clear) and the idiosyncrasies of the game and those who play it. The book moves from setting up the balls and the break, right through to the end of the game and concludes that "snooker, then, is a bit more complicated than it looks as you watch those immaculate professionals running up their century breaks and shaking hands with the sponsor". Bryan Flaherty's cartoons are drawn with verve and dash and complement the text nicely.

Value   £3 - £5

3.15   **How to be Really Interesting**

Steve Davis / Geoff Atkinson
1988   Penguin Books, London
ISBN   0140113061
Paperback   96pp, ill. (some col.), plates (some col.), ports. (some col.), 30 x 21cm
Notes   Brian Moody (photog.)

Davis was dubbed Steve 'Interesting' Davis by the satirical TV show 'Spitting Image'[8] and this book is a zany send-up of Davis' lifestyle and persona. Some gems include 'The Joy of Socks', 'Steve's Racy Fashion Tips' ('Hush Puppies' obligatory), 'Catching Gudgeon – with Steve Davis', and 'Motorways are Interesting'. The style and layout of this publication gives it the feel of a magazine and whatever the reader may think of it, it is certainly one of the more 'interesting' snooker books for the collector!

Value   £5 - £8

3.16   **John Ireland's Snooker Characters**

John Ireland (Ill.) / text by Ted Lowe
1989   Queen Anne Press, London
ISBN   035617932X
Hardback   94pp, ports. (mostly col.), 35 x 25cm

There is one small b & w cartoon of Ted Lowe at the end of the Introduction to this book and the remainder of the volume comprises full-page colour cartoons that are exceptionally well drawn. Ireland and Lowe have split the book into four sections – 'Recent World Champions', 'The Contenders', 'The Referees' and 'Hall of Fame'. A cartoon is included on almost every odd numbered page while the text sits on the even pages. Every reader will have their own favourite but the cartoon of Kirk Stevens on page 57 resplendent in white shoes, trousers, waistcoat and tie, plus cerise shirt and with a flowing mane of hair is particularly appealing. The book, probably the largest snooker book in terms of dimensions, has snooker-cloth

---

8   A show that ran for 21 series from 26th February 1984 until 18th February 1996.

green endpapers and pastedowns, black boards and a terrific dustjacket picturing a cartoon of Dennis Taylor raising his cue in triumph after winning the 1985 World Championship.

Value   £8 - £12

3.17   **John Virgo's Book of Snooker Trick Shots**

John Virgo / Jim Maloney
1994   Boxtree, London
ISBN   075220999X
Hardback   126pp, ill., plates (some col.), ports. (some col.), 26 x 20cm
Notes   Introduction by Jim Davidson; Colin Loughrey (ill.); John Clarke (photog.)

1994   Boxtree, London
ISBN   075220999X
Paperback   126pp, ill., plates (some col.), ports. (some col.), 25 x 19cm
Notes   As above

1995   Boxtree, London
ISBN   0752207091
Paperback   128pp, ill. (some col.) 25cm
Notes   New edition [description based on British Library catalogue]

'Snooker Trick Shots' originally sold for £9.99 and features over 100 trick shots, many of them performed by Virgo on the TV show 'Big Break'. After a brief overview of basic techniques the book is split into 3 sections – 'For Absolute Beginners', 'Trickier Trick Shots' and 'Try 'Em if you Dare'. Each shot is fully explained and illustrated and there are plenty of photos of Virgo on and off the set of 'Big Break', most of them picturing him in the rather lurid waistcoats he wore on the show.

Value   £4 - £8

Two variant covers of Stancliffe's 'Fun on the Billiard Table', first published by C. Arthur Pearson in 1899. The 1st edition now sells for £40-£60 in very good condition. See entry 3.0.

Front and back covers of 'Billiards in Mufti' published by the Billiard House, Glasgow in 1919. The book is very scarce and sells for £200-£300. See entry 3.1.

Newman Mond's work has a vibrant green and white dustjacket and normally sells for £15-£20. See entry 3.2.

Snooker was so popular during the 1980s that an enormous number of books were published on the sport. Pictured here are four humorous works published between 1985 and 1987. They all now sell for between £2-£5.

~ SNOOKER – INSTRUCTIONAL ~

~ Pre 1945 ~

4.0 **How to Play Snooker Pool**

Wallace Ritchie
[1911] Burroughes & Watts, London
Hardback 106pp, ill., 19 x 13cm

Burroughes & Watts were founded in 1836 and had premises in London's Soho Square where their famous matchroom was located. The enterprise grew to a considerable size and had offices in most major UK cities, as well as some in Canada and South Africa. The firm was taken over in 1967 when it was purchased by the Hurst Park Syndicate, and E. J. Riley took over the repair side of the business. Ritchie says in his Introduction that Snooker Pool is now on a level of popularity with billiards and because of this he feels that a treatise fully covering the game is warranted. The book is amply illustrated and has a dark grey-green cover depicting a player about to break off.

Value £30 - £50

4.1 **Snooker**

Tom Reece
[192?] No publisher details given
[Paperback] 8pp, [8]pp, 14 x 11cm

In this slim booklet, Reece takes the reader through the basics of snooker with the aid of line diagrams arranged after the numbered pages. Due to the brevity of the publication, and the fact no publisher details are given, it may well have been given away free with a miniature billiards/snooker table. [description based on a photocopy].

Value £150 - £200

4.2 **How to Play Snooker and Other Pool Games**

Willie Smith
1924 C. Arthur Pearson, London
Hardback 122pp, ill., 19 x 13cm

Willie Smith's book was issued with the almost standard green boards of snooker books, this one featuring the title in black on the upper half of the front board and a picture of a player, about to play a stroke, blocked onto the lower half. The jacket is orange and green and contains a photo of Smith but, unfortunately, most copies no longer have the jacket. Chapter headings include 'How to Pot a Ball', 'Potting Practice', 'Doubles', 'Tactics' and so on. The last few chapters deal with volunteer snooker, pyramids, and slosh - "slosh has many names. It is known officially as 'Russian' Pool, Indian Pool, Toad-in-the-Hole, slosh, and is essentially a chummy sort of game for cuemen who like to score". As with other Pearson publications of this era the book includes adverts and a publisher's catalogue at the rear. The volume appears regularly on Abe and eBay, although collector's hoping for a copy with the elusive dustjacket may have to pay double the price of a copy without.

Value £10 - £15

4.3 Snooker : How to Improve Your Play

The 'Bos'un'(pseud. of Osworth & Beeson)
[1926]	Athletic Publications, London
Paperback	64pp, ill., 19 x 13cm
Notes	Contains Errata

[1947]	Athletic Publications, London
Paperback	64pp, ill., 19 x 13cm
Notes	2nd edition; contains Errata slip attached to page 11

[1952]	Athletic Publications, London
Paperback	64pp, ill., 19 x 13cm
Notes	3rd edition

The Introduction to this book reflects on the decline of billiards and the growth of snooker and puts forward reasons for that growth. Namely, that snooker is a more sociable game, players compete on more equal terms, and it is "... pleasant and easy to play before an audience ...", although I'm sure a lot of players would disagree with the last two points. Full-page diagrams illustrate the book and it could be argued that with this publication the seeds of all modern day instructional snooker books were sown. Chapter headings include 'Balls on the Cushion', 'Evading the Snooker' and 'Methods of Potting'. Rather surprisingly, there are two chapters devoted to 'Doubles', a subject that would probably cover a page in modern day manuals.

Value £15 - £20

4.4 My Snooker Book

Joe Davis	
1929	John Long, London
Hardback	160pp, ill., plates, 1 port., 20 x 13cm

This rather plain looking volume is bound in dark green cloth and has the title on the spine rather than the cover. There are numerous contemporary adverts throughout, including ones for Thurston's 'Stanfast' cushions and 'Janus' billiard cloth, plus some adverts for various books at the rear. A few photos and plenty of illustrations guide the reader through Davis' lessons on opening the game, potting a ball, how to practise, and the gentle art of 'snookering'.

Value £35 - £50

4.5 **How to Play Snooker**

Stanley Newman / C. D. Dimsdale
1936   Sir Isaac Pitman & Sons, London
Hardback   xvi, 81pp, ill., plates, 1 port., 18 x 13cm
Notes   Introduction by Tom Newman; includes Index

1948   Golden Galley Press, London
Hardback   x, 53pp, ill., plates, 22 x 14cm
Notes   Re-issue; as above

Originally selling for 1/6, this offering from Stanley Newman has thick card covers, predominantly green, with a photo of the author at play in the middle and was issued with a dustjacket replicating the photograph. The frontispiece includes a b & w plate of Tom Newman, Stanley's brother, who wrote the Introduction. Printed on glossy paper, and with an abundance of illustrations, this work takes the reader through the basics of holding the cue and stance, right through to snookers and doubles. There are also sections entitled 'How Professionals Play' and 'The Rules Explained'. One quirky part is 'Playing the Game', where Newman states "... nothing is more unpleasant than a bad-tempered and nagging opponent ... who cannot accept the misfortunes of the game ...". The back of the book has a catalogue of Pitman's publications and the book frequently appears for sale via the usual sources.

Value £15 - £20

4.6 **Improve Your Snooker**

Joe Davis
1936   Methuen & Co., London
Hardback   viii, 93pp, ill., 1 port., 19 x 13cm

1946   Methuen & Co., London
Hardback   viii, 87pp, ill., 1 port., 19 x 13cm
Notes   2nd edition; reprinted 1956

In the Preface of this book Davis says that the rise in popularity of snooker has been "...the most astonishing happening ..." in recent years in the billiard world. Never one to miss a trick, Davis capitalised on the boom with this, his second snooker book, and the expected subject matter follows over the 93 pages. The book was issued with a white dustjacket with green typography and a table diagram sitting in the centre and the book has white boards with green lettering. The frontispiece to the book features a terrific b & w photo of Joe Davis looking more like a Chicago gangster than a snooker player! 1st editions of 'Improve Your Snooker' have sold for as little as £12 on eBay in recent years and for as much as £41.

Value £20 - £30

4.7 How to Play and Win at Snooker

W. G. Clifford
[1938] W. Foulsham & Co., London
Paperback 62pp, ill., 19 x 13cm
Notes One of Foulsham's 'New' Popular Handbooks; three Wartime reprints were issued

[n.d.] W. Foulsham & Co., London
Paperback 62pp, ill., 19 x 13cm
Notes One of Foulsham's 'New' Popular Handbooks

The design on the orange card covers of this book is the same as Clifford's [1927] book 'Billiard Table Games' also published by Foulsham (see entry 6.101). There are not so many illustrations in this volume as other snooker books but Clifford talks the reader through various aspects of play, including 'Doubles and Pots', 'How to Make Breaks' and 'The Art of Snookering'.

As with many of Foulsham's books there is no date of publication given but the British Library copy has a British Museum stamp dated October 1938. The 1st edition has a richly coloured jacket and collectors should have no problem locating a copy. The undated edition has a different dustjacket which is a rather garish red and yellow with dozens of small red dots surrounding a large star. Collector's wishing to own all editions should note there were also three Wartime reprints, one costing 1/-, one 1/3 and the other 1/6.

Value £10 - £15

57

~ Post 1945 ~

4.8 **How I Play Snooker**

Joe Davis
1949   Country Life, London
Hardback   176pp, ill., plates, 1 port, 24 x 16cm
Notes   Reprinted 1950

1956   Country Life, London
Hardback   174pp, ill., plates, 22 x 14cm
Notes   Revised edition

1964   Country Life, London
Hardback   174pp, ill., plates, 22 x 14cm
Notes   2nd (revised) edition; reprinted 1967

1975   Star Books / W.H.Allen & Co., London
ISBN   0352300574
Paperback   174pp, ill., plates, 1 port., 22 x 14cm
Notes   Reprint of the 2nd edition; reprinted 1976 (twice), 1977, 1978 and 1981

On page 11 of this book Davis states that "... this is not merely a book on how to play snooker, but a book which describes in the greatest possible detail exactly *how I myself play snooker*". This mode of playing may well be out of date but at the time there was no better tutor than Joe Davis and this book was a classic in its day. The book is well illustrated with diagrams and photos and many areas are covered, including the all important 'Match-Winning Mentality'. The book has very attractive bright green boards with the outline of a snooker table framing the white letters of author and title. The book was issued with a dustjacket and most copies appear to still have this intact. Collectors should note that there were two variants of the Star Books edition – one with a white cover and one with blue. There have been signed and presentation copies of the 1st edition on Abe over the past few years priced rather optimistically at £350-£400 but a standard 1st edition sells for far more modest sums.

Value   £20 - £30

4.9 **Advanced Snooker**

Joe Davis
1954   Country Life, London
Hardback   112pp, ill., plates, 1 port., 22 x 14cm
Notes   J. Allan Cash (photog.)

	[1966][9]	Country Life, London
	Hardback	112pp, ill., plates, 1 port, 23 x 15cm
	Notes	Re-issue; new title **'Advanced Snooker for the Average Player'**; J. Allan Cash (photog.); title page printed on blue paper

Davis' fourth snooker book, like his others, is a rather plain book to look at, with its dark red boards and silver title running down the spine. However, the contents more than make up for the outer plainness. There are lots of photos in the book, most featuring Joe at play but also his younger brother Fred, Walter Donaldson, John Pulman and the former commentator Ted Lowe. Davis' snooker books became 'bibles' to aspiring players and you can see why with this volume, packed as it is with information, advice and tips. As the title hints the book is aimed at the more accomplished player and the chapters on 'The Use of Screw', 'Unusual Plants and Kiss Effects', and 'Splitting the Pack' bear testimony to this. A copy of this book, signed by Joe Davis, fetched the bargain price of £14.50 on eBay in 2007; although it must be noted most dealers price the book slightly above the £20 mark and a good 1st edition, with torn dustjacket, fetched £25 on eBay in November 2007.

Value   £15 - £20

4.10 Tackle Snooker This Way

	John Pulman	
	1965	Stanley Paul & Co., London
	Hardback	144pp, ill., plates, 19 x 13cm
	1974	Stanley Paul & Co., London
	ISBN	0091212707
	Hardback	142pp, ill., plates, 20 x 13cm
	Notes	Revised edition; reprinted 1977, 1981, 1983 and 1984; revised title of **'Tackle Snooker'**
	1974	Stanley Paul & Co., London
	ISBN	0091212715
	Paperback	144pp, ill., plates, 19 x 12cm
	Notes	Revised edition; reprinted 1977, 1981, 1983 and 1984

This publication is bound in black cloth with the author's name in green on the spine and the title and publisher in gilt and was one of only a handful of snooker

---

9	'Complete Snooker for the Amateur' (see entry 4.11) states this re-issue with extended title was published in 1967, however the British Library copy is date stamped 10.10.66 so a 1966 publication date is more likely.

books published in the 1960s. Every aspect of snooker is covered over the eighteen chapters and the growing sophistication of shots and techniques is confirmed in chapters with titles such as 'The Swerve and Potting along the Cushion', 'The Nap of the Cloth and its Effect', 'The Plant, and Use of Side' and so on. One interesting chapter is 'Black Complex', where Pulman urges the reader to play for the easiest colour to continue the break, not to constantly play to get on the black. Collectors should insist on 1st edition copies having the dustjacket, featuring a b & w picture of Pulman with a green band across the lower portion. The 1974 revised edition, 'Tackle Snooker', has a different dustjacket photograph, different photos in the book and green boards with gilt lettering to the spine.

Value £10 - £15

4.11   Complete Snooker for the Amateur

Joe Davis	
1967	Country Life, London
Hardback	vii, 174pp, 111pp, [16] pp, ill., plates, 1 port., 23 x 15cm
Notes	Contains–'How I Play Snooker', 'Advanced Snooker for the Average Player' and 'Shots You Must Know'; J. Allan Cash (photog.)
1969	Country Life, London
SBN	600316432
Hardback	vii, pp[4]-174, pp[4]-111, [16]pp, ill., plates, 1 port., 23 x 15cm
Notes	Revised edition; as above
1974	W. H. Allen, London & New York
ISBN	0491015216
Hardback	vii, 174pp, 128pp, 16pp, ill., ports., 22 x 14cm
Notes	As above; reprinted 1975, 1976 (twice), 1977 and 1978; revised title of '**Complete Snooker**'; Foreword by Eddie Charlton

This 3-in-1 book weighs in at just over 300 pages and comprises two of Davis' previous books, plus a 16 page supplement entitled 'Shots You Must Know'. All aspects of snooker are covered and the book is illustrated throughout by line drawings and photos, some featuring a young Ted Lowe. The jacket of the 1974 edition, designed by Lesley Banks, is unusual for snooker books in that yellow (rather than red or green) dominates the colour scheme.

Value £15 - £20

4.12 Spencer on Snooker

John Spencer
1973　　　　　　　Cassell & Co., London
ISBN　　　　　　 030493898X
Hardback　　　　 137pp, ill., 1 port., 22 x 14cm
Notes　　　　　　 2nd impression May 1974, 3rd impression February 1976; Duncan Mil (ill.); includes Index

1978　　　　　　　Cassell & Co., London
ISBN　　　　　　 0304301191
Paperback　　　　137pp, ill., 22 x 14cm
Notes　　　　　　 2nd, revised edition; Duncan Mil (ill.); includes Index

John Spencer, the three times World Champion, begins this book with a chapter entitled 'How it all Happened', that details his introduction to snooker and ends with his defeat to Alex Higgins in the 1972 World Championship final. There then follows hints on the basics, positional techniques and play, safety play, doubles, the rest, tips, and matchplay. In the final chapter Spencer takes the reader through every amateur players dream – a century break. There are plenty of illustrations throughout the book and it has plain green boards with the title in black on the spine.

Value　　　　　　　　　　　　　　　　　　　　　　　　　　　　£8 - £10

4.13 Snooker

Ted Lowe
1975　　　　　　　EP Publishing, Wakefield
ISBN　　　　　　 0715805851
Hardback　　　　 111pp, ill., plates, 1 port., 21 x 21cm
Notes　　　　　　 Reprinted in hardback 1979; part of the EP Sport Series; Foreword by Clive Everton; Joe Jay (photog.)

1979　　　　　　　EP Publishing, Wakefield
ISBN　　　　　　 071580703X
Paperback　　　　111pp, ill., plates, 1 port., 20 x 20cm
Notes　　　　　　 Reprinted 1981, 1982, 1983, 1984 and 1985; part of the EP Sport Series; an 'Official BSCC Publication'; Foreword by Clive Everton; Joe Jay (photog.)

1988　　　　　　　A & C Black, London
ISBN　　　　　　 0713655984
Paperback　　　　95pp, ill., plates, ports., 20 x 20cm
Notes　　　　　　 4th edition; part of the EP Sport Series; an 'Official BSCC Publication'; includes Index

This book, an official Billiards & Snooker Control Council publication, has bright red and green pictorial boards and is almost square in shape (the exact dimensions are 20.6 x 20.3cm). Ted Lowe was manager of Leicester Square Hall, the home of professional snooker in the '40s and '50s, but most readers will remember him chiefly as a TV commentator. There are no surprises in this book and the expected subject matter is illustrated with line drawings and photos of Rex Williams, Eddie Charlton and Fred Davis. There are also plenty of photos of amateur players showing the reader how not to do things! Other sports in the 'EP Series' included badminton, judo and basketball and the series was later published by A & C Black in paperback format.

Value   £3 - £5

4.14   **Snooker : How to Become a Champion**

Rex Williams
1975   William Luscombe, London
ISBN   0860020096
Hardback   144pp, ill., plates, 22 x 14cm
Notes   Part of the 'Challenge' Series; Peter F. Chaplin (ill.); M. Athar Chaudhry (photog.)

1975   William Luscombe, London
ISBN   086002136X
Paperback   144pp, ill., plates, 22 x 14cm
Notes   As above

Bound in the almost obligatory green cloth, this book sees the former World Billiards Champion Rex Williams give his take on how to play snooker. There are also a couple of chapters at the end covering billiards called 'Billiards : Some Standard Shots' and 'Billiards : Top of the Table is Easy'. All sections of the book are amply illustrated to help steer the reader through the various lessons and instructions. The book has an attractive green dustjacket picturing a triangle of ten red balls plus the pink and black, and a cue dividing this picture from the title and author lettering at the top.

Value   £3 - £5

4.15   **Classic Snooker**

Ray Reardon
1976   David & Charles, Newton Abbot
ISBN   0715372440
Hardback   128pp, ill., 23 x 15cm

Notes	2nd impression 1977, 3rd impression 1978, 4th impression 1979, 5th impression 1979, 6th impression 1982, 7th impression 1983, 8th impression 1984, 9th impression 1988; includes Appendix
1978	Coronet Books, Sevenoaks
ISBN	0340231122
Paperback	156pp, ill., 18 x 11cm
Notes	3rd impression 1981, 4th impression 1981, 5th impression 1983; includes Appendix

The first 18 pages of this book give a brief autobiographical account of Reardon's introduction to the game of snooker, his life as a miner and then a policeman, and his subsequent career as a snooker player. This first section takes the reader up to the 1976 World Championship, where Reardon clinched his fifth World title, beating Alex Higgins 27-16 in the final. The majority of the book, however, is an instructional guide to the game with over 150 diagrams and illustrations. Chapter headings include 'Striking the Cue-Ball', 'Potting', 'Safety Play', 'Playing with Side' and so on. There is also an Appendix detailing two breaks made by Reardon; a 142 compiled at Pontardulais Conservative club and a 147 made at Pontin's Broadreeds Holiday Camp.

Value £4 - £8

4.16 Winning Snooker : with Eddie Charlton

Eddie Charlton	
1976	Macmillan, London
ISBN	0333210638
Hardback	112pp, col. ill., col. ports., 25 x 18cm
Notes	Foreword by Joe Davis; includes the text of the Billiards & Snooker Control Council's 'Rules of Snooker' and 'General Rules'; includes 'List of Lessons'
1978	Pan Books, London
ISBN	0330254839
Paperback	112pp, col. plates, 1 col. port., 25 x 18cm
Notes	As above; includes Snooker Terminology and Index

The 1st edition of this offering from Eddie Charlton has green boards with the title in silver on the spine and was published in hardback by Macmillan. There is a nice colourful photo spread over the frontispiece and title page of Charlton practicing the 'line-up' routine, with some of his trophies in the background. The book is heavily illustrated with colour photos and features all the expected topics as well as a 'Rules' chapter.

Value £4 - £8

4.17   **Snooker**

Fred Davis
1977   Adam & Charles Black, London
ISBN   0713617403
Hardback   95pp, ill., plates, ports., 22 x 14cm
Notes   One of Black's 'Picture Sports' series; includes Glossary

1983   A & C Black, London
ISBN   0713623608
Hardback   95pp, ill., plates, 21 x 13cm
Notes   2nd edition; as above

The majority of 'Snooker' by Fred Davis is an instructional guide to the game but also included are brief sections entitled 'History of the Game' and 'Useful Information' (comprising a book list and details of various snooker organisations). There are plenty of b & w photos of Davis and selected amateur players helping to illustrate the text where one useful tip is to "avoid shoes with slippery soles, as you often have to balance delicately on one leg". Black's 'Picture Sports' series included subjects such as fly fishing, badminton, skiing, volleyball etc.

Value   £3 - £5

4.18   **Winning Snooker**

W. G. Clifford / Geoff Martin (Ed.)
1981   W. Foulsham & Co., Slough
ISBN   0572011482
Paperback   64pp, ill., 19 x 13cm

'Winning Snooker' is a slim paperback that deals with tactics, doubles and pots, plants, building a break and so on. The final chapter, 'Snooker and more snooker', briefly describes the games of 'Short Snooker', 'Volunteer Snooker', and 'Real Snooker' – a game where after all the reds have been potted a player may take the yellow and then a colour, the green and then a colour and so on. The text is rather plain looking and is sparsely illustrated.

Value   £4 - £8

4.19   **How to Play Snooker**

Rex Williams
1982   Hamlyn, London
ISBN   0600350134
Hardback   61pp, ill., plates, ports., 25 x 18cm

Notes	Slightly amended version of **'Snooker : How To Become a Champion'**(see entry 4.14); Peter F. Chaplin (ill.); M. Athar Chaudhry (photog.); ISBN is incorrectly printed as 0600350135 on title page	
1988	Treasure Press, London	
ISBN	1850513031	
Hardback	61pp, ill., plates, 25 x 18cm	
Notes	As above; part of the 'How to Play Series'	

Rex Williams' instructional guide contains plenty of photos and illustrations to steer the amateur through the various lessons outlined in this publication. Tips for playing against the 'nap', plants and sets, safety play etc. are all featured, along with the basics such as stance and cue delivery.

Value £3 - £5

4.20 Successful Snooker

Steve Davis / Julian Worthington (Ed.)
1982	Charles Letts & Co. (in collaboration with World of Sport), London
ISBN	0850974372
Paperback	95pp, ill. (some col.), plates (some col.), 22 x 21cm
Notes	Reprinted 1982, 1985 and 1986; a 'Letts Guide'; Hayward Art Group (ill.); includes Index

Steve Davis won his first World Championship in 1981 and lost no time in getting some publications onto the nation's bookshelves. The 'Letts Guide' series were produced in collaboration with ITV's 'World of Sport' programme, retailed at £2.95 and included sports such as table tennis, track athletics and swimming. Davis breaks his snooker guide into five chapters – 'Equipment', 'Basic Techniques', 'Advanced Techniques', 'Planning' and 'Tactical Play' and all these are illustrated with colour diagrams and photographs. To engage the reader further, scattered throughout the chapters are text boxes called 'Hints on practice' where Davis describes various practice drills for the reader to attempt.

Value £3 - £5

4.21 The Complete Book of Snooker : incorporating Winning Snooker and Trick Shots

Eddie Charlton
1983	Macmillan, South Melbourne (Australia)
ISBN	0333356705
Hardback	191pp, ill., col. plates, col. ports., 25 x 19cm

Notes	Foreword by Les Wheeler; includes Index

1987	David & Charles, Newton Abbot
ISBN	0715387359
Hardback	191pp, col. ill., col. plates., 1 col. port., 25 x 19cm
Notes	As above

If you're going to buy a book on how to play snooker you might be better advised to opt for one written by Stephen Hendry or Steve Davis rather than 'steady' Eddie Charlton. However, this book is very comprehensive and incorporates two previous books by Charlton and is well illustrated in colour throughout. There is a 'Rules of Snooker' chapter at the rear of the book plus a brief list of honours under the headings 'My Life With Snooker' and 'Eddie Charlton's Record'.

Value　　　　　　　　　　　　　　　　　　　　　　　　　　　　　£4 - £8

4.22   Complete Snooker

Terry Griffiths / Julian Worthington
1984	Pelham Books, London
ISBN	0720715024
Hardback	128pp, ill. (some col.), plates (some col.), ports. (some col.), 29 x 22cm

1984	Pelham Books, London
ISBN	0720715024
Paperback	128pp, ill. (some col.), plates (some col.), ports. (some col.), 29 x 22cm
Notes	Reprinted 1985 and 1988

A photo of a smiling Terry Griffiths leaning on the baulk cushion of a snooker table adorns the frontispiece of this 'how-to-play' book published by the popular snooker publisher Pelham. Griffiths takes the reader through all aspects of the game with the aid of plenty of full-page table illustrations and a mixture of colour and b & w photos. The book begins with a brief history of the game (look out for a marvellous photo of Joe Davis and Tom Newman) and ends with the self-explanatory chapter 'The Future', where Griffiths generally talks about the growth of the sport, the increase in prize money, increased TV coverage and his hope that the women's game can develop further.

Value　　　　　　　　　　　　　　　　　　　　　　　　　　　　　£4 - £8

4.23   Dewch i Chwarae Snwcer (Come to Play Snooker)

Bob Dorkins
1984	Y Lolfa, Talybont

ISBN	0862430712
Paperback	84pp, ill. (mostly col.), plates, ports., 19 x 17cm
Notes	Reprinted 1987; part of the 'Come to Play' series; Introduction (Cyflwyniad) by Terry Griffiths; Glyn Rees (ill.); Marian Delyth (photog. and designer); David Muscroft (photog.); includes Glossary (Geirfa)

This Welsh language publication was written by Bob Dorkins who was North Wales Snooker Champion in 1978 and 1979 and the book was supported by the Welsh Books Council and the Arts Council for Wales. The book is mainly aimed at young children and youths who wish to learn about snooker through the medium of Welsh. The book is split into eight chapters – 'The Game', 'Standing Correctly', 'Pocketing', 'Cueing Difficulties', 'Spinning the Ball and Playing for Position', 'Snookering', 'Playing Safe', and 'Conclusion'. The first chapter outlines the history of snooker, explains the rules of the game and finally the importance of choosing an appropriate cue. The remaining chapters describe simply and clearly how to develop various skills and techniques. The text is supported by a large number of diagrams, cartoons and photos all reflecting the book's target audience, and the 'Come to Play' series featured other sports such as tennis, horse riding, netball and athletics.

Value £2 - £4

4.24 Snooker

Rex Williams
1984   Hamlyn, London
ISBN   0600347664
Paperback   61pp, ill., plates, 24 x 17cm
Notes   Originally published as **'How to Play Snooker'** (see entry 4.19); slightly amended version of **'Snooker : How to Become a Champion'**, (see entry 4.14); part of Hamlyn's 'Play the Game' series; Peter F. Chaplin (ill.); M. Athar Chaudhry (photog.)

This book is a fairly slim volume featuring many b & w photos and copious illustrations demonstrating all aspects of snooker. The book was part of Hamlyn's 'Play the Game' series that featured books on sports such as golf, tennis and squash.

Value £3 - £5

4.25 Teaching Material : No. 8 Snooker

The Two Can Project
1985   Two-Can Project, Derby

ISBN	095098518X
Unbound	53 leaves, ill., 30 x 21cm
[n.d.]	[Two-Can Project], [Derby]
ISBN	0948328118
Notes	2nd edition [data taken from subsequent editions]
[1987]	Two-Can Project, Derby
ISBN	0948328185
Unbound	53 leaves, ill., 30 x 21cm
Notes	3rd edition
1998	Two-Can Project, Derby
ISBN	094832838X
Spiral bound	52 leaves, ill., 30 x 21cm
Notes	4th edition

The Two-Can Project (whose logo was, predictably, a toucan), started in March 1982 and was jointly funded by Derbyshire County Council and the Manpower Services Commission. Its aim was to "assist profoundly deaf adults achieve greater independance [sic] and integration by obtaining literacy and information". Their 'Teaching Material' on snooker is certainly one of the quirkiest and most interesting series for the snooker fan to add to their collection but is extremely scarce. The first few editions had illustrated card covers and were bound by treasury tags and featured rather rudimentary drawings complete with special sign-language drawings for the deaf. The 1998 edition has bright yellow, illustrated card covers and is spiral bound. This edition has updated and improved drawings and has a slicker, more professional feel to it.

Value £20 - £30

4.26 Snooker

John Spencer / Clive Everton (Ed.)
1986	Teach Yourself Books, Sevenoaks
ISBN	0340393661
Paperback	147pp, ill., 20 x 13cm
Notes	Revised edition; previous edition published 1973 as **'Spencer on Snooker'** (see entry 4.12); 2nd impression 1986, 3rd impression 1987, 4th impression 1988; part of the 'Teach Yourself' Series; Duncan Mil (ill.); includes Index
1992	Hodder & Stoughton, London
ISBN	0340393661
Paperback	147pp, ill., 20 x 13cm
Notes	Reissue; includes Index

'Snooker' is a revised edition of Spencer's previous snooker book detailed in the Notes above. This paperback edition has ten extra pages and includes copious table diagrams and well drawn illustrations by Duncan Mil. The chapter entitled 'How it all Happened' included in the 1973 edition is absent from this revised edition. The book moves from the initial fundamental techniques through to a full discussion of the principles of shot selection, break-building, and safety and tactical play.

Value £2 - £4

4.27   Ten Steps to Snooker Success

[A. H. Smeeton]
[1986]   Apex Publishing, Southend-on-Sea
ISBN   None given
Paperback   69pp, [18]pp, ill., 22 x 15cm
Notes   Includes four Appendices – 'Glossary of Terms'; 'Tables'; 'The Rules'; and 'An Illustrated Frame'

This book by Smeeton has no title on the cover, is spiral bound and has orange card covers and is illustrated throughout with table diagrams. In the Introduction the author says whilst reading through a snooker manual he noted that the author claimed a player's cue action was better when playing a double than a normal pot. Taking this theory and applying it to his own game he quickly progressed from a high break in the 30s to one of 75! This quirky and lively manual has fourteen chapters covering the usual instructional material. But one interesting piece is the author's "Magic Method" - revealed as closing your eyes when making the final backswing when about to strike the ball. This book is very difficult to get hold of and rarely appears for sale.

Value £10 - £20

4.28   Cliff Thorburn's Snooker Skills

Cliff Thorburn / Peter Arnold (Ed.)
1987   Hamlyn, Twickenham
ISBN   0600552101
Paperback   127pp, ill. (mostly col.), plates (mostly col.), ports. (some col.), 27 x 20cm
Notes   2nd impression 1987; Peter Dazeley (photog.); includes Glossary and Index

Another former World Champion gives his instructions on how to play the game in this publication from Hamlyn. This book has all the usual topics and in addition features a brief section on trick shots. There is also a Glossary and a section called 'Some Points in the Rules'.

Value £3 - £5

4.29   **Improve Your Snooker**

Edward Horton / Clive Everton
1987   Willow Books, London
ISBN   0002182556
Hardback   144pp, col. ill., col. plates, col. ports., 29 x 25cm
Notes   Phil Evans (ill.); David Muscroft (photog.); includes Glossary and Index

1990   Willow Books, London
ISBN   0002183617
Paperback   144pp, col. ill., col. plates, col. ports., 28 x 24cm
Notes   1990 printing of the 1987 edition; reprinted 1992

1994   Willow Books, London
ISBN   0002183617
Paperback   144pp, col. ill., col. plates, col. ports., 28 x 24cm
Notes   1994 printing of the 1987 edition; Introduction and break analyses by Clive Everton; includes Glossary and Index

This instructional book from Willow Books is well illustrated and supported with table diagrams and colour photos from the David Muscroft Picture Library. On the reverse of the title page it states that the text was by Edward Horton with the Introduction and break analyses being supplied by Clive Everton. Apart from the standard elements there are sections on matchplay temperament, the mental game, and snooker rules. The book is bound in green cloth with gilt lettering to the spine and the dustjacket is predominantly white with colour pictures of Steve Davis, Jimmy White, Alex Higgins and Cliff Thorburn.

Value   £8 - £10

4.30   **Jimmy White's Snooker Masterclass**

Jimmy White / Charles Poole
1988   Queen Anne Press, London
ISBN   0356155838
Hardback   158pp, ill., 24 x 19cm
Notes   Foreword by Jimmy White

Jimmy White wrote his 'Masterclass' with his friend, Charlie Poole[10], and in the Foreword White states that they wanted their book to be different to other

---

10   On page 40 of his autobiography (see entry 1.19) White says of Charlie Poole that he rates him as one of the three greatest players ever – along with Patsy Houlihan and Alex Higgins - although Poole never played professionally.

instructional books and not to focus on the basics of the game. Because of this there are only a handful of pages devoted to the stance, cue action etc. and the remainder concentrates on more complicated shots and table positions. Given the above, the reader will find a lot of the table illustrations to be a lot more complex than those in most instructional manuals. One unusual chapter is called 'I Don't Know What to Practice', where White offers the reader over twenty different practice drills. This heavy book has black boards with gilt lettering to the spine and a picture of a smiling White on the jacket.

Value £4 - £8

4.31   Master Snooker

[N. A. Mitchell]
[1988]   [N. A. Mitchell], [Stafford]
ISBN   None given
Paperback   [15]pp, 21 x 15cm

This self-published book is wrapped in pale green card covers and simply stapled together. The contents include 'Causes of Movement' – "three-quarters of all missed shots are due to one fault; HEAD movement"; 'Cue Grip', 'Stance' and so on. The 'Cue Action' chapter states "the one thing that distinguishes a good player from an ordinary player is the cue action"; a view generally held to be true by all coaches and professionals. This is another of those slim paperback books (along with Brian Halter's 'How to Beat Your Dad at Snooker' – see entry 7.54) self-published in the 1980s that rarely, if ever, appear for sale.

Value £10 - £20

4.32   Matchroom Snooker

Julian Worthington
1988   Pelham Books, London
ISBN   0720718260
Hardback   168pp, col. ill., col. plates, ports., 29 x 22cm
Notes   Introduction by Barry Hearn; Guy Smith (ill.); Terry Trott (photog.); includes Appendices of 'Fact File' and 'Career Record'; includes Index

This is another snooker publication from Pelham, this time a heavy, chunky volume of 168 pages originally costing £14.95 and with a jacket picturing the Matchroom players wearing formal attire. After chapter introductions by Steve Davis, each of the Matchroom players takes the reader through various facets of snooker. The most fascinating part of the book is the Fact File chapter, where each player is quizzed on topics such as the cue they use and the snooker books they have read.

Value £4 - £8

4.33   **Play to Win : Snooker**

Jim Meadowcroft / John Hennessey
1988   Octopus Books, London
ISBN   0706431588
Hardback   80pp, ill. (mostly col.), col. plates, col. ports., 25 x 20cm
Notes   Includes a contribution from Frank Sandell; Klim Forster and Oxford Illustrators (ill.); includes Glossary and Index

In the Introduction to this book Jim Meadowcroft says "snooker is the easiest game in the world to play badly". In order for the reader to avoid playing badly the authors have covered the game completely, right from the equipment and basics to competing with pressure. Some sections are very in-depth (there are 3 pages devoted to choosing a cue and 6 to competing with pressure) and there are plenty of b & w line drawings and colour table diagrams to illustrate the points made. The last section is specifically dedicated to coaching juniors and this is written by Frank Sandell, a coach based near Worthing in Sussex.

Value   £3 - £5

4.34   **Frank Callan's Snooker Clinic**

Frank Callan / John Dee
1989   Partridge Press, London
ISBN   1852250690
Hardback   128pp, ill., plates, ports., 24 x 19cm
Notes   Preface by Steve Davis

The hugely respected snooker coach Frank Callan covers all aspects of the sport in this 1989 publication from the grip, via cue action, right through to the effect of the nap on the run of the balls. Perhaps the most readable sections are 'Davis v Davis', where Callan debates whether Joe or Steve Davis was the greater player, and 'The Doug Mountjoy Story', where Callan describes Mountjoy's remarkable renaissance after he approached the author for help in 1988. The book has plain black boards with the title in gilt running down the spine.

Rather astonishingly, a superb signed copy of this book realised £51 on eBay in May 2007; whereas another signed copy, described as very good with a very good dustjacket, made £16 in July 2007. A further copy available on eBay, also described as very good with a very good dustjacket, sold for £32 in September 2007.

Value   £15 - £20

4.35 **How to Play Snooker : a Step-by-Step Guide**

Liz French	
1990	Jarrold Publishing, Norwich
ISBN	0711705046
Paperback	47pp, col. ill., 17 x 16cm
Notes	Reprinted 1993 and 1995; technical consultant Albert Stewart; Malcolm Ryan (ill.); includes Glossary

There have been hardly any snooker books written by women and the last was this colourful book by Liz French published by Jarrold in 1990. As the author states in the Introduction, "this book takes you step by step through all the basics of the game, from how to choose a cue and how scoring works to developing your accuracy and practising to improve your technique". All this is demonstrated by plentiful colour diagrams (some featuring female players) and a Glossary on the final page. This is one of the scarcest modern snooker books and may take a bit of finding, although prices do not reflect its scarcity.

Value £3 - £5

4.36 **Play Snooker with Dennis Taylor**

Dennis Taylor / Clive Everton (Collab.) / Gordon Menzies (Ed.)	
1990	BBC Books, London
ISBN	0563360372
Paperback	119pp, ill., plates (some col.), ports. (some col.), 25 x 19cm
Notes	Foreword by Steve Davis; Mike Gilkes (ill.); includes Glossary and Index

Dennis Taylor's book was based on the BBC TV series[11] and all the usual topics are dealt with; plus there are brief pieces on wearing spectacles, the mental approach and coping with tension. The text is accompanied by diagrams and photos, the outstanding centre page double-spread photo of a packed Crucible Theatre being especially pleasing.

Value £3 - £5

4.37 **Snooker : the Fine Art Method**

Daniel Marner	
[1991]	[Daniel Marner], [Goole]

---

[11] In these programmes Dennis Taylor introduced the game of snooker in three series comprising six episodes each. The three series were shown on BBC2 and began on 8th April 1990, 25th October 1990 and 27th October 1992.

ISBN	0951708902
Paperback	82pp, ill., plates, 21 x 15cm
Notes	Geoff Moore (ill.); Graham Wragg (photog.); includes Index

The author of this book describes himself as "a frustrated old snooker player that only "sussed" it out after retirement". It's a pity he didn't "suss it out" a little earlier as this quirky, somewhat tongue-in-cheek instructional book offers an alternative view on how to play the game. Marner's principal tenet is that the cue ball should be 'speared', hence the abundance of illustrations throughout the work of a cue striking through an apple to remind the reader of this point. There are plenty of b & w photos in the book to aid the reader but sadly the blurb on the cover boasting that "the Fine Art Method of coaching snooker, will in time be the basis of all snooker coaching" has not come true. This book may prove difficult to track down and does not appear very often on eBay, Amazon or Abe due, I would imagine, to a small print run and the fact it was self-published.

Value £5 - £10

4.38 Snooker

Ken Williams	
1995	A & C Black, London
ISBN	0713636807
Paperback	48pp, col. ill., col. plates., 14 x 21cm
Notes	Part of the 'Know the Game' Series; Sylvio Dokov (photog.); includes Glossary and Index

2000	A & C Black, London
ISBN	0713652659
Paperback	48pp, ill. (mostly col.), col. plates, col. ports., 14 x 21cm
Notes	2nd edition; part of the 'Know the Game' Series; includes Glossary and Index

2002	A & C Black, London
ISBN	0713660015
Paperback	48pp, col. ill., col. plates., 14 x 21cm
Notes	3rd edition; Dave Saunders (ill.) / Ron Dixon (ill.); Sylvio Dokov (photog.); includes Glossary and Index

2006	A & C Black, London
ISBN	071367699X
Paperback	64pp, col. ill., col. plates, 20 x 13cm
Notes	4th edition; as above

The 'Know the Game' series of books began to feature snooker exclusively from 1995 onwards when the 1st edition was published and are one of the few instructional books still in print. Illustrated with colourful diagrams, they analyse all aspects of play and include a Glossary and Index. The latest (4th) edition published in 2006 has been given a complete revamp. The rather awkward oblong shape has been replaced by a more practical size and the book has added subject matter. These new sections include 'A Brief History of Snooker', details of the World Champions 1927-2005, details of maximum breaks made between 1992-2005, and a 1 page feature on the W. P. B. S. A and World Snooker.

Value out of print eds. £2 - £3
in print (2006 ed.) £6.99

4.39 Snooker Masterclass

Stephen Hendry
1995   Bloomsbury Publishing, London
ISBN   074751870X
Hardback   128pp, col. ill., col. plates, col. ports., 25 x 20cm
Notes   Includes Glossary

1996   Bloomsbury Publishing, London
ISBN   0747531439
Paperback   128pp, col. ill., col. plates, col. ports., 24 x 19cm
Notes   As above

Before Bloomsbury launched the publishing phenomena that are J. K. Rowling's 'Harry Potter' books, part of their list included instructional snooker books! Stephen Hendry gives his own take on how to play the game and, apart from the usual subjects, there are chapters dedicated to 'The Tactical Approach' and 'The Mental Approach'. The text is fully supported throughout with colour diagrams and there is a lovely photo of Hendry on page 47 playing against Steve Davis in the desert with a man and his camel looking on. Collectors should note that there is also an undated paperback edition that the British Library catalogue as a 1995 publication with a 1996 printing.

Value £3 - £5

4.40 Just One Frame : Your Key to Playing Better Snooker

David Jenner
1998   David Jenner, Maidstone
ISBN   0955085101
Ring Bound 83pp, ill. (mostly col.), 19 x 14cm / 16 x 11cm
Notes   Foreword by Dave Brocking

This highly unusual and imaginative book is held in a ring bound folder rather like a Filofax, the folder measuring 19 x 14cm but the book itself 16 x 11cm. The package also includes a pen and a 'Snooker Targets' card where the player can record, for example, the number of blacks potted off the spot and improve this over time. Chapter headings include 'Back to Basics', 'Sharpen Your Technique' and 'Playing for Position'. The different sections of the publication are printed on different coloured pages and there are a few diagrams scattered throughout. Incidentally, the author at the time of publication was Chairman of the Kent County Billiards & Snooker Association. For more information on how to purchase this book, see www.justoneframe.com.

Value in print £20

4.41 The Audacia Performance Plan : the Definitive Snooker Manual for Players of All Ages

Darren Copp
2001   Audacia, Swansea
ISBN   None given
Ring bound   109pp, ill. (mostly part col.), 30 x 21cm
Notes   Reprinted 2002

'The Audacia Performance Plan' was designed to help all snooker players improve their game and is a ring bound publication of 109 pages. The Plan is divided into six programmes, each one named after the six colours used in the game. The first programme, 'Yellow', takes in aspects of snooker such as break-building and safety play; whilst the final programme, 'Black', deals with topics including judgement of pace and playing with the rest. There are numerous exercises right through the book and progress sheets to monitor development.

Value £10 - £15

4.42 The Snooker Exercise Challenge

F. C. Adamson
2001   F. C. Adamson, [Bristol]
ISBN   None given
Paperback   23pp, col. ill., 30 x 21cm

'The Snooker Exercise Challenge' was written and published by Frank Adamson and, as the title makes clear, contains numerous snooker exercises for the reader to make his or her way through. Each exercise is illustrated with a colour diagram and is accompanied by clear instructions.

Value £10 - £15

4.43 The Audacia Junior Blueprint

Darren Copp
2002   Audacia, Swansea
ISBN   None given
Ring bound   149pp, ill. (mostly part col.), col. plates, col. ports., 30 x 21cm

'The Audacia Junior Blueprint' "contains everything that a young player would need in order to start becoming successful at snooker". So says the author in his second instructional snooker publication. The manual uses two Welsh Junior players, Perry Foster and Nathan Biggs, to demonstrate aspects of play such as gripping the cue, stance, the bridge hand, and using the spider. However, the bulk of the publication is a series of exercises to guide the player right through all aspects of the game.

Value   £10 - £15

Pictured is 'Dewch i Chwarae Snwcer', the only Welsh language snooker guide published to date. Even though copies appear to be relatively uncommon they only sell for £2-£4 when they do appear for sale. See entry 4.23.

'How to Play Snooker and Other Pool Games' was published by C. Arthur Pearson in 1924. The book now sells for £10-£15 without the dustjacket, considerably more if the jacket is present. See entry 4.2.

'Snooker : How to Improve Your Play' is a common early snooker title that was issued by Athletic Publications of London. The book now commands £15-£20 in very good condition. See entry 4.3.

'How to Play and Win at Snooker' was first published by W. Foulsham in the late 1930s. Copies with the brightly coloured dustjacket now sell for a modest £10-£15 in very good condition. See entry 4.7.

Joe Davis had several billiards and snooker titles published and this effort was first published by Country Life in 1949. The book has a very attractive dustjacket and very good copies with this present now command £20-£30. See entry 4.8.

John Pulman's 1965 book 'Tackle Snooker This Way' was published by Stanley Paul and copies can easily be picked up for £10-£15 complete with the jacket. See entry 4.10.

Numerous World Champions have had instructional snooker guides published. Pictured here is Cliff Thorburn's 1987 book 'Cliff Thorburn's Snooker Skills', and Stephen Hendry's 1995 work 'Snooker Masterclass'. Both sell for £3-£5 in very good condition. See entries 4.28 and 4.39.

~ Billiards & Snooker – Instructional ~

~ Pre 1945 ~

5.0   **Billiards and Snooker**

Arthur F. Peall
1928	Frederick Warne & Co., London
Paperback	64pp, ill., 19 x 13cm
Notes	Reprinted 1932, 1933, 1935, 1936 and 1939; one of Warne's 'Recreation' Books (no. 16)

1943	Frederick Warne & Co., London
Paperback	64pp, ill., 19 x 13cm
Notes	8th edition; one of Warne's 'Recreation' Books

1947	Frederick Warne & Co., London
Paperback	64pp, ill., 19 x 13cm
Notes	9th edition; one of Warne's 'Recreation' Books

1949	Frederick Warne & Co., London
Paperback	64pp, ill., 19 x 13cm
Notes	10th edition; one of Warne's 'Recreation' Books

This instructional guide from Arthur Peall is very similar in size, length and original price to Joe Davis' 'How to Pot a Ball' (see entry below), although Peall's book has a wider scope and more detail. The colourful cover, drawn by Gordon Robinson, shows a player at the table and the rear cover has a wonderful period advert for 'Ovaltine'. Peall's book is split into six chapters - 'Preliminary Hints', 'Striking a Ball', 'Hazard-Striking', 'Cannons', 'Using Side and Screw', and 'Snooker Pool'. The book achieves the aim of the 'Recreation' series which was to "give a brief outline of the main principles and rules of each [sport or pastime] ... and also give hints on points of etiquette customary with the game".

Collectors should note that reprints from either 1936 or 1939 onwards had a new cover to previous editions. Peall's book was number 16 in Warne's 'Recreation' Books series, a series that included golf, cricket, football and boxing. Incidentally, Frederick Warne is most closely associated with the works of Beatrix Potter, the company publishing the first trade edition of 'Peter Rabbit' in 1902.

Value   **£20 - £25**

5.1   **How to Pot a Ball**

Joe Davis
[1932]   Wright & Brown, London
Paperback   61pp, ill., 19 x 13cm

This slim paperback volume originally sold for 6d. and has a bright red, white and green cover. The reverse of the front cover features an advert for 'The Joe Davis Snooker Cue' and the back cover has adverts for the publisher's books. The simple premise of the book is contained in the title and Davis states in his Introduction that "I have no space here to go into such important matters as stance, bridge, cue-hold and cue-delivery". The book covers both billiards and snooker and each shot described is accompanied by an illustration.

Value   £15 - £25

5.2   **Learn to Become a Good Billiards and Snooker Player : by Following the Instructions Given Here**

Tom Newman
[1935]   No publisher details given
Paperback   30pp, ill., 1 plate, 1 port., 18 x 12cm
Notes   Cover title is 'How to Play on your Home-size
                Billiard Table'

Originally selling for 1/-, this slim volume has an attractive green, black and white cover. No publisher details are given so it may well have been included with the 'Tom Newman Billiard Table' (as the cover title would suggest) an advert for which features on page 5. Alternatively, as the book had a 1/- price it may also have been sold separately for players who already owned home tables. The book is firmly focussed on Home-size tables – "small-table billiards and snooker are great home games" – and the text is supported by a few illustrations to help the reader along.

Value   £30 - £50

5.3   **Billiards and Snooker for Amateur Players**

Horace Lindrum
1937   Penguin Books, Harmondsworth
Paperback   119pp, ill., 18 x 12cm
Notes   Introduction by Melbourne Inman; Penguin Books no. 119

Penguin books was set up in 1935 by Allen Lane after his employer, The Bodley Head, rejected his idea of publishing cheap paperback imprints. Penguin's first titles were sold for sixpence, and Lindrum's book is no exception. The use of different colours was adopted to signify different subject matter – orange for fiction, green for crime etc. This book is in the rarer lemon yellow colour, a famous example of which is 'The Compleat Angler' by Izaak Walton published in 1939. There are two standard book sizes used for paperbacks, A and B Format, and this book is a Format A type (measuring exactly 181 x 111mm). This book includes the original 'Penguin' logo, the tripartite division of the cover (devised by Edward Young) and employs a Bodoni Ultra Bold type-face for the publisher's name and Gills Sans for the remainder of the cover and spine information.

'Billiards and Snooker for Amateur Players' was number 119 in the Penguin series and followed the early pattern of having a thin dustjacket replicating the information found on the card covers (although the price was printed on the dustjacket only). Penguin also used any spare pages at the end of books to advertise their own books and in keeping with this there are 6 pages of lists of Penguin titles at the rear. Illustrated with 40 diagrams this book is a real gem for the collector and perhaps the reason it is not more valuable is that early Penguins proved so popular they had massive print runs - according to Phil Baines early fiction titles sold 40,000 copies in 3-4 months and political 'Specials' 100,000 copies in weeks.

Value   £5 - £10

5.4   **Billiards and Snooker : Volunteer Snooker-Pool-Russian Pool-Pyramids : How To Play Well**

B. Scriven
[1938]   Universal Publications, London
Paperback   90pp, ill., 17 x 11cm

[1940]   Universal Publications, London
Paperback   90pp, ill., 17 x 11cm
Notes   Universal Publications book no. 39

[1941]   Universal Publications, London
Paperback   90pp, ill., 17 x 11cm
Notes   Universal Publications book no. 39

[1956]   Universal Publications, London
Paperback   90pp, ill., 17 x 11cm
Notes   Re-issue of 1938 edition; Universal Publications book no. 39

No date of publication is given on the title page of the 1st edition so I assume the British Library have got the probable date of 1938 from the publisher's catalogue included in the book. Scriven's book is last on this list and the preceding three titles were all published in 1938 so their estimate would appear to be correct.

This is a pocket-sized book with fifteen chapters covering, amongst other subjects, 'The Equipment', 'The Play', 'How a Game is Played', and 'Attitude and Position'. The chapter on snooker begins with the lines "it is easy to see why snooker is so

83

tremendously popular. First, it demands almost all the skill of billiards and it offers a good deal more variety". This sentence could sum up the gradual demise of billiards and the rise of snooker, variety being the key word. The snooker section covers 11 pages and after that volunteer snooker, pool, Russian pool and pyramids are examined.

There are some adverts for intriguing products at the rear of the book, including the games of Snooker-Dice, the U.P.L. Beetle Game (in the 1956 edition it claims that 6.3 million of these have been sold), Scats and a book entitled 'School Yarns and Howlers'. The 1st edition has card covers and was issued with a predominantly green and blue jacket. Some later editions were printed on bright pink paper, and some editions were issued with a richly coloured red, white and blue dustjacket.

Value £15 - £25

5.5 Billiards and Snooker Strokes

Riso Levi
[1940]   R. Levi, Wilmslow
Hardback   260pp, ill., 22 x 14cm

'Billiards & Snooker Strokes' is bound in green cloth, has the title and author in gilt in the top left corner and has a white dustjacket that, unfortunately, the collector will find very elusive; virtually every copy coming up for sale does not include the jacket. There are 43 short chapters in the book and Levi states in the Preface his reason for writing it is "... because allied to my enthusiasm for the game, there is, to me, a very real pleasure in writing about it". Levi certainly must have gained pleasure from writing about billiards and snooker because it would appear from the sheer volume of his work on the games that he spent most of his adult life engaged in writing about them.

The first snooker chapter, 'The Popularity of Snooker', begins with a piece called 'How to Kill Safety Play' and is included because the Doncaster player, Sidney Smith, warns that "I am very much afraid that unless the professionals wake up to the fact that excessive safety play can turn a great entertainment into a drab imitation of a spectacle, the popularity of snooker will quickly fade". The remainder of the snooker section features tips on snooker strokes and snooker problems; and the billiards material is standard Levi fare.

A lot comprising two copies of Levi's work, with the cloth a little rubbed, realised a price of £250 at the Dominic Winter July 2006 auction, against a rather low estimate of £70-£100.

Value £80 - £120

~ Post 1945 ~

5.6 **Billiards and Snooker for Amateurs**

    Horace Lindrum
    1948   Sir Isaac Pitman & Sons, London
    Hardback   xvii, 119pp, ill., 1 plate, 1 port., 20 x 13cm
    Notes   Reprinted 1955, 1957 and 1962 (the latter with a revamped dustjacket); part of the 'Games and Recreations' series; includes a chapter by Melbourne Inman

This book is a fully revised and re-arranged version of Lindrum's earlier book 'Billiards and Snooker for Amateur Players' published by Penguin in 1937 (see entry 5.3). This edition, with slightly shortened title, has pale blue boards with the title and author printed on the cover and spine in a darker blue and a simple yet effective green and white dustjacket. The rear of the book has a short listing of Pitman's other sports and leisure titles.

The Introduction by C. D. Dimsdale has a useful discussion of billiards and snooker and a few anecdotes, the subjects of which are chiefly Joe Davis and Horace Lindrum. Chapter one, entitled 'A Veteran's Tribute to Youth', is by Melbourne Inman and includes brief pieces on John Roberts ("the greatest showman I have ever seen in the game"), big breaks and nursery cannons. Perhaps the highlight of this section is the splendid cartoon of Inman drawn by Tom Webster the former Daily Mail cartoonist. The rest of the book has instructional text and full-page table diagrams covering all the various facets of both games.

Value   £15 - £20

5.7 **Billiards and Snooker**

    [Billiards Association & Control Council]
    1954   Educational Productions, London
    Paperback   32pp, ill. (some part col.), 1 plate, 14 x 21cm
    Notes   Foreword by P. B. Fisher; part of the 'Know the Game' series; produced in collaboration with the Billiards Association & Control Council

    1955   Educational Productions, London
    Paperback   32pp, ill. (some part col.), 1 plate, 14 x 21cm
    Notes   2nd edition; as above; print run of 10,000

    1956   Educational Productions, London
    Paperback   32pp, ill. (some part col.), 1 plate, 14 x 21cm
    Notes   3rd edition, revised; as above; print run of 10,000

    1959   Niblick Publishing, [London]

Paperback	32pp, ill. (some part col.), 1 plate, 14 x 21cm
Notes	4th edition; as above; Foreword by W. E. Chappell; published by Niblick for Educational Productions

1965	E. P. Publishing, London
SBN	715801066
Paperback	36pp, ill. (some part col.), 1 plate, 14 x 21cm
Notes	5th edition; as above; Foreword by Harold Phillips (later printings of the 5th edition had a Foreword by Jack Karnehm)

1972	E. P. Publishing, Wakefield
ISBN	0715801066
Paperback	36pp, ill. (some part col.), 14 x 21cm
Notes	6th edition, revised; Foreword by Len Oldham; part of the 'Know the Game' series; produced in collaboration with the Billiards & Snooker Control Council

1973	E. P. Group, Wakefield
ISBN	0715801066
Paperback	36pp, ill. (some part col.), 14 x 21cm
Notes	8th edition; reprinted 1974; Foreword by W. H. Cottier; part of the 'Know the Game' series; produced in collaboration with the Billiards & Snooker Control Council

1974	E. P. Publishing, Wakefield
ISBN	0715801066
Paperback	36pp, ill. (some part col.), 14 x 21cm
Notes	9th edition; reprinted 1976, 1978, 1979 and 1980; Foreword by W. H. Cottier; part of the 'Know the Game' series; produced in collaboration with the Billiards & Snooker Control Council

1982	E. P. Publishing, Wakefield
ISBN	0715808214
Paperback	36pp, ill., plates, 14 x 21cm
Notes	3rd revised edition; reprinted 1984 with new ISBN of 0713625708; also reprinted 1985, 1986 and 1987; Foreword by W. H. Cottier and Stan Brooke; part of the 'Know the Game' series; produced in collaboration with the Billiards & Snooker Control Council

Most collectors and dealers refer to this book as 'Know the Game' and a large number of different sports were covered in the series including netball, cycling, show jumping and fencing. The book is oblong in shape and has a wonderful period cover illustrated in red, green, black and white showing a player about to pot a red ball. There are an abundance of illustrations scattered right through the book, all helping to explain the shot-to-nothing, snookering, the opening shots etc. that are all referred to in the book.

This book went through numerous editions and reprints but the contents changed remarkably little throughout. The bibliographic data is shown on the rear cover of early editions and the 1954 edition had a print run of 15,000. This high figure probably explains why it comes up for sale so regularly on eBay. The 1959 (4th) edition comprised four different printings with the covers being the main difference. The first printing states the total copies printed was 47,000, the 2nd printing stating 53,000, the 3rd printing stating 66,000 and the 4th printing has a proper title page and has been expanded to 36 pages. Later printings of this 4th edition have the price of 2/6 Net in the bottom right corner and an illustration of a footballer on the reverse of the rear cover. There were also three printings of the 1965 (5th) edition, with the total copies printed numbered on the respective editions as 122,000, 150,000, and 162,000. The 1974 edition has a fantastic advert on the reverse of the rear cover featuring a game called 'Snooker Express' manufactured by Subbuteo and following the same flicking principles as the football version.

Value   £2 - £3

5.8 Teach Yourself Billiards and Snooker

Richard Holt
1957   The English Universities Press, London
Hardback   x, 214pp, ill., plates, 18 x 12cm
Notes   Reprinted 1961, 1963, 1964 and 1967; part of the 'Teach Yourself Books' series; includes Billiards Index and Snooker Index

1969   The English Universities Press, London
SBN   340055235
Hardback   xi, 214pp, ill., 18 x 11cm
Notes   Revised impression; new impressions published 1970 and 1972; part of the 'Teach Yourself Books' series; includes Billiards Index and Snooker Index

1974   Teach Yourself Books, London
ISBN   0340190825
Paperback   xi, 212pp, ill., 18 x 11cm
Notes   2nd edition; 2nd impression 1975, 3rd impression 1977, 4th impression 1978, 5th impression 1980, 6th impression 1981, 7th impression 1982, 8th impression 1983, 9th impression 1983; part of the 'Teach Yourself Books' series; includes Billiards Index and Snooker Index

The 'Teach Yourself' series of books, originally published by The English Universities Press (EUP), cover a wide range of subjects and are still in print today. The 1st edition of Holt's work has blue boards with the EUP logo embossed onto the front board with a green jacket with white lettering that features a b & w shot of Robert

Marshall, three times World Amateur Billiards champion. Holt was an Editor of 'The Billiard Player' and 'Billiards and Snooker' magazines, and has packed a considerable amount of information and knowledge into this instructional book. Luckily, the two indexes make it easy for the reader to pick and choose areas to study. This book has gone through several editions and revised impressions, each book normally in a different format and with a new cover. For example, the 1974 2nd edition is a paperback with a cover photograph of Ray Reardon at play against Eddie Charlton. The editions of the late 1960s and early 1970s are especially attractive, having striking yellow and black dustjackets. A very good 1st edition, with a dustjacket with slight foxing, edge wear and small tears, realised £14 on eBay in August 2007.

Value £10 - £15

5.9   **Official Coaching Guide to the Games of English Billiards and Snooker**

Billiards Association & Control Council
[1970]   B. A. & C. C., London
ISBN   None given
Paperback   [24]pp, ill., 13 x 9cm
Notes   Authorised by the B. A. & C. C.

As the title suggests, this small booklet was intended for coaches "taking part in the National Coaching Scheme put into operation by the Billiards Association and Control Council on February 2nd, 1970". The purpose of the scheme was to teach young people the fundamentals of the game and encourage participation in billiards and snooker. The 16 pages of illustrations help the coach with ideas on what to include in their instructional sessions with the youngsters. The book has pale green card covers and for a relatively modern book is quite scarce.

Value £15 - £25

5.10   **Billiards and Snooker**

Jack Karnehm
1973   Pelham Books, London
ISBN   0720703603
Hardback   119pp, ill., plates, 23 x 14cm
Notes   2nd impression April 1973, 3rd impression December 1973, 4th impression January 1975, 5th impression June 1979; Foreword by the Earl of Mexborough

Jack Karnehm was a former Chairman of the Billiards Association and Control Council and was also responsible for founding a National Coaching Scheme for billiards and snooker. This volume is a very detailed study of both games all amply illustrated with 24 photos and 30 line drawings interspersed throughout the text.

The final chapter is called 'The Billiards-Snooker Partnership' and contains some reminiscences of Karnehm's frequent overseas trips to play and coach.

Value £4 - £8

5.11 Horace Lindrum's Snooker, Billiards and Pool

Horace Lindrum
1974	Paul Hamlyn, Dee Why West (New South Wales, Australia)
ISBN	0600072843
Hardback	144pp, ill., plates (some col.), ports., 29 x 21cm
Notes	Title is '**Pool, Snooker and Billiards**'; includes Index and Glossary

1974	Paul Hamlyn, Dee Why West (New South Wales, Australia)
ISBN	0600072843
Hardback	144pp, ill., plates (some col.), ports., 29 x 21cm
Notes	Reprinted 1975

1977	Paul Hamlyn, Dee Why West (New South Wales, Australia)
ISBN	0727101056
Paperback	144pp, plates (some col.), ports., 29 x 21cm
Notes	4th impression; includes Index

1979	Hamlyn, London
ISBN	0600384071
Hardback	156pp, ill., plates (some col.), ports., 29 x 21cm
Notes	Revised edition; reprinted 1980; includes Index

1980	Hamlyn, London
ISBN	0600384071
Hardback	156pp, ill. (some col.), 29cm x 21cm
Notes	Reprint of the revised edition (see above)

This book was originally published in Australia in 1974, the year that Horace Lindrum died, with the title of "Pool, Snooker and Billiards". Hamlyn published the 1979 revised edition and the white boards they chose to bind the book are, unfortunately, prone to discolouration. The predominantly green dustjacket features a photo of an ageing Lindrum that is repeated in b & w on the title page. As well as the 'how to play' aspect other chapters include an informative 'Origin & History', 'the Great Snooker Players', 'American Billiard games', and 'Billiards & Snooker around the World'. In addition, there is a rules section that was not included in the 1st edition. There are some fascinating photos in the book, picturing players of the past such as Clark McConachy, Sidney Smith and Walter Donaldson. [description based on 1979 revised edition].

Value £4 - £8

5.12   **Better Billiards and Snooker**

Clive Everton
1975   Kaye & Ward, London
ISBN   0718214412
Hardback   90pp, ill., plates, 23 x 19cm
Notes   Peter F. Chaplin (ill.); includes General Glossary, Snooker Glossary and Billiards Glossary, and Useful Addresses

1981   Kaye & Ward, London
ISBN   0718214412
Hardback   90pp, ill., plates, 23 x 19cm
Notes   As above; revised edition

1985   Kaye & Ward, London
ISBN   0718214803
Paperback   90pp, ill., plates, 23 x 19cm
Notes   As above; revised edition; reprinted 1986

Clive Everton's book begins with a chapter on 'Basic Rules' and ends with one called 'Snooker : Doubles, Sets, Plants and Hints on Match Play'. In between the reader is guided through all aspects of billiards and snooker and the text is amply illustrated by line drawings and photos of the author and Willie Thorne at the table. The book is bound in burgundy cloth and has silver lettering to the spine. Some copies of the 1981 revised edition have an ISBN of 0718214722 but this would appear to be a misprint as other copies have a sticker placed over them with the correct ISBN printed on them.

Value   £4 - £8

5.13   **Understanding Billiards and Snooker**

Jack Karnehm
1976   Pelham Books, London
ISBN   0720708605
Hardback   127pp, ill., plates, 26 x 20cm
Notes   Part of the Pelham Pictorial Sports Instruction Series; Roger Blake and Tom Finnane (photogs.)

1983   Pelham Books, London
ISBN   0720714559
Paperback   127pp, ill., plates (some col.), 25 x 19cm
Notes   2nd edition; reprinted 1984 and 1988; as above; as adopted by the Billiards & Snooker Foundation

There are only 28 pages of this book devoted to billiards, reflecting the decline of the game and the rise of snooker as a popular sport during the 1970s. This is an annual-sized hardback with pictorial boards, illustrated with b & w photos, that should not prove too difficult for the collector to track down. Other sports featured in the series included rugby, boxing, table tennis, soccer, golf, cricket, women's hockey and squash rackets.

Value   £4 - £8

5.14   **Billiards and Snooker**

Ian Morrison
1988   Ward Lock, London
ISBN   0706366581
Paperback   80pp, ill., plates, ports., 23 x 17cm
Notes   Reprinted 1989, 1990 and 1992; Foreword by Stan Brooke; part of Ward Lock's 'Play the Game' series; Peter Bull Art (ill.); includes Index and Useful Addresses

Ian Morrison's publication was endorsed by the Billiards & Snooker Control Council and was part of Ward Lock's 'Play the Game' series that encompassed such sports as American football, badminton, squash and bowls. 'Billiards and Snooker' is split roughly equally between the two games and covers equipment and terminology, and technique and rules. A nice feature is that the rules sections are arranged in a Q & A format. There are plenty of illustrations and photos throughout and the pictorial cover is a mixture of bright yellow, green, red and blue.

Value   £2 - £4

5.15   **Snooker, Billiards and Pool**

Ian Morrison / Terry Smith
1988   Hamlyn, London
ISBN   0600557375
Paperback   32pp, col. ill., col. plates, 27 x 21cm
Notes   Part of the Hamlyn 'Colourfax' series; Karel Feuerstein (ill.); ISBN is incorrectly printed as 0600557383 on page 32; includes Index

This charming book is firmly aimed at younger readers and the text is accompanied by colour photos of children playing on a 6ft x 3ft table. The decision to include billiards is somewhat surprising but this section only comprises 2 pages as does the pool section. There were a further ten titles in the 'Colourfax' series and this publication can be difficult to hunt down, presumably because many children didn't look after their copies or threw them away, but does not command high prices.

Value   £2 - £3

5.16 **Snooker and Billiards : Technique · Tactics · Training**

Clive Everton
1991   The Crowood Press, Marlborough
ISBN   1852234806
Paperback   124pp, col. ill., col. plates, col. ports., 25 x 19cm
Notes   Part of the Crowood Sports Guides Series; Taurus Graphics (ill.); Eric Whitehead (photog.); includes General Glossary and Snooker Glossary; Appendix – 'Snooker & Billiards Tournaments'; and Index

2002   The Crowood Press, Marlborough
ISBN   1852234806
Paperback   124pp, col. ill., col. plates, col. ports., 25 x 19cm
Notes   As above; 2002 impression

This offering from Clive Everton was first published in 1991 and over 15 years later is one of the few instructional books still in print. The book is a standard run-through of the equipment, rules, and technique and skills of snooker and billiards; and numerous colour photos and illustrations guide the reader through the various shots and practice drills recommended by the author. Crowood publish numerous books covering a wide range of sports.

Value   in print £9.99

5.17 **Some Basics of Billiards and Snooker**

Peter J. Payne
2001   Mark E. Mytton, [Huntingdon]
ISBN   None given
Spiral bound 32pp, col. ill., 1 port., 30 x 21cm
Notes   Includes Glossary of Terms

In the Introduction to this book it says that the diagrams and notes were first made by Peter Payne in 1979 and have since been updated and computerised. Throughout the book the text is accompanied by well-presented colour diagrams and there are sections on billiards and snooker practice, basic billiards, behaviour of the balls etc. The author was born in Bedford in 1924 and first started playing billiards and snooker in 1974 and was present when Joe Davis made a 147 break at snooker in 1955.

Value   £5 - £10

Joe Davis published numerous billiards and snooker books and pictured above is his 1932 book 'How to Pot a Ball'. The volume now sells for £15-£25. See entry 5.1.

Scriven's book was first published in 1938 with a brightly coloured blue, green and white dustjacket. Later editions have an even brighter jacket in red, white and blue. The first edition now sells for £15-£25 complete with the jacket. See entry 5.4.

Tom Newman's slim paperback book has a colourful cover in black, green and white and is valued at £30-£50. See entry 5.2.

~ BILLIARDS ~

~ 18th Century ~

6.0   **A Treatise on Billiards, With Instructions and Rules**

John Dew
1779   J. F. & C. Rivington[12] et al, London
Hardback   52pp, ill., 16 x 10cm
Notes   2nd edition published in 1808

The title page of this book says of the author that he is a marker, "well known to be experienced in the practical as well as theoretical Parts of Billiards, upwards of Thirty Years"; and that certainly made John Dew well placed to pen one of the earliest books concerning billiards. Reading through this book takes a bit of getting used to as the language and spelling are, understandably for a book almost 230 years old, somewhat antiquated. The book is primarily a rule book with the white winning and losing games, and Carambole winning and losing games detailed. On page 30 the rules of a rather bizarre game called Fortification Billiards begins. These rules are illustrated by two copper plates showing where the 'forts' (or castles) should be placed on the table. Each of the forts has an arch cut into it large enough for a ball to pass through and the game proceeds from this starting point. The final third of the book is taken up with 'Odds at Billiards' tables and the final page states that the author "may be heard of, by enquiring at the Half Moon, Clipftone [Clipstone] Street, near Portland Road".

The British Library copy of this small, pocket-sized book has faded red, white and blue marbled effect boards with a brown calf spine. I imagine this copy has been re-bound at some point as the book is in remarkably good condition for its age. According to 'The Amateur Billiard Player' of November 1997 there is probably only one other copy of this book surviving and that sold for £1,035 (including the 15% premium) at Bloomsbury Book Auctions in 1997. Because of the recent buoyancy in the sports memorabilia market if it came up for sale again it would almost certainly exceed that price.

Value   £1,000+

---

12   For more information on Charles Rivington and his sons, John and James, see en.wikipedia.org/wiki/Charles_Rivington

~ 19th Century ~

6.1   Game of Billiards

'An Amateur'
1801   T. Hurst, London
Hardback   72pp, ill., 14 x 9cm

This book has a fabulous fold-out frontispiece showing a group of gentlemen enjoying a game of billiards whilst another is asleep on a chair in the corner of the room. Probably the most interesting section of the book for the collector is the short 'Historical Description of the Game of Billiards'. After this the standard rules and instruction follows, plus Tables of Odds. The British Library copy has been re-bound in dark green boards with leather trim.

Value   £800 - £1,000

6.2   A Philosophical Essay on the Game of Billiards

'An Amateur'
[1806]   No publisher details, [Bath] or [London?]
[Hardback]   iv, pp5-59, [2]pp, pp2-44, 22 x 13cm
Notes   Includes Errata

There is no date of publication in the copy of this book that I have seen but most libraries seem to date it at 1806. On library catalogues it also normally states that the work is signed by Philobill but the photocopy I have seen wasn't. There are also no publisher details available in the book but it does state that it was *printed* by W. Meyler of Bath. The author says in the Introduction that "it is not supposed, that a perusal of the following pages can be of any use to a *good player* . . . neither is it expected, that a *novice* in the game will derive much advantage from it". This was rather a strange statement to make as it naturally begs the question of who exactly the book was intended for?! The text is a rather scientific discussion of the sport and there are a few diagrams at the rear to illustrate the points made. [description based on a photocopy].

Value   £800 - £1,000

6.3   A Practical Treatise on the Game of Billiards

E. White
1807   W. Miller, London
Hardback   vii, 212pp, ill., 19 x 13cm

1818   T. M'Lean, London
Hardback   vii, [40]pp, 212pp, ill., 20 x 13cm
Notes   New edition

That this is one of the earliest billiards books is demonstrated by the author saying on page v. that "... no work on the game of Billiards had hitherto made its appearance in this country ..." The 16 pages of illustrations are placed separately from the text at the end of the volume so there is a lot of flicking between pages for the reader who wishes to master the white winning game or learn about angles and hazards. There are quite a few mathematical equations towards the back of the book and several 'what if' scenarios. There is also a 4 page catalogue for William Miller books at the rear of the 1st edition. The British Library copy of this book may have been re-bound and has dark brown boards with black leather corners and a black spine. There are also copies with marbled boards, marbled endpapers and a leather spine. There appear to be two variant editions of the 1818 publication as some have the 40 un-numbered pages at the front and others at the back.

A copy of the 1st edition sold at a 'buy it now' price of £575 on eBay in August 2006, although the seller may have regretted their decision as copies would normally sell for substantially higher than that.

Value   **£850+**

6.4   **A New Guide and Companion to the Billiard Table**

'An Amateur'
1829   Effingham Wilson / Madeley, London
[Hardback]   vii, [2]pp, pp10-34, ill., 19 x 13cm

The cover title of this publication is just 'Billiards' with a date of 1830 above and it was published jointly by two publishers. However, the title page shows a much longer title (only the first part of which is noted above) with a date of 1829. The decorative frontispiece shows the interior of a billiard room with several well-attired gentlemen either watching the game in progress or else milling around talking. After two brief pieces entitled 'Introduction' and 'Historic Account of the Game of Billiards', there then follows an extensive rules section. This part of the publication includes accounts of the White Losing Game, Bricole, Carambole, the Bar Hole, the Four Game, and others. There is one tiny illustration in the book on page 33 that depicts where the ball should be struck to execute certain strokes; after this follows a series of table diagrams further demonstrating various strokes of play. [description based on a photocopy].

Value   **£800 - £1,000**

6.5 The Noble Game of Billiards

Monsieur Mingaud / translated by John Thurston
1830   John Thurston, London
Hardback   7pp, [1]p, 40pp, ill., 30 x 20cm

1831   John Thurston, London
Hardback   7pp, [2]pp, 40pp, ill., 30 x 20cm
Notes   2nd edition

1834   John Thurston, London
Hardback   7pp, [2]pp, 40pp, ill., 30 x 20cm
Notes   2nd edition; folding ill. frontispiece

1835   John Thurston, London
Hardback   7pp, [3]pp, 40pp, ill., 30 x 20cm
Notes   2nd edition

1836   John Thurston, London
Hardback   7pp, [3]pp, 40pp, ill., 30 x 19cm
Notes   3rd edition; folding ill. frontispiece

Captain Mingaud was a French infantry officer whose 'Noble Game of Billiards' went through several editions but was originally published in Paris in 1827 as 'Noble Jeu de billard'. The British Library copy of the 1830 edition is bound in dark brown cloth with leather trim and has a superb fold-out frontispiece protected by tissue paper that depicts a game of billiards taking place in the match room at Thurston's Catherine St. premises c.1829. There are also 40 splendid full-page illustrations, after John Thurston's Preface, setting out various strokes. In this Preface Thurston says that M. Mingaud "...justly claims the merit of the most brilliant discoveries of modern times". One of these discoveries is the leather tip that Mingaud experimented with whilst in prison in Paris in 1807. On his release he rendered speechless those who witnessed the superior cuemanship the tip afforded him. Incidentally, John Thurston had set up a cabinet making business in 1799 and from 1814 began to concentrate production solely on billiard tables and the company name has been synonymous with billiards and snooker ever since.

A 3rd edition of Mingaud's work, with some water staining and a defective spine, sold for £440 against an estimate of £150-£200 at the Bloomsbury auction of May 2007. And another 3rd edition of 1836 – described as in original half sheep and marbled boards, heavily rubbed with recent reback - sold for an impressive £820, against a rather low estimate of £200-£300, at the Dominic Winter sale of July 2007.

Value   **£900+**

6.6   The Game of Billiards Clearly Explained, and the Scientific Principles of the Side Stroke

J. Tillotson
1836   Thos. Tegg & Son, London
Hardback   iii, pp1-10, [4]pp, pp1-8, [2]pp, pp1-62, ill., 13 x 8cm

This Thomas Tegg & Son publication is actually two books in one as it features the 1836 2nd edition at the front and the 1835 1st edition at the rear of the volume. However, I have not been able to track down a copy of the 1835 edition as a separate publication. There is a title pasted onto the front cover dated 1835 but this may have been added and may not necessarily be a standard feature of all copies. Tillotson's offering contains a Pool Rules & Regulations section, Rules & Regulations for the winning and losing Game (by S. Hunt), as well as advice on playing billiards. The book is amply illustrated and the page edges are nicely tipped in gilt and the book in bound in blue cloth.

Value   **£500 - £800**

6.7   The Game of Billiards Scientifically Explained

Edwin Kentfield (aka Jonathan Kentfield)
1839   Smith, Elder & Co., London
Hardback   viii, vi, 48pp, 93 plates, 35 x 22cm
Notes   Includes Rules and Errata

1848   Smith, Elder & Co., London
[Hardback]
Notes   4th edition; [information taken from Craven]

1850   John Thurston, London
Hardback   vi, 54pp, ill., 93 plates, 35 x 22cm
Notes   5th edition

1886   Thurston & Co. / Alfred Boot & Son, London
Hardback   xv, 93pp, ill., 93 plates, 23 x 15cm
Notes   6th edition

This volume has an extraordinarily long title only the first part of which is listed above[13]. The book has dark blue boards with a scroll pattern in each corner of a rectangle with 'Kentfield On Billiards With Illustrations' blocked in gilt in the centre. The frontispiece is a lovely fold-out plated entitled 'The Interior of a

---

[13]   The full title is 'The Game of Billiards : Scientifically Explained, and Practically Set Forth, in a Series of Novel and Extraordinary Strokes; and Illustrated by Numerous Appropriate Diagrams. To which is added the Rules and Regulations which govern the Numerous Games as they are played at the Present Day in all Countries of Europe'.

Billiard Room : with Thurston's Table, Improved Revolving Lamp, and Furniture Complete', that depicts several gentlemen watching two players at play in a well furnished billiard room. Some old style 'mace' cues can be seen in the two racks present in the room. This frontispiece illustration is very similar to the one in Mingaud's 'The Noble Game of Billiards' of 1830 (see entry 6.5).

Kentfield is viewed as the first professional billiard player and the first to be acknowledged as champion, so this work must have been well regarded when it was first published. In the author's Preface he states that the book is primarily aimed at beginners and that he feels all billiard books published in the last twenty or thirty years have "now become comparatively useless, in consequence of the many alterations and improvements that have been successively introduced". There is also a 'Proprietor's Address' by John Thurston dated September 1839, extolling the virtues of the game. The book then goes on to detail such areas as Cannons, Winning Hazards, Losing Hazards etc., which are illustrated via plates after the numbered pages finish and several of these plates are protected by fine tissue paper. There is an 'Opinions of the Press' page at the rear and also a full-page advert for John Thurston Billiard Table Manufacturers, complete with a vibrant lion and unicorn royal crest. There are only 48 numbered pages in the 1st edition but there are plenty of un-numbered pages covering Games of Pool and Foreign Games (such as the French, Russian and Spanish Games).

At the Dominic Winter sale in July 2006 a copy of the 1839 1st edition, with slight yellowing to pages, attained a price of £240 against an estimate of £200-£300. Another 1st edition at the Dominic Winter sale of July 2007, described as "with some splits to folds and subsequent tape repairs . . . final engraved leaf torn with loss, some light staining and marks", sold for £230 against an estimate of £200-£300; and finally a copy on eBay recently fetched £180.

Value £200 - £250

6.8 A Hand Book to the Game of Billiards

B., Colonel
1841 T. & W. Boone, London
Hardback 72pp, ill., 15 x 9cm

1842 T. & W. Boone, London
Paperback 80pp, ill., 15 x 10cm
Notes 2nd edition to which is added pool

[1850] William Tegg, London
Paperback 80pp, ill., 15 x 10cm
Notes Revised title of **'How to Play Billiards and Pool : Showing the Laws of the Game'**

This is another pocket-sized book that has discussion of the development and spread of the game, the evolution of tables, and a brief overview of billiards. The text that follows takes the reader through the various winning and losing games (mentioning Fortification Billiards – see entry 6.0), and then a whole bunch of Odds Tables. Finally, there are 44 diagrams depicting various aspects of play. The British Library volume has almost certainly been re-bound and has pale green boards and a dark green spine with gilt lettering. The William Tegg edition has thin reddish-brown cloth covers, the title in gilt and pages edges tipped in gilt.

Value £300 - £500

6.9 Billiards : Game, 500 Up

Edward Russell Mardon, Dr.
[1844]   W. Leppard, Brighton
Hardback   116pp, ill., 28 x 23cm

1849   No publisher details given, London
Hardback   ii, 290pp, ill., 22 x 14cm
Notes   2nd (extensively enlarged) edition

1858   No publisher details given, Brighton
Hardback   vi, 431pp, ill., 22 x 14cm
Notes   3rd (extensively enlarged) edition; includes Erratum

This volume details the last nine breaks of a game between the author and a Mr. Porker at Mr. Kentfield's room on 18th January 1844. Following the illustration of these breaks comes some further illustrations of tips for players who have already made some progress in the game; the illustrations being full-page with the text sitting opposite. The last sections details 'General Observations', which includes 'Laws of the Game', and an interesting piece called 'Gold Cue' where a game is arranged between a Gentlemen [sic] and a Noblemen [sic], the winner receiving the gold cue. Both the 2nd and 3rd editions are bound in red cloth with the title in gilt and page edges nicely tipped in gilt. A copy of the latter, in generally very good condition, realised £180 on eBay in January 2007; and a copy of the 2nd edition sold for a disappointing £120 at the Dominic Winter sale of July 2007.

Value £950+

6.10 That Grand and Practical Game Billiards

H. Turner
1849   J. T. Burgess, Northampton
Hardback   ii, 6pp, [91]pp, ill., no measurements available

H. Turner was for many years the proprietor of billiard tables at the University of

Cambridge and on the page preceding the Preface it states that "H. T. will be happy to give instructions to any Gentleman who may be desirous of his services". The instructions in his work only actually cover 4 pages and there then follows 41 plates demonstrating a variety of strokes and positions. The author also states "there are some who, not having the least idea of Theory, yet play a good game by Practice; the Theory, however, in this case, as in all others, achieves nothing; but when *fine Practice is based upon Sound Theory*, the most brilliant results are sure to follow"! [description based on a photocopy].

Value £500 - £800

6.11   **The Science of Billiards : Explaining the Theory and Principles on which the Game is Founded**

Reuben Roy
[1850]   Henry Kent Causton, London
Paperback   iv, 102pp, ill., 14 x 10cm
Notes   Includes Index

This book has green card covers with the title in black and a drawing in the centre of a billiard player playing a fancy stroke with the cue behind his back. Roy begins his treatise with a description of the billiard table and a discussion on billiard balls, cues and maces. The book then moves onto the scientific side of the sport with much talk of motive power, elasticity, concussion and velocity. There then follows ten 'problems' that Roy shows the reader how to solve with the aid of diagrams. After this come details and rules of nineteen billiard games ending with the obsolete game of 'Fortification' billiards.

Value £600 - £800

6.12   **Billiards : its Theory and Practice**

Captain Rawdon Crawley (Pseud. of George Frederick Pardon)
[1856]   C. H. Clarke, London
[Hardback]   xii, 164pp, 8pp of adverts, ill.
Notes   [Description based on Crawley's Bibliography in 'The Billiard Book' 1877, Crawley & Cook – see entry 6.16]

[1857]   C. H. Clarke, London
Hardback   xii, 160pp, ill., 15 x 10cm
Notes   2nd edition

[1857]   C. H. Clarke, London
Hardback   xii, 160pp, ill., 15 x 10cm
Notes   3rd edition

[1858]	C. H. Clarke, London	
Hardback	iv, viii–xii, 160pp, ill., 15cm x 10cm	
Notes	4th edition	
[1859]	Bickers & Bush, London	
Hardback	vi, 180pp, ill., 15 x 10cm	
Notes	5th edition [?]; there is an anomaly here as the title page says '5th edition' but the Preface says 'Preface to the Seventh edition'	
[n.d.]	C. H. Clarke, London	
[Hardback]		
Notes	6th edition; [description based on Crawley's Bibliography–see notes to 1856 edition]	
[1859]	S. O. Beeton, London	
Paperback	vi, 180pp, ill., 14 x 10cm	
Notes	7th edition	
[n.d.]	S. O. Beeton, London	
Paperback	vi, 180pp, ill., 15 x 10cm	
Notes	8th edition	
[n.d.]	C. H. Clarke, London	
Hardback	vi, 180pp, ill., 15 x 10cm	
Notes	9th edition	
[1876]	Ward, Lock, & Tyler, London	
Hardback	x, 154pp, ill., 19 x 13cm	
Notes	10th edition; thoroughly revised; 40 diagrams; ill. frontispiece; publisher's catalogue at rear; brown boards with title and crossed cues motif in gilt	
[n.d.]	C. H. Clarke, London	
Hardback	vi, 180pp, ill., 15 x 10cm	
Notes	11th edition; red boards with crossed cues motif	
[1876]	Ward, Lock & Co., London	
Hardback	x, 154pp, ill., 19 x 13cm	
Notes	11th edition; as 10th edition; green boards with crossed cues motif and title etc. in black	
[1876]	Ward, Lock & Co., London	
Hardback	x, 154pp, ill., 17 x 11cm	
Notes	11th edition, thoroughly revised	

Pocket-sized billiard books seemed to be popular in the 19th century as was the picture of two crossed cues that is blocked in gilt onto the front boards of the various editions of this book. Originally selling for 2/6, this book was first published in 1856 and remained in print till at least 1876, when it was published by Ward, Lock & Co. The illustrations in the book are not quite so plentiful as other volumes but the text more than makes up for that. There are several adverts at the rear of the book, the most fascinating of which is one for 'The Gorget Patent Self Adjusting Shirt'. George Frederick Pardon (1824-1884) was a compiler of books on games as well as a journalist, and for the 9th edition of the 'Encyclopaedia Britannica' he wrote articles on billiards and bagatelle. According to Craven the pseudonym Pardon chose for his billiards books "was inspired by Thackeray's dissolute billiards player in Vanity Fair [1848], Captain Rawdon Crawley".

Collectors should note that there are several variants of the 11th edition. One has the cover title as 'Billiards and Bagatelle' and has a picture of playing cards, a chess set and billiard balls on a billiard table and the rear board carries an advert for Hennig Bros. Other variants have separate coloured bindings of brown, blue, pale green and olive green with the crossed cues motif and title in gilt; with the blue binding being especially attractive.

Value £120 - £140

6.13 Billiards : its Theory and Practice Set Forth and Explained

William White
1858   William White, Dublin
Hardback   vii, 128pp, ill., 15 x 10cm
Notes   Includes Errata slip attached to page 128

1865   R. J. Kennett, London
Hardback   ill.
Notes   2nd edition; reprint of 1858 edition with 2 pages added [description based on Crawley's Bibliography–see entry 6.16]

This small book is bound in red cloth with 'White on Billiards' and the price of 2/6 in gilt on the cover. The double page frontispiece illustration shows a game taking place in the author's billiard room in Lower Abbey St., Dublin. This drawing is very similar to the frontispiece of both 'The Noble Game of Billiards' by Mingaud (see entry 6.5) and 'The Game of Billiards Scientifically Explained' by Kentfield (see entry 6.7), and they may well have been drawn by the same artist. White's treatise is a standard run-through of the game encompassing rules, how to learn the game, winning and losing hazards and so forth, all profusely illustrated. Finally there is 'A Card' at the rear of the book, stating that the author is available for tuition at extremely moderate terms. Rather interestingly, this book is mentioned in the 'Bibliography' contained in the 1877 edition of 'The Billiard Book' by Crawley and Cook. Of White's 1858 edition Crawley says "this book – a piracy on my first treatise, which it imitated in size, style, & C. – was withdrawn from circulation on law proceedings being commenced". Crawley also says that the 1865 edition was withdrawn from circulation and this fact almost certainly contributes to the scarcity of the volume.

Value £300 - £500

6.14 A Handbook of Billiards, With the Theory of the Side-Stroke, the Rules of the Games, and a Chapter on Bagatelle

George Frederick Pardon
1862	Routledge, Warne, & Routledge, London
Hardback	viii, 96pp, ill., 14 x 9cm
Notes	One of Routledges' Sixpenny Handbooks

1863	Routledge, Warne, & Routledge, London
Hardback	vi, 96pp, ill., 14 x 10cm
Notes	As above; new edition

1868	George Routledge & Sons, London
Hardback	viii, 96pp, ill., 14 x 10cm
Notes	As 1863 edition

[n.d.]	George Routledge & Sons, London
Hardback	viii, 96pp, ill., 15 x 10cm
Notes	Title is '**A Handbook of Billiards and Bagatelle**'; one of Routledges' Sixpenny Handbooks

In the Preface to this book the author admits that he is not a professional billiard player but wrote this work because he is fond of the game and because he feels there is need of a cheap elementary treatise on the subject. There is an awful lot packed into the 96 pages, not least the bewildering variants of billiards and pool described, and the diagrams are far more detailed than most found in other books. This book is a real gem for the collector, its yellow pictorial boards featuring drawings of two games taking place in a billiard saloon and the rear board featuring an advert for Messrs. Thurston & Co. The undated volume, entitled 'A Handbook of Billiards and Bagatelle', has two variants. One has dark green boards with the title in red and the crossed cues motif in the centre; whilst the other has the same yellow pictorial boards as mentioned above.

Value £150 - £180

6.15 The ABC of Billiards

F. Hardy
1866	Frederick Warne & Co., London
Paperback	vi, 95pp, ill., 1 col. plate, 10 x 7cm
Notes	One of Warne's Bijou Books

[1866]	Frederick Warne & Co., London	
Hardback	vi, 95pp, ill., 1 col. plate, 10 x 7cm	
1868	Frederick Warne & Co., London	
[Hardback]	vi, 95pp, ill., 10cm	
Notes	One of Warne's Bijou Books [information taken from Craven]	

This delightful miniature book was number 10 in a 28 volume series of Bijou Books published by Frederick Warne. The dated, paperback volume, has deep red cloth covers with a lovely gilt billiard player along with the title in the centre. The hardback of 1866 is bound in dark green cloth and has a small colour picture of two players at the table to the right of the cover. The author states in his Preface that "this little book pretends to be no more than the simple Alphabet of Billiards. It has been stripped as far as possible of all pretentious phraseology and made as simple and as practical as possible". The book contains the expected instructional material and finishes with the rules of various games.

Value £300 - £500

6.16 The Billiard Book

Captain Crawley (pseud. of George Frederick Pardon)
1866   Longmans, Green & Co., London
Hardback   xv, 261pp, ill., plates, 24 x 16cm
Notes   Includes Index and Appendices

Captain Crawley / William Cook
1877   Ward, Lock & Co., London
Hardback   xvi, 344pp, ill., 25 x 16cm
Notes   New edition, enlarged and revised; John Proctor (ill.); 29 woodcuts; includes Index

Another billiards book with dark green boards and the crossed cues and three billiard balls motif on the cover, this effort was written due to the favourable reception accorded to Crawley's previous treatise on the sport. This is a very detailed study that has plenty of full-page illustrations and there is a rules section, a chapter on how to fit up a billiard room, plus two Appendices where a mathematical approach to play is explored. The British Library copy of the 1877 edition is in exceptionally clean and bright condition and has the title and authors' names, framed by a billiard table and accessories, stamped in gilt on the cover. A copy of the 1877 edition sold for £105 at the Dominic Winter sale of July 2006, although the 1866 edition is much more valuable and eagerly sought after by collectors. The 1877 edition is also important because it includes an Appendix called 'Bibliographical Catalogue of the Chief Printed Books on Billiards' that is invaluable for determining bibliographical data, especially dates of publication.

Value £250+

6.17   **Practical Billiards**

William Dufton / Frederic Hardy
1867   George Routledge & Sons, London
Hardback   xi, 242pp, ill., 22 x 14cm
Notes   Includes Index

1870   George Routledge & Sons, London
Hardback   xi, 242pp, ill., 22 x 14cm
Notes   2nd edition; includes Index

1873   George Routledge & Sons, London
Hardback   xiv, 242pp, ill., 22 x 14cm
Notes   Includes Index

Frederic Hardy prepared a considerable proportion of this book but unfortunately died before its publication. William Dufton had been assisting Hardy, chiefly with the diagrams, and happily took over the full project when the publisher's approached him after Hardy's death. The result is a mixture of both men's work but the description of the method of playing Handicap Billiards and the Rules Appertaining to that Game are exclusively Dufton's. There is rather a tragic history to this book as Crawley says in his Bibliography that "poor Dufton died, by his own hand, two days after the match for the championship, in May, 1877".

The publisher's should be congratulated for including so many fantastic woodcuts in the volume (32 in total), those showcasing designs for billiard rooms on pages 11 and 13 being particularly enjoyable. The woodcut at the bottom of page 13 is especially splendid, picturing as it does a Tudor design billiard room complete with smoking tower. The chapter including these woodcuts is called 'The Billiard-Room and Appurtenances' and features discussion on tables, lighting, cloth, how to spot a table etc.

The 61 diagrams included in the book help to illustrate the various chapters on Winning Hazards, Losing Hazards, Cannons etc. The final two chapters include 'Recent Matches at Billiards', where the Oxford and Cambridge University match of 1865 is one of the matches described, plus an extensive 'Rules for Billiards' section. The British Library copy contains a dedication to John Davis of Leicester and has green boards with the familiar crossed cues design on the spine in gilt.

Value   **£550+**

6.18   **White on Billiards : a Practical Manual, Containing the Most Recent Rules and Regulations Relating to the Game**

[William White]
1867   F. Pitman, London

Hardback	vii, 143pp, ill., 15 x 10cm
Notes	Includes a numbered 6 page Appendix

This 1867 publication by William White is a revised edition of 'Billiards: Its Theory & Practice Set Forth & Explained (see entry 6.13) and the furore surrounding that particular book was probably the reason White's name is not mentioned on the title page. The book has green boards with 'Billiards by Cox & Yeman' in gilt sitting in a decorated square in the middle of the cover. The title page also states that it is a "New edition – revised and improved for Messrs. Cox & Yeman". The work includes an Appendix detailing matches that had recently been played by some of the leading players of the day.

Value £300 - £500

6.19 Billiards for Beginners

Captain Rawdon Crawley (pseud. of George Frederick Pardon)

[1868]	Griffin & Co., London
Hardback	viii, 90pp, ill., 17 x 11cm

[n.d.]	C. H. Clarke, London
Hardback	viii, 90pp, ill., 17 x 11cm

[1873]	The Graphotyping Co. / Simpkin, Marshall & Co., London
Paperback	64pp, ill., 17 x 11cm
Notes	New and revised edition; one of the 'Champion' Handbooks

The British Library have catalogued this pocket-sized hardback as being printed in 1868, although there is no date on the title page and Crawley in his Bibliography mentioned above dates it as 1867. Craven lists an edition published by Darton & Hodge of London but I have not been able to verify that this edition exists. The 1st edition is bound in dark red cloth with the title and author on the front in gilt, plus the original price of 1/-, whereas the C. H. Clarke edition has dark green boards. Crawley's book is amply illustrated and covers all aspects of the game over its five chapters. There is a separate section on bagatelle at the end of the volume, followed by an advert for Thurston & Co.

Value £250 - £350

6.20 Roberts on Billiards

John Roberts Senior / Henry Buck (Ed.)

[1868]	Stanley Rivers & Co., London
Hardback	370pp, col. ill., 21 x 14cm

[1869] Stanley Rivers & Co., London
Hardback xvi, 368pp, col. ill., 20 x 13cm
Notes 2nd edition, revised and enlarged

This heavy book has very dark brown boards and the much used crossed cues design embossed in gilt, along with the title, on the front cover. There is a 4 page advert for Thurston's at the back of the book, one advert featuring 'The New Game of Battue', a cross between billiards and bagatelle. Interestingly, for a 19th century book, the twenty diagrams featured in the book are all in colour. The tome is divided into two parts; the first, called 'The Game', features the English, American and French games, 'Incidents in my Career', 'Players I Have Met' ("J. Roberts jun. plays a dashing game, with great power of cue"), and so on. The second part is entitled 'How to Play It' and includes the usual subject matter. This second part also includes a 'Rules' section and details of celebrated matches played between 1850–1868. I assume this latter date guided the British Library in the date of publication because the book has no publication date on the title page. Captain Crawley also gives the volume a probable date of 1868 in the Bibliography contained in 'The Billiard Book' of 1877 (see entry 6.16). He also goes on to add that "in 1870 Stanley Rivers & Co. failed, and the stock was sold off in sheets" and this was presumably the reason why a 3rd edition was not published.

A copy of the 1868 1st edition, described as "slightly rubbed to extremities", sold for £70 against an estimate of £70-£100 at the Dominic Winter auction held in July 2006; another copy, although it is not explicit whether the 1st or 2nd edition, sold for £65 at Bloomsbury's auction of February 2007. Copies on eBay have fared slightly better, with a very good 1st edition fetching £72 in June 2006, and a copy of the 1869 2nd edition achieving an impressive £104 in March 2007.

Value   £70 - £100

6.21 The Handy Book on Billiards

William Cook Junior
[1870] No details given
Paperback 66pp, 15 x 9cm

This book has 'Cook on Billiards' as the title on the brown cover and contains a series of articles originally written for the 'Sporting Life' of January 1870. As well as pieces on the spot stroke and losing hazards, there are descriptions of matches recently played between the star players of the day. It seems the book was reprinted or revised at a later date as I have seen photocopies of a title page showing another edition published by H. E. Harberd & Co. of Red Lion Court, Fleet St. This edition has a b & w frontispiece signed underneath 'Yours Truly' W. Cook.

Value   £400 - £600

6.22 The Spot-Stroke

Joseph Bennett / 'Cavendish' (pseud. of Henry Jones) (Ed.)
1871   Thos. De La Rue & Co., London
[Hardback]   27pp, ill., 16 x 12cm [description based on a photocopy]

1872   Thos. De La Rue & Co., London
Paperback   27pp, ill., 16 x 11cm
Notes 2nd edition

In the Historical chapter of this book, Bennett states that the spot stroke is a modern invention and goes on to add that "a stroke which offers such chances of scoring is worth study". Bennett then goes on to examine all aspects of the spot stroke with the aid of almost one diagram per page. The 2nd edition has pink, glossy card covers and the page edges are tipped in gilt. I assume the 1st edition of 1871 is a hardback but I have only been able to see a photocopy.

Value   £400 - £600

6.23 Billiards

Joseph Bennett / 'Cavendish' (pseud. of Henry Jones) (Ed.)
1873   Thos. De La Rue & Co., London
Hardback   483pp, ill., 22 x 15cm
Notes   Contains Errata

1873   Thos. De La Rue & Co., London
Hardback   483pp, ill., 22 x 14cm
Notes 2nd edition; as above

1881   Thos. De La Rue & Co., London
Hardback   483pp, ill., 20 x 13cm
Notes 3rd edition; ill. frontispiece; adverts and publisher's catalogue at rear; dark green boards with title and author framed in a scoreboard motif

1884   Thos. De La Rue & Co., London
Hardback   483pp, ill., 20 x 13cm
Notes 4th edition; as 1881 edition

1889   Thos. De La Rue & Co., London
Hardback   483pp, ill., 20 x 13cm
Notes 5th edition

1894   Thos. De La Rue & Co., London
Hardback   xi, 475pp, ill., 20 x 13cm
Notes 6th edition; as 1881 edition

1899	Thos. De La Rue & Co., London
Hardback	xi, 475pp, ill., 20 x 13cm
Notes	7th edition; as 1881 edition

There is an illustration on practically every other page of this very heavy volume by Joseph Bennett. The page edges are tipped in gilt, the boards are dark green and the cover has the common device of a billiard table framing the title, author and publisher details. The same information has been stamped onto the rear board. This is another book that follows the pattern of history of billiards, the table and the implements, followed by instructions on how to play the various billiard strokes. At the rear of the book is a section on Championship Rules with notes by the editor. There are numerous adverts at the back of the book from the publisher's, plus Thurston & Co., Cox & Yeman, Orme & Sons, and finally Cooper & Holt advertising their reversible dining and billiard table.

A lot comprising the 1st edition of 1873, along with the 5th and 6th editions, fetched £95 at the Dominic Winter Sale in July 2006. A further 1st edition copy, in superb condition, sold for an impressive £122 on eBay in 2007.

Value £60 - £75

6.24 Billiards Made Easy : With the Scientific Principles of the Side-Stroke and the Spot-Stroke Familiarly Explained

'Winning Hazard' (pseud. of Albert de Vere)

[1873]	Houlston & Sons, London
Hardback	viii, 83pp, ill., 17 x 11cm

[n.d.]	Houlston & Sons, London
Hardback	viii, 83pp, ill., 17 x 11cm
Notes	2nd edition

This pocket-sized book has decorative dark green, stiff cloth covers that lend the book the feel of a paperback. The title sits in the centre in gilt framed by the ubiquitous crossed cues motif and there is a nice frontispiece of a lady playing billiards with a gentleman whilst another couple look on. Under the frontispiece illustration is the famous Shakespeare quotation "let us to billiards", taken from 'Anthony and Cleopatra'. The 2nd edition has black boards with the same design sitting in the centre as the 1st edition, only in white rather than gilt. There is also an undated version, in addition to the 2nd edition listed above, which is bound in puce coloured cloth. This may be a variant binding of the 1st edition, that doesn't include a date on the title page, or alternatively a later edition.

There is no date of publication given in the 1st edition but the British Library date of 1873 concurs with the Bibliography contained in 'John Roberts' Billiards Annual, 1909' (see entry 8.3) and also Crawley's Bibliography (see entry 6.16). According to Crawley "the text of this book first appeared in chapters contributed to the 'Gentleman's Journal', published in 1870-2 by Messrs. Harrison, Salisbury Square".

In the first chapter of the book, the author mentions E. White's book of 1807 ('A Practical Treatise on the Game of Billiards' – see entry 6.3) and says the side-stroke was not even invented then and that nor had slate-topped tables, India-rubber cushions or leather-tipped cues. Thus de Vere brings the instructional side of the game up to date with the aid of several illustrations. There is a 'Laws' (or Rules) section at the front and a separate chapter dedicated to Bagatelle. The rear of the book features a publisher's catalogue.

Value £200 - £300

6.25 **Prize Essays on "Billiards as an Amusement for all Classes, Especially in Reference to its use in Clubs, Literary Mechanics', and Other Institutes"**

[Thomas Orme & Sons] (Corp.)
1873 James Galt & Co., [Manchester]
Hardback xvi, 113pp, ill., 29 x 22cm
Notes Published for Orme & Sons, Billiard Table Makers, Manchester

This beautifully designed volume features five essays on billiards, chosen from 21 entries, written by Mr E. L. Davies, J. P., W. M. D., Mr D. L. Kirkpatrick, and Mr D. W. Gilchrist; for which Orme & Sons presented £25 together with "one Gold-Mounted cue & Two Silver-Mounted Cues". After the essays there follows a rules section and various bits and pieces including a list of those whom Orme & Sons had the privilege of supplying billiard tables to. There are some superb engravings throughout and the book is bound in pale green cloth with a leather spine.

Value £500 - £800

6.26 **Armistead's Patent Billiard Angle Measurer**

Armistead (Corp.)
[1881] [Simpkin, Marshall & Co.], [London]
Hardback [6p], ill., 39 x 24cm

This book details a billiard angle measurer, including two full-page illustrations, of which Armistead says he has found "this simple instrument very useful in improving his game at billiards". He then goes on to say that "the instrument is founded on Prop. XV, first book Euclid – if two straight lines cut one another the vertical or opposite angles shall be equal". There then follows details of 'fixed pointer', 'moveable pointer' and 'the block', instruments that help the angle measurer perform its function. The British Library copy has a British Museum stamp dated

13.12.1881 but the book itself contains no clues as to why it has been catalogued as being published by Simpkin, Marshall & Co.

Value £200 - £300

6.27   **Billiards**

William Cook Senior / A. G. Payne (Ed.)
[1883]	Burroughes & Watts, London
Hardback	xxxii, 332pp, colour ill., plates, 1 port., 20 x 13cm
Notes	Contains Errata

[1885]	Frederick Warne & Co., London
Hardback	xxxii, 332pp, [64]pp, col. ill., 1 port, 20 x 13cm

[1891]	Burroughes & Watts, London
Hardback	xxxii, 292pp, col. ill., plates, 20 x 13cm
Notes	There is no mention of A. G. Payne on the title page of this edition

[1891]	Burroughes & Watts, London
Hardback	xxxii, 292pp, [79]pp, col. ill., plates, 20 x 13cm
Notes	As above

The 1st edition of this book is bound in dark green cloth with the author and title in gilt on the cover as well as an embossed gilt picture of two players at the table in the centre. The frontispiece has a plate of William Cook. There is no date of publication in the work but the final chapter describes certain matches played in 1882 and a Burroughes & Watts advert mentions a Gold Medal award of 1883. Collectors wishing to make sure they purchase a 1st edition have one unique rule to follow – the book must be published by Burroughes & Watts and have 332 numbered pages. All other combinations of publishers and page numbers signify later editions!

At 332 pages this is a lengthy and heavy book covering virtually all aspects of the game, including an extensive section on pool and pyramids and their variants. Unusually for a book of this date, the full-page table diagrams are in colour. An intriguing chapter is one called 'How to Train for a Billiard Match' where the author talks us through his routine of plenty of exercise, plain living and his daily walk up to Lord's (cricket ground). The last chapters detail the history of billiards since 1861 by A. Payne, and matches between the top players, complete with scorecards, are covered. As with many other publications of this era, Burroughes & Watts has some adverts at the front and rear. Collector's should note that there are two variants of the 1891 edition; one having a 79 page 'Price List, 1891' at the back of the volume. At the Dominic Winter auction of July 2006 a copy of the 1st edition, along with an 1891 edition, sold for £125 against an estimate of £70-£100.

Value £60 - £80

6.28 Billiards Simplified : or, How to Make Breaks

Burroughes & Watts (Corp.)
[1884] Burroughes & Watts, London
Hardback iv, 181pp, ill., plates, 19 x 13cm

[1889] Burroughes & Watts, London
[Hardback] vi, 217pp, ill.
Notes 11th thousand; includes adverts and b & w ill. catalogue [description based on microfilm copy]

[1890] Burroughes & Watts, London
Hardback vi, 239pp, ill., 20 x 13cm
Notes 20th thousand; 83 diagrams; dark green boards with title etc. in black framed by a billiard table

This book has a great cover, the dark green boards having a billiard table in gilt round the edges and the title of the book inside the table. Rather unusually, the title has been repeated on the rear by stamping the words into the board. The page edges are also tipped in gilt to produce a lovely vibrant looking book. There is no date of publication given in the book but on page 2 it mentions a high break of 1,989 made "this year" by Peall at Cambridge. Then on page 78 the break is mentioned again with a full date of May 19th 1884. There are many more editions of this book and it is notoriously difficult to date any edition so I have only listed the three copies I have actually seen.

There are some great photographic plates included in the book featuring players such as John Roberts, Joseph Bennett, W. J. Peall and others, and several chapters illustrate some of their breaks in detail using full-page diagrams. In addition, there is a section on rules featuring billiards, pool, pyramids, cork pool and shell out.

Perhaps the best part of this book though, certainly for the collector, is the 60 plus page Burroughes & Watts catalogue at the rear. This includes price lists for seats, table covers, gas fittings, cues and rests, interchangeable 'Cottage Billiard and Dining Tables' etc. All of these items are fully illustrated in the catalogue and make intriguing viewing. The catalogue also includes press notices and testimonials. Various copies have sold on eBay recently and later editions sell for around £50 in very good condition.

Value £60 - £80

6.29 The Art of Practical Billiards for Amateurs

A. W. Drayson, Major General
1889 George Bell & Sons, London
Hardback viii, 112pp, ill., 18 x 12cm
Notes Part of the 'Club Series'; approved by W. J. Peall

1892	George Bell & Sons, London
Hardback	xii, 112pp, ill., 18 x 12cm
Notes	As above

1895	George Bell & Sons, London
Hardback	xii, 115pp, ill., 18 x 12cm
Notes	As above

1897	George Bell & Sons, London
Hardback	xii, 115pp, ill., 17 x 12cm
Notes	As above

1901	George Bell & Sons, London
Hardback	xii, 115pp, ill., 17 x 12cm
Notes	As above

1909	George Bell & Sons, London
Hardback	xii, 115pp, ill., 17 x 12cm
Notes	As above

1912	George Bell & Sons, London
Hardback	xii, 115pp, ill., 17 x 12cm
Notes	As above

1918	George Bell & Sons, London
Hardback	xii, 115pp, ill., 17 x 12cm
Notes	As above

1919	George Bell & Sons, London
Paperback	xii, 115pp, ill., 18 x 12cm
Notes	As above

1923	George Bell & Sons, London
Paperback	viii, 115pp, ill., 18 x 12cm
Notes	As above

Bell's 'Club Series' of books featured card and table games and covered whist, chess, draughts and backgammon, bezique and cribbage, and so on. This charming book originally retailed at 1/- and has red boards (that are unfortunately prone to fading) with illustrations of the games featured in the series on the cover. Apart from the usual billiards topics there is an interesting chapter on the 'Etiquette of the Billiard Room', where the author expounds on a previous article he had written for the journal 'Land and Water'[14]. There is a 3 page chapter called 'The Game of

---

14 A journal principally covering field sports, sea and river fisheries, and practical natural history that ran from 27th January 1866 until 27th May 1905.

Snooker' at the end of the work and interestingly this may be the first significant discussion of snooker in a billiards book. The opening lines state "the game, which is not as yet generally known, or much played, is an amusing extension of the game of pyramids". The extra 3 pages of the book from 1895 onwards comprises added material entitled 'The Rules of the Game of Snooker's Pool'. As the books progressed over the ten editions the only real changes were a move to paperback format and differing adverts throughout the pages.

Value £60 - £75

6.30 The Billiard Note Book

R. R. W.
[1889]   A. Webster & Co., London
[Hardback]   [144]pp, 28 x 17cm

This note book, almost certainly by Reginald Rimington-Wilson, had a diagram of a billiard table on every other page and included a pencil and a 4 inch measure. The idea behind it was that the amateur player could draw on the pages containing billiard table diagrams and make notes on the opposite, blank, pages. The book would appear to have had a decorative, swirling, marble effect cover. Due to the nature of this note book pages would have been torn out once they had been used and, indeed, the whole book would probably have been discarded once full. Therefore, if any copies of this book survive they must be incredibly scarce and would command high prices at auction. [description based on microfilm copy].

Value £100 - £150

6.31 Tables for Ascertaining the Factor of a Billiard Player

The Earl of Crawford (James Ludovic Lindsay)
1890   R. Platt, Wigan
Hardback   14pp, [138]pp, 22 x 15cm
Notes   Includes fold-out chart inserted into a pocket attached to reverse of rear board entitled 'Table Showing the Odds to be given to the Weaker of Two Players in a Game of 100 Points'

The British Library copy of this volume is a fine specimen complete with near perfect dark blue boards[15], gilt lettering to the cover, marbled endpapers and the page edges tipped in gilt. The first 14 pages of the book are taken up by the various explanations and formula concerning how to ascertain the factor (number of

---

15   The British Library copy may have been re-bound as I have also seen a copy with burgundy boards and their copy is surely in too good a condition for the book to have survived so well after more than 100 years.

points scored divided by number of visits to the table) of a billiard player. Lindsay got this idea from Drayson's 'The Art of Practical Billiards for Amateurs' published the previous year (see entry 6.29). After the 14 numbered pages come 138 pages of tables showing various games won at a certain number of points and the tables associated with such a winning score. There is another copy of the folding chart listed in the Notes above attached to one of the rear endpapers. There were only 50 copies of this book published so any surviving copies coming up for sale would almost certainly exceed the record paid previously for a billiards publication. Incidentally, James Lindsay (1847-1913) was the 26th Earl of Crawford and the 9th Earl of Balcarres, an astronomer and book collector who originally lived at Haigh Hall in Wigan. He eventually became MP for Wigan in 1874 and held that seat until 1880 when he succeeded to his father's earldom and sat in the upper house as Lord Wigan.

Value £2,400 - £2,600

6.32 Hints on Billiards

J. P. Buchanan
1895   George Bell & Sons, London
Hardback   vi, 208pp, vi, ill., 19 x 13cm
Notes   Includes Appendix–'The Rules of Billiards'

1902   George Bell & Sons, London
Hardback   vi, 152pp, ill., 17 x 12cm
Notes   2nd edition; as above; one of the 'Club Series' of Card and Table Games

John Penruddocke Buchanan states in his Preface that this volume is aimed at players who are only able to devote a few hours a week to the game, purely as recreation. He then goes on to discuss the table, rudiments of the game, cannons, the spot-stroke and so forth. The 1895 edition contains 36 diagrams and has a few contemporary adverts at the rear and is bound in blue cloth with a player's bridge hand set in the middle of the front cover. The 2nd edition of 1902 has red pictorial boards that feature the same attractive design as 'The Art of Practical Billiards for Amateurs' by A. Drayson published in 1889 by the same publishing house (see entry 6.29). The 1902 edition has considerably less pages because chapters on miscellaneous strokes, the spot-stroke and billiard players and billiard records have been dropped.

A copy of the 1st edition, in only fair condition and with staining and repairs to the cover, sold for a respectable £91 on eBay in February 2007; whereas an earlier auction of the 1st edition saw a sale price of £80. And a further copy appearing for sale in November 2007, in very good condition, fetched a healthy £92.

Value £70 - £90

6.33 Billiards

W. Broadfoot, Major, R.E.

1896	Longmans, Green & Co., London & Bombay
Hardback	xii, 455pp, ill., plates, 20 x 14cm
Notes	Part of the 'Badminton Library' series of Sports and Pastimes; Lucien Davis (ill.); includes Index

1897	Longmans, Green & Co., London & Bombay
Hardback	xii, 455pp, ill., plates, 20 x 14cm
Notes	New edition; part of the 'Badminton Library' series of Sports and Pastimes; includes Index

1901	Longmans, Green & Co., London & Bombay
Hardback	xii, 455pp, ill., plates, 20 x 14cm
Notes	Part of the 'Badminton Library' series of Sports and Pastimes; Lucien Davis (ill.); includes Index

1902	Longmans, Green & Co., London & Bombay
Hardback	xii, 455pp, ill., plates, ports., 20 x 14cm
Notes	New impression; as 1897 edition; Lucien Davis (ill.)

1906	Longmans, Green & Co., London & Bombay
Hardback	xii, 454pp, ill., plates, ports., 20 x 14cm
Notes	New edition; as 1897 edition; Lucien Davis (ill.)

This heavy book, with brown pictorial cloth and a lovely gilt picture of a billiard player at the foot of the spine, includes contributions by A. Boyd, Sydenham Dixon, W. Ford, Dudley Pontifex, Russell Walker, and Reginald Rimington-Wilson. The Badminton Library of Sports & Pastimes was published by Longmans between 1886 and the 1920s and was edited by the Duke of Beaufort and A. E. T. Watson and there were 70-odd volumes published in the series.

In the Introduction the author says that "no treatise or manual exists in which modern developments are considered" and that the science of making breaks has altered considerably since the older manuals were published. This volume includes some evocative period plates, including a chivalrous gentleman resplendent in evening dress chalking a young lady's cue for her. Most of the plates are protected by tissue paper and many picture female players.

The chapter on Implements by Archibald Boyd is particularly fine, covering as it does the billiard room ("the position of the fireplace is also important. A flickering light in the eyes of the players interferes seriously with good play"), the table, cues and billiard balls. The section on cues illustrates the splicing of the butt, tips, choice of wood etc. There is a good 'History of Billiards' chapter by Sydenham Dixon spanning nearly 50 pages that will appeal to historians of the game and the rest of the book is taken up by instructional material. Most collectors will want to acquire the 1st edition of 1896 but an eye-catching alternative is the 1906 edition with its colourful marbled endpapers, pastedowns and page edges. There are also variant editions available bound in orange cloth with a blue leather spine and corners.

Value £80 - £100

6.34 Billiards

William Mitchell / A. W. Cooper (Ed.)
[1897] Dean & Son, London
Hardback 64pp, ill., 1 port., 18 x 12cm
Notes One of Dean's 'Champion Hand Books'

[1897] Dean & Son, London
Paperback 64pp, ill., 18 x 12cm
Notes As above

William Mitchell / W. H. Robbins and S. Mussabini (Eds.)
[1897] Dean & Son, London
Hardback 64pp, ill., 1 port., 19 x 13cm
Notes As above

There are numerous full-page table illustrations in this publication, all helping to illustrate the topics covered – winning and losing hazards, cannons etc. Mitchell offers advice throughout the book and the novice should note that "there are many pitfalls which surround the footsteps of the tyro, and they are mostly born either of ignorance or self-confidence". The book includes an essay on billiards, an explanation of technical terms and the rules of the game.

The paperback volume has green card covers and a red drawing of the familiar crossed cues emblem complete with a pack of red balls. The hardback edition has three un-numbered pages at the rear advertising Dean's 'Shilling Plays', as well as 2 pages of Dean's books at the front and a frontispiece of William Mitchell. Finally, the text 'Dean's Champion Hand Books' is in black on the cover of the hardback, whereas it is red on the paperback. The edition edited by Robbins and Mussabini, that may well have been published after 1897, has a chapter entitled 'Our Foremost Players' from pages 58-64 that does not feature in the other two volumes.

A very good, clean copy of the 1st hardback edition sold on eBay in January 2007 for £84; whilst another very good copy fetched £72 in March 2007.

Value £70 - £85

6.35   **Billiards**

A. G. Payne
[1897]   George Routledge & Sons, London
Hardback   95pp, ill., 19 x 13cm
Notes   One of the 'Oval' Series of Games

There are plenty of full-page table diagrams in this book to take the avid reader through the chapters on striking the ball, position, the spot stroke and so on. Also included are the National Rules of Billiards and a useful Dictionary of the Billiard Language, and there is a short list of billiards books at the back. The book has exquisite, deep red boards with the front board carrying a gilt design of a table and two players.

Value   £100 - £200

6.36   **The Game of Billiards and How to Play It**

John Roberts Junior
[1897]   The John Roberts Billiard Co., London
Paperback   xvi, 142pp, ill., plates, 22 x 14cm
Notes   Includes Index

[1897]   The John Roberts Billiard Co., London
Paperback   xvi, 142pp, ill., plates, 22 x 14cm
Notes   2nd edition; includes Index

[1897]   The John Roberts Billiard Co., London
Paperback   xvi, 142pp, ill., plates, 22 x 14cm
Notes   3rd edition; includes Index

Many dealers and collectors believe the 1905 edition of this book to be the 1st but in fact the 1st edition was published in 1897. This date is further reinforced by the fact that in his 1901 book, 'Billiards for Beginners' (see entry 6.39), Roberts mentions 'The Game of Billiards and How to Play It'. Having said the above, it is no surprise there is confusion regarding this particular book. The 1905 edition (which I have treated as a separate publication – see entry 6.52) contains revised text and diagrams and the text is arranged in a different order to the 1897 edition and is much more user-friendly, with plenty of sub-headings. To confuse matters further, the diagrams were also renumbered for the 1905 edition and the book was published by C. Arthur Pearson!

This offering from Roberts is a reprint of twelve articles that he had previously contributed to 'The Billiard Review'[16] and covers all aspects of the game with

---

16   This journal ran from October 1895 – February 1898 and continued as a new series in February 1899 and ran until May 1901.

232 diagrams of strokes to guide the reader through the book. The 1st edition has wonderfully vibrant green and red card covers with a picture of Roberts in the centre. The book has some fabulous contemporary adverts for a wide range of products including Greenlees Brothers Highland Whisky, 'Three Castles' cigarettes made by W.D. & H.O. Wills, and Hamley's Grand Magical Saloons. There is also a 4 page catalogue for The John Roberts Billiard Co. printed on brown paper near the back of the volume. Lastly, there is a fantastic advert on the final page for Pears Soap that featured in 'Punch' in April 1884.

Rather extraordinarily a copy of this book, which I presume was the 1st edition, described as "seen better days with some wear and tear", only made £41 when it came up for sale on eBay in July 2007.

Value £120 - £150

6.37 **Hints on Billiards**

John P. Mannock / Sydenham Dixon (Ed.)
1897   Bradley & Co., London
Paperback   29pp, plates, 1 port., 22 x 15cm
Notes   Introduction by Sydenham Dixon

This pamphlet (as it is described in the Introduction) contains roughly ten hints on play and is illustrated with four full-page b & w plates. Subjects briefly covered include 'Side, Screw, and Top Side', 'Position', 'Aiming and Striking' etc. Dixon says in the Introduction that ". . . my friend Mr. Mannock and myself have constantly found ourselves of late years working together as members of the Billiard Association, and fighting shoulder to shoulder against anything and everything that appeared likely to decrease the popularity of the game we both love". They certainly did a good job as it was many years before the popularity of billiards began to wane. It also states in the Notes section "twenty years or so ago, professional matches were much more interesting to watch than now". The cover carries a b & w plate of Mannock in the centre and has vibrant red type-face and originally sold for the fairly standard price of 1/-.

Value £100 - £200

6.38 **Billiards Mathematically Treated**

George Wirgman Hemming
1899   Macmillan & Co., London
Hardback   45pp, ill., 28 x 19cm

1904	Macmillan & Co., London	
Hardback	61pp, ill., 28 x 19cm	
Notes	2nd edition; includes Errata and folding Appendix	

The 1st edition of this book has the ubiquitous dark green boards of many billiards books and the title in gilt on the cover, and the 2nd edition has blue boards. As the title makes clear, a mathematical approach to the game is examined in this slim volume by George Hemming. There are plenty of mathematical equations and diagrams in the book, all explaining the effects of friction, velocity, acceleration, impact and so on. This is a rather dry billiards book, especially for those who are not mathematically or scientifically inclined, but it could be argued that every collector should have one book of this type on their bookshelf. Indeed, Willie Smith in his book, 'Match-Winning Billiards' (see entry 6.93) says "I refer to G. W. Hemming ... whose 'Billiards Mathematically Treated' is the one classic in our language on the pure science of billiards". George Hemming (1821-1905) was a mathematician and law reporter who wrote several books on those subjects, most notably 'An Elementary Treatise on the Differential and Integral Calculus' of 1848. Collectors should note that Hemming's book is now available as a print on demand service via Abe; a viable alternative to the expensive and elusive 1st edition.

Value £300 - £500
print on demand copies £16 - £25

~ 1900 – 1914 ~

6.39 **Billiards for Beginners**

John Roberts Junior / F. M. Hotine (Ed.)

1901	Sands & Co., Edinburgh & London
Hardback	70pp, ill, 19 x 13cm
Notes	2nd and 3rd editions also published in 1901

1903	Sands & Co., Edinburgh & London
Hardback	70pp, ill., 19 x 13cm
Notes	4th edition

1905	Sands & Co., Edinburgh & London
Hardback	70pp, ill., 19 x 13cm
Notes	5th and 6th editions also published in 1905

1909	Ward, Lock & Co., London
Hardback	70pp, ill., 19 x 13cm
Notes	Includes 4 pages to record 'Scores' at rear

1911	Ward, Lock & Co., London
Hardback	70pp, ill., 19 x 13cm

This attractive publication by Sands & Co. is bound in grey-green cloth with the title and price (1/-) on the cover in white typography. The rear board features a full-page advert for the omnipresent Burroughes & Watts and the volume is a reprint of articles contributed by the author to the 'Billiard Review'. Roberts in his Introduction says that his previous book was too advanced for beginners so he has covered that ground in this publication. The book examines all the expected topics and is profusely illustrated and also includes numerous contemporary advertisements. The dustjacket, that unfortunately most copies do not have, is white and features a crossed cues motif and several red balls scattered around.

Value £20 - £30

6.40   **Billiards for Everybody**

Charles Roberts ('Vivid')
1901	Simpkin, Marshall, Hamilton, Kent & Co., London
Hardback	128pp, ill., plates, 1 port., 19 x 13cm
1901	Simpkin, Marshall, Hamilton, Kent & Co., London
Paperback	128pp, ill., plates, 19 x 13cm
1906	George Routledge & Sons, London
Hardback	x, 129pp, ill., plates, 1 port., 19 x 13cm
Notes	2nd edition
1908	George Routledge & Sons, London
Hardback	x, 129pp, ill., plates, 1 port., 19 x 13cm
Notes	3rd edition
[1915]	George Routledge & Sons, London
Hardback	x, 129pp, ill., plates, 1 port, 19 x 13cm
Notes	4th edition
[1917]	George Routledge & Sons, London
Paperback	x, 129pp, ill., plates, 19 x 13cm
Notes	5th edition
[n.d.]	George Routledge & Sons, London
Paperback	x, 129pp, ill., plates, 18 x 13cm
Notes	6th edition
[n.d.]	George Routledge & Sons, London
Paperback	viii, 88pp, ill., plates, 19 x 13cm
Notes	7th edition

As the title makes clear, this book is for all standards of players but veers heavily towards the beginner. The more experienced player may be more interested in the chapters called 'Strokes of Great Players' and 'Leading Professionals in 1901', both of which are found towards the end of the book. Chapter eighteen, 'Noteworthy Facts' is packed with information and statistics on the leading players of the day (e.g. Charles Dawson, John Roberts, W. J. Peall etc.). There are about 20 adverts dispersed throughout the book, ranging from T. W. Willis & Co. Electrical Engineers, through Geo. Edwards billiard tables, to The Swan Hotel, Thames Ditton, Surrey.

Collectors should note that two variants of the 1906 2nd edition exist. There is one with "second edition" clearly stated on the title page and one without; thus, this latter book could be confused with the 1st edition. However, they are both dated 1906 so collectors wishing to purchase a 1st edition must make sure they look for the 1901 book published by Simpkin, Marshall, Hamilton, Kent & Co. rather than a George Routledge copy.

Value £40 - £50

6.41 Side and Screw : Being Notes on the Theory and Practice of the Game of Billiards

Charles Dealtry Locock
1901   Longmans, Green & Co., London
Hardback   xiv, 182pp, ill., 20 x 14cm

The Preface of this offering from Charles Locock states that it is for "moderately advanced amateurs. A knowledge of the laws of the game and of the more elementary strokes is presumed". There is an interesting diagram on page viii, where the pockets and various points on the table have been marked out with compass points and the author refers to these compass points throughout the text. Aside from the usual chapters there is an uncommon one called 'The Billiard-Clock', where top-of-the-table play is illustrated with reference to the 12 hour marks of the clock. The book has maroon boards with gilt lettering to the spine and the front and rear endpapers have a green marbled effect, although the British Library copy may have been re-bound.

Value £80 - £120

6.42 Billiard Secrets

Wallace Ritchie
[1902]   W. Ritchie, Liscard
[Hardback]   70pp
Notes   [Information taken from British Library catalogue]

1929   G. Bell & Sons, London
Hardback   xii, 156pp, ill., 18 x 11cm

1929	G. Bell & Sons, London
Paperback	xii, 156pp, ill., 17 x 11cm

The British Library lists this book as first being self-published by Ritchie in 1902 and I have listed this edition but have not been able to see a copy (the British Library copy was destroyed during the Second World War). However, it would seem unlikely that Ritchie's book would be re-published a full 27 years later and with double the number of pages. Therefore, the 1902 copy would almost certainly have had different contents than the 1929 editions.

This small-sized compact book kicks off with a chapter called 'The ABC of Billiards' and continues with chapters named 'Side', 'Screw', 'Cannons', 'Losing Hazards', etc. The 'ABC of Billiards' chapter features the basics of the game, the 'A' being the correct stance; 'B' the proper method of holding the cue; and 'C' the formation of a correct bridge. Full-page table diagrams illustrate the points the author makes in the text and the final chapter in the book, 'Snooker', is a 12 page guide to the game including four diagrams. Ritchie admits in his Preface that he has given only the bare outlines of the game and refers the reader to his book called 'How to Play Snooker Pool', published by Messrs. Burroughes & Watts (see entry 4.0). The book is bound in plain green cloth with gilt lettering to the spine and has a green dustjacket promoting the work. [description based on 1929 edition].

Value £15 - £20

6.43 Modern Billiards

John Roberts Junior & Others / F. M. Hotine (Ed.)
1902	C. Arthur Pearson, London
Hardback	xiii, 321pp, ill., plates, 1 port., 22 x 14cm
Notes	Includes the complete text of John Roberts' book **'The Game of Billiards and How to Play It'** 1897; includes Index

1902	C. Arthur Pearson, London
Hardback	xiii, 321pp, ill., plates, 1 port., 22 x 14cm
Notes	2nd edition; as above

1910	C. Arthur Pearson, London
Hardback	xiii, 321pp, ill., plates, 1 port., 22 x 14cm
Notes	3rd edition; as above

1919	C. Arthur Pearson, London
Hardback	viii, 320pp, ill., 22 x 14cm
Notes	4th impression; as above

'Modern Billiards' has the common dark green boards of so many billiards and snooker books and the 1919 edition has a green jacket (as earlier editions most likely had too). The cover has a gilt rectangle in the top left corner containing the title, author and two crossed billiard cues. This is a real miscellany of a book, including a potted biography of Roberts and matches he played in; breaks made by W. Mitchell, Charles Dawson and H. Stevenson (there are often 27 diagrams to a page in this section); celebrated matches; and details of matches played between John Roberts and Charles Dawson between March 20th 1899 and April 3rd 1899. The prize money consisted of £100 plus the gate receipts of £2,154, which must have been an extraordinary sum in 1899! This book represents good value for collectors, containing as it does the text of one of Roberts' other publications 'The Game of Billiards & How to Play It', 1897 (see entry 6.36).

Value £25 - £35

6.44   **Practice Strokes at Billiards : for Tables of all Sizes**

Frederick Martin Hotine
| [1902] | C. Arthur Pearson, London |
| Hardback | 77pp, ill., 19 x 13cm |

1905	C. Arthur Pearson, London
Hardback	77pp, ill., 19 x 13cm
Notes	2nd edition

1913	C. Arthur Pearson, London
Hardback	91pp, ill., 19 x 13cm
Notes	3rd and enlarged edition

1919	C. Arthur Pearson, London
Hardback	91pp, ill., 19 x 13cm
Notes	4th edition; reverse of title page mistakenly says the 3rd enlarged edition was published in 1912

There is at least one illustration on virtually every page of this book, ranging from losing hazards, to opening play, to cushion cannons. Each illustration is accompanied by a few lines of text telling the reader how to play the particular shot pictured. The volume has lovely bright red and green pictorial boards featuring a billiard player at the table on the front and an advert for Burroughes & Watts on the rear. Contemporary adverts at the front and back of the book include miniature tables made by J. R. Mally & Co., the book 'Fun On The Billiard Table' by 'Stancliffe', miniature and full-size tables by Kent & Co., 'Modern Billiards' by John Roberts and Others, A. W. Gamage Ltd. (billiard tables and accessories), 'Billiards for Everybody' by Charles Roberts, plus a 4 page catalogue of Pearson's publications.

The extra material featured in the 1913, enlarged edition is two chapters – 'A Losing Hazard Break by W. Mitchell' and 'A Billiard 'Patience Game'. Overall this book is very similar in size, content and feel to 'The Game of Billiards and How to Play It' by John Roberts Junior, also published by Pearson three years later (see entry 6.52).

A copy of Hotine's book, with an incorrect publication date of 1906 quoted by the seller, in very poor condition (the cover picture was virtually obliterated) fetched a very healthy £48 on eBay in December 2007.

Value £40 - £50

6.45   Cue Tips : Hints on Billiards for 100 Up-pers and Owners of Bijou Tables

William Mitchell / Frederick Martin Hotine (Ed.)
[1903]   R. A. Everett & Co., London
Paperback   128pp, ill., 17 x 11cm

The author states in his Preliminary Remarks that he feels "... that there is not only room for, but an absolute want of a popular manual of billiards which should cater for the ordinary player ...". Mitchell then goes on to deliver this manual by illustrating a series of positions that an ordinary player may come up against in the course of a game. The book does this by a page of text on the even numbered pages and a diagram of play on the odd. The Conclusion recommends further study in the form of Roberts's 'Modern Billiards' (see entry 6.43), an obvious plug for F. M. Hotine as he also edited that particular book. This book was originally published in paperback format but as the covers are so fragile many copies have been re-bound.

Value £100 - £200

6.46   Billiards Expounded : to all Degrees of Amateur Players

J. P. Mannock / S. A. Mussabini
Vol. 1 : The Elementary Side of Billiard-Playing
1904   Grant Richards, London
Hardback   viii, 437pp, ill., plates, 21 x 14cm

Vol. 2 : The Advanced Side of the Game
1904   Grant Richards, London
Hardback   vi, 415pp, ill., plates, 21 x 14cm

Vol. 1 : The Elementary Side of Billiard-Playing
[1908]   John F. Shaw & Co., London
Hardback   viii, 437pp, ill., plates, 19 x 13cm

Vol. 2 : The Advanced Side of the Game
[1908]   John F. Shaw & Co., London
Hardback   vi, 424pp, ill., 19 x 13cm

The early years of the 20th century was a good time for publishing billiards books with Riso Levi's 3-volume set, 'Billiards : the Strokes of the Game' (see entry 6.49), totalling nearly 800 pages and this effort reaching 852 pages over two volumes. The usual green boards, crossed cues motif and gilt lettering are used on the 1st edition set and the same adverts appear in the back of both volumes. John Patrick Mannock (credited with the discovery of the anchor cannon) was a tutor of billiards and S. A. Mussabini was Editor of 'The New World of Billiards'[17] and all the expected areas of the game are covered in this vast, encyclopaedic publication.

Each volume of the 1st edition sells for around £70-£75 on eBay and copies of the 1908 edition usually command £50-£55. Indeed, a 2 volume 1st edition set, described as very good with no faults or markings and in clean condition, made £165 on eBay in October 2007. A further set, bound in contemporary half green morocco with marbled endpapers and minimal rubbing to the bindings and in excellent clean condition, sold for £167 on eBay in December 2007.

Value each vol. **£60 - £75**

6.47   **Billiards : the Strokes of the Game Volume I**

Riso Levi
1904   R. Levi, Manchester
Paperback   76pp, ill., 22 x 16cm

1904   [R. Levi], [Manchester]
Paperback   76pp, ill., 22 x 16cm
Notes   2nd edition

This publication has green & white card covers with a cartouche containing a billiard table sitting in the centre and the rear cover carries an advert for Crystalate Billiard Balls. Volume I of this IX volume series addresses topics such as 'Potting the White', 'Potting the Red & Cannoning (or vice versa) in One Stroke', 'Bringing the White out of Baulk', 'Potting the Red to Leave an In-off from the White', 'the Long In-off from the White – after the Balls are Touching', 'The Cannon – after the Balls Touch', and 'Various In-offs'.

Collectors should note that there are several variant copies of Volume I, some including advertisements at the front and back of the book and each variant copy advertising different business concerns on the front cover. The page numbers in the series followed on from the previous volume; so for example, Volume I ended at page 76 and Volume II began at page 77.

Value **£20 - £40**

---

17   A journal that ran from 2nd October 1907 to 12th January 1910.

6.48   **Practical Billiards**

Charles Dawson
1904   C. Dawson, Surbiton
Hardback   ii, 233pp, ill., plates, ports., 22 x 14cm
Notes   Includes Index

This self-published book by Charles Dawson (four time winner of the World Professional Billiards Championship) brings together a number of pieces associated with the game including player biographies, illustrated hints to beginners and how-to-play instruction; plus details of the Billiard Championship and Amateur Championship, Burroughes & Watts Tournaments, and Miscellaneous Cuttings, plus a small section on Record Breaks. This is rather a heavy book that is printed on good quality paper. The book is bound in green cloth with the title and crossed cues motif on the spine and the front board carries a gilt design of a billiard player at the table.

A superb signed copy of Dawson's book made a highly respectable £165 on eBay in June 2006; although a later copy reached £127 but didn't meet the seller's reserve. A further signed copy, in good condition throughout, realised £103 in December 2007.

Value   £100 - £120

6.49   **Billiards : the Strokes of the Game**

Part 1
Riso Levi
[1905]   Riso Levi, Manchester
Hardback   264pp, ill., 1 port., 22 x 16cm

Part 2
[1909]   Riso Levi, Manchester
Hardback   xii, pp.265–500, ill., 22 x 16cm

Part 3
[1912]   Riso Levi, Manchester
Hardback   xii, pp.501–786, ill., 22 x 16cm

Unfortunately, as with most of Levi's books, there are no dates of publication in these three volumes. However, in the Preface to Part 3 (p. x) it states "... red ball break of 453 ... made this year (1912) by Henry Taylor"; in Part 2 it says on p. iv., "Diggle stands at the table in the most unorthodox manner, and yet to-day (1909) ..."; and the latest date in Part 1 appears to be 1905 where Levi states "Stevenson .. . break of 802, on February 17th 1905". I have used these dates as my guide although it must be noted that Seddon dates these books all at 1912 and Craven puts them as being published between 1907–1916.

This extraordinary 3-volume set must surely have been a labour of love for Levi, encompassing virtually every aspect of the game over an astonishing 786 pages. The volumes are profusely illustrated (over 1,000 in total) and the text is incredibly detailed. Any collector who owns these three volumes will certainly have an in-depth billiards encyclopaedia at their disposal by a man of whom W. G. Clifford stated "let it be said at once that Riso Levi has done more than any other man in the world to popularize the playing of billiards". The British Library copies are in exceptional condition, the dark green cloth and gilt title and gilt billiard table on the covers being almost pristine. Collectors should note that Part 1 was issued with a plain red jacket, Part 2 with a green jacket, and Part 3 with a blue jacket but copies with these present are incredibly rare and fetch premium prices.

Value　　　　　　　　　　　　　　　　　　　　　　　　　　the set £180+

6.50　　**Billiards : the Strokes of the Game Volume II**

Riso Levi
[1905]　　　　Riso Levi, Manchester
Paperback　　pp77-170, ill., 22 x 16cm

Volume II of Levi's series has the same cover design as Volume I except that this volume is red & white and carries different front cover advertisers, although there is no difference in the advertisements in the book itself. The contents include – 'Side', 'Run-Throughs', 'Screw & Reverse Rotation'.

Value　　　　　　　　　　　　　　　　　　　　　　　　　　£20 - £40

6.51　　**Billiard Tips : the Strokes Made in a Hundred Break**

'A Forty Years' Player'
1905　　　　　　Forster Groom & Co., London
[Paperback]　　[78]pp, ill., 14 x 10cm
Notes　　　　　2nd edition

'Billiard Tips' has dark green covers and consists of 78 un-numbered pages. The book has a Contents page, plus 4 pages of text, and the remainder of the publication consists of diagrams illustrating the strokes made in a 100 break. The last few pages have blank table diagrams printed on them, presumably for the reader to draw their own shots on them whilst practicing. [description based on a photocopy].

Value　　　　　　　　　　　　　　　　　　　　　　　　　　£350 - £450

6.52　　**The Game of Billiards and How to Play It**

John Roberts Junior
1905　　　　　　C. Arthur Pearson, London

Hardback	124pp, ill., 19 x 13cm
Notes	2nd impression 1909, 3rd impression 1913 (hb), 4th impression 1917 (hb and pb), 5th impression 1919 (pb); includes Index
1922	C. Arthur Pearson, London
Hardback	124pp, ill., 18 x 12cm
Notes	6th impression; includes Index
1933	C. Arthur Pearson, London
Hardback	124pp, ill., 19 x 13cm
Notes	7th impression; includes Index

This book is basically a revised and updated edition of Roberts' 1897 work with the same title (see entry 6.36), with the text arranged in a different order to the earlier edition and is much more user-friendly, with plenty of sub-headings. The diagrams were also renumbered for the 1905 edition. The book has superb bright green, red and white pictorial boards featuring a picture of a billiard table and this is the edition collectors should look out for as the 1897 edition is scarce. However, the 1905 edition is difficult to value as copies have sold for as much as £120 on eBay and as little as £20. Due to the number of copies that have appeared for sale lately a more conservative estimate of value would seem appropriate. However, copies with the green dustjacket may achieve slightly higher prices than that listed below.

Value £25 - £35

6.53   Billiards : the Strokes of the Game

R. Levi
[1906]   R. Levi, Manchester
Hardback   420pp, ill., 22 x 16cm

A one cloth volume of Levi's classic work, this book covers all aspects of billiards over a mammoth 420 pages and is amply illustrated with small line diagrams. Subjects covered include – 'Potting the White', 'Bringing the White out of Baulk', and 'the Cannon-after the Balls Touch'.

Value £50 - £100

6.54   Billiards : the Strokes of the Game Volume III

Riso Levi
[1906]   Riso Levi, Manchester
Paperback   pp171-264, ill., 22 x 16cm

Volume III of Levi's series has blue & white card covers and has variant adverts, both on the cover and inside the book itself, to the previous two volumes. Contents are

– 'Drag', 'Top', 'Fine Strokes', 'Forcing Strokes', 'Jennies', 'Kiss-Cannons', and 'Kiss In-offs'.

Value £30 - £50

6.55 The Top-of-the-Table Game

H. W. Stevenson
1906 Cox & Yeman, London
Hardback 64pp, ill., plates, 1 port., 14 x 17cm
Notes 1/- edition

1906 Cox & Yeman, London
Hardback 64pp, ill., plates, 1 port., 14 x 17cm
Notes 2/- edition

This scarce book by Stevenson has stiff green boards with an oval portrait of the player on the cover. There are some fascinating b & w plates at the front showing scenes from a billiard table maker's workshop depicting tables, cushions and cues being crafted. The rest of the book is amply illustrated with small line diagrams and there are plenty of period advertisements. The 2/- edition has stiffer boards and is a darker green than the 1/- edition and the title and author are stamped in gilt on the cover. Both editions carry the same oval portrait of Stevenson of whom Riso Levi stated "he was second to none in his mastery of the intricacies of the top-of-the-table play". A copy of this book, with boards creased down the middle and corners slightly bumped, fetched £265 on eBay in October 2006.

Value £250 - £300

6.56 The Whole Art of Billiards

F. M. Hotine
1906 Sands & Co., Edinburgh & London
Hardback 117pp, ill., 23 x 15cm
Notes Includes contributions from W. Spiller and W. Mitchell

1906 Sands & Co., Edinburgh & London
Paperback 117pp, ill., 23 x 15cm

The author in his Introduction states that "...this book is for the most part reprinted from a magazine which had a very small circulation, and it is now among the things that were". Unfortunately, the magazine is not named. Hotine's book includes illustrations (16 to a page) of a match between Roberts and Stevenson; a Professional 300 Up; and a 367 break by Edward Diggle. There are also more talkative aspects to the book, particularly in 'Tips from an Old Cue', 'Some Practical Instructions', and 'American View of Origin of Billiards'. Originally selling for 1/6, this fairly slim volume is bound in dark olive cloth with a substantial picture of a player at the table in the centre.

Value   £60+

6.57   **The A.B.C. of Billiards**

Sydenham Dixon
[1907]   Henry J. Drane, London
Hardback   86pp, ill., 14 x 11cm

Dixon was the Billiards Association president between 1906-1919 and his delightful pocket-sized book is essentially a guide to billiards for beginners containing all the usual chapter headings – 'Cues', 'Striking the Cue-Ball', 'Losing Hazards', 'Winning Hazards' etc. There is also a 5 page list of 'Terms Used in Billiards'. The publication includes an advert for Crystalate billiard balls as well as one for other ABC books on subjects including solo whist, chess, palmistry and graphology. The book has red boards with white lettering and placed in three of the four corners are small pictures of two billiard cues, a triangle and a set of billiard balls.

Value   £100 - £120

6.58   **Potting the Red Ball (Volume IV of Billiards : the Strokes of the Game)**

Riso Levi
[1907]   R. Levi, Manchester
Paperback   pp265-346, ill., 22 x 16cm

As the title suggests the contents of this volume are very slender and contain only one chapter, entitled 'Potting the Red Ball'. The design of the cover is different from the previous three volumes and is dark green & white.

Value   £40 - £60

6.59   **The Board of Green Cloth**

Cecil Harverson
[1908]   Eveleigh Nash, London
[Paperback]   15pp, 11 x 7cm

'The Board of Green Cloth' has a 1 page section on snooker and the remainder of the tome encompasses various aspects of billiards. The billiards section includes hints for amateurs where Harverson says "never practise unless you feel in the mood for it. When you tire, and play carelessly, put your cue away". Also included are tables of 'Championships' and 'Records' of Amateur Championship winners from 1896-1908, plus Billiard Association winners from 1899-1903. The book has green wrappers depicting two gentlemen at play stamped onto the cover. [description based on a photocopy].

Value £100 - £200

6.60   **The Game of Billiards : With a Special Treatise on Nursery Cannons**

William Cook
[1908]   The New World of Billiards, London
Paperback   124pp, ill., ports., 19 x 13cm

Another instructional billiards book featuring the expected chapters all amply illustrated with line drawings. There is an advert for Thurston's of Leicester Square, plus an interesting advert stating that the author, world record break holder with 42,746, is available "to play Exhibition Matches in Town or Country; or to teach Billiards to Ladies and Gentlemen". This book has very thick card covers and the publication date can be gleaned from an advert in the book that is dated 1908. A copy with a frayed and chipped spine sold for an impressive £210 against an estimate of £70-£100 at the Dominic Winter sale of July 2006 but most copies sell for less than that figure.

Value £100 - £150

6.61   **The In-off Game (Volume V of Billiards : the Strokes of the Game)**

Riso Levi
[1908]   R. Levi, Manchester
Paperback   pp341-427, ill., 22 x 16cm
Notes   The extra numbered pages of this edition carry adverts

[1908]   R. Levi, Manchester
Hardback   pp341-420, ill., 22 x 16cm

Levi's 1908 publication, 'The In-off Game', continued his 'Billiards : the Strokes of the Game' series and had a blue & white cover that carried the same design as Volume IV. The numerous 'in-off' chapters include – 'Cross In-offs', 'In-offs from the Red on the Spot', 'Centre-Pocket In-offs', and 'Top-Pocket In-offs'. Collectors should be aware that there is a variant hardback edition where the page numbers stop at 420 and the subsequent, un-numbered, 4 pages contain contemporary advertisements.

Value £50 - £80

6.62 **Suggested Amended Billiard Rules for Amateur Players**

P. H. Emerson
1908   P. H. Emerson, Southbourne-on-Sea
[Hardback]   8pp

Peter Henry Emerson's short book is an examination of the various billiard strokes and the rules of the game and includes discussion of J. P. Mannock and Rimington-Wilson and their theories. In his summing up, the author argues that the amateur should "go for scientific losing hazard play, and all the billiard world will profit by it, and amateurs will increase in numbers and keenness". Emerson was part of the Foxwold Billiard Circle whose publications held by the British Library were unfortunately destroyed during the Second World War. [description based on microfilm copy].

Value   £50 - £80

6.63 **Cannons (Volume VI of Billiards : the Strokes of the Game)**

R. Levi
[1909]   R. Levi, Manchester
Hardback   pp421-500, ill., 22 x 16cm

[1909]   R. Levi, Manchester
Paperback   pp421-504, ill., 22 x 16cm
Notes   The extra numbered pages of this edition carry adverts

This volume is bound in plain green cloth, and stamped in gilt on the cover is the inscription "With the Compliments of Thos. Padmore & Sons, Billiard Table Manufacturers, 118 Edmund St., Birmingham". The contents are as follows – 'Cannons to Leave an In-off', 'Cannons in Baulk', 'Cannons off the Red on the Spot', 'Cannons off the Top Cushion', 'Cannons off the Side Cushion', and 'Cross Cannons'.

Value   £50 - £80

6.64 **How to make a Hundred Break, Billiards Made Easy**

John Roberts Junior
1909   Simpkin, Marshall, Hamilton, Kent & Co., London
Hardback   86pp, ill., 1 port., 19 x 13cm
Notes   Includes 'Billiardaria', a Collection of Anecdotes and Reminiscences connected with my Billiard Career'

In this book Roberts gives the reader a lesson in the art of making breaks because he feels "this is where the average amateur fails so lamentably". The first part, 'A

Hundred Break', takes up 65 pages and the next section, 'Billiardaria', relays various anecdotes. The final chapter is called 'The Future Government of Billiards', a section where Roberts attacks the Billiard Association in a ferocious manner and states his belief that the future of the sport lays firmly in the hands of the Billiards Control Club and Union.

A couple of copies of this book have sold on eBay recently. The first, rather a poor copy with damage to the spine, made almost £79 in April 2007; whilst the second copy, described as generally good with the spine lightly cracked and some marks and stains on the cover, achieved £72 in July 2007.

Value £70 - £80

6.65 **Cannons : Part II : (Volume VII of The Strokes of the Game)**

R. Levi
[1910] R. Levi, Manchester
Paperback pp501-588, ill., 22 x 16cm

1910 R. Levi, Manchester
Paperback pp501-594, ill., 22 x 16cm
Notes Additional pages contain adverts

'Cannons : Part II' of Levi's series has blue & white card covers and contains the following instructional content – 'Screw Cannons from the D', 'Long-Distance Cannons – Object Balls Close Together', 'Cannons – Hitting a Cushion First', 'Gathering Cannons', 'Cannons off Double Baulks', 'Nursery Cannons and Close Cannons', 'Rocking Cannons', 'Pendulum Cannons', 'Cradle Cannons', and 'The Jam Stroke'.

Value £100 - £120

6.66 **Useful Strokes for Billiard Players**

Wallace Ritchie
[1910] George Routledge & Sons, London
Hardback vi, 101pp, ill., 19 x 13cm

Ritchie's book has fantastic deep red pictorial boards with the title in black at the top and a picture of a player leaning over the table whilst his opponent looks on in the centre. In his Introduction, the author states that the strokes included within the pages are "in all cases such as can be made by any ordinary player" and that "it is not, however, to the expert cueist that I specially appeal, but rather to the average player". Ritchie makes this appeal by detailing 50 strokes, each one described on even numbered pages and illustrated on odd. This book, whilst not especially valuable, is worth owning for the superb cover alone!

Value £40 - £50

6.67   **Billiard Hints**

Charles Roberts ('Vivid')
[1911]   Dawe & Son, London
Paperback   16pp, ill., 19 x 13cm

[1922]   The Sydenham Press, London
Paperback   16pp, ill., 19 x 13cm
Notes   2nd edition

The 1st edition of 'Billiard Hints' has orange card wrappers and originally sold for 3d., but unfortunately is not dated. However, the rear cover mentions three of Roberts' previous publications the last of which, 'The Complete Billiard Player', was published in 1911. This is a slim volume portraying the basics of billiards – cues, the bridge, easy positions – through to losing hazards, half ball cannons and so forth. The book is amply illustrated and includes the Rules of the Game of Billiards. The 2nd edition originally cost 8d., has green card covers, and includes the Rules of the Game of Snooker Pool.

Value   **£140 - £160**

6.68   **Billiards Simplified**

Wallace Ritchie
[1911]   Burroughes & Watts, London
Hardback   xviii, 72pp, plates, 19 x 13cm
Notes   Revised edition; Preface by Edward Diggle; includes
                  Appendix

This volume has nice looking grey boards with a decorative b & w picture on the cover. After the 8 page Preface, Ritchie takes the reader through the usual instructional topics. To keep the reader engaged the author then includes chapters on the 'Billiard Temperament', 'Averages' and an Appendix reprinted from an April 14th 1909 article contributed by Ritchie to 'The New World of Billiards' that concerns the revolutionary replacing of wooden beds with slate on a billiard table.

Value   **£25 - £35**

6.69   **Billiards in Twelve Lessons**

Wallace Ritchie
[1911]   Burroughes & Watts, London
Hardback   143pp, ill., plates, 22 x 14cm

The twelve lessons in Ritchie's book cover the expected instructional topics and are illustrated by line drawings and photos. In the chapter called 'Tenth Lesson

– Cushion & All-Round Cannons', Ritchie states "I am not, as you are aware, by any means an advocate of the elaborate and showy style of play affected by many amateurs, but pin my faith wholly and solely to the axiomatic truth that the simpler you can make your game the better". This philosophy runs right through the book and the simplicity of Ritchie's message must have appealed to readers. The volume originally cost 2/6 and has a colourful picture, in orange and green, of a lady and gentleman at play stamped onto the front cover. Copies of this book, one in poor condition, sold recently on eBay for £27 and £36 but copies in very good condition realise higher prices than that.

Value £35 - £50

6.70 **The Complete Billiard Player**

Charles Roberts ('Vivid')
1911 Methuen & Co., London
Hardback x, 284pp, ill., plates, 1 port., 23 x 15cm
Notes Includes 31 page publisher's catalogue at rear

1921 Methuen & Co., London
Hardback vii, 208pp, ill., 1 plate, 23 x 15cm
Notes 2nd (revised) edition; 8 page publisher's catalogue at rear

In his Preface the author states that "an attempt is made in this book on billiards to teach the game thoroughly to those who have never handled a cue". After a few preliminary chapters discussing the origins of the sport and the billiard room and its accessories, Roberts takes the reader through all aspects of play and thus instructs those readers who have indeed never handled a cue. There is a 'Glossary of Billiard Terms' near the start of the volume and a rules section, tables of records and a brief section on 'Snooker Pool and Other Games' at the rear. There are plenty of table diagrams (very often 4 to a page) plus b & w photos of Roberts demonstrating aspects of play.

Value £150 - £180

6.71 **Drop Cannons and Getting Position for Top-of-the-Table Play (Volume VIII of The Strokes of the Game)**

R. Levi
[1911] R. Levi, Manchester
Paperback pp589-656, ill., 22 x 16cm

This book has a brown & white cover and the contents include - 'Getting Position for a Drop Cannon', 'Drop Cannons', and 'Getting Position for Top-of-the-Table Play'.

Value £110 - £130

6.72   The Practical Science of Billiards and Its "Pointer"

Charles Maximilian Western, Colonel
1911   Simpkin, Marshall, Hamilton, Kent & Co., London
Hardback   iv, 153pp, ill., 1 plate, 23 x 15cm
Notes   Contains Errata attached to page 3

This book, consisting of dark green boards with gilt lettering, is a fascinating look at billiards from a scientific angle. The 'pointer' of the title is an instrument that points out on the table the direction that both balls will follow under every possible condition. This 'pointer' is illustrated in a superb fold-out diagram attached to page 113. For those who are not scientifically minded this book may prove to be a struggle as there are plenty of mathematical tables illustrating angles of trajectory, force of the object ball etc. There are two tables at the rear of the volume where players can fill in their own angles of shots. There are also a couple of tear-out order forms where the reader could order a 'Pair of Breeches Position Indicator' from Odhams of Long Acre, London, and 'The Billiard Pointer' from Aston & Mander of Soho, London, at 3s. 6d. and 15s. respectively. The frontispiece is a plate called 'The Law and the Magic Spot', that shows a billiard table with a diagram that is explained on pages 145 and 146. Copies of Western's book do not appear for sale often but a copy sold for £180 on eBay in June 2006.

Value   £150 - £200

6.73   **Red Ball Play**

George Gray
1911   Cassell & Co., London
Paperback   viii, 128pp, ill., plates, 1 port., 19 x 13cm
Notes   Foreword by George Nelson

As the title suggests, and George Nelson's comments in the Foreword state, this is not a general treatise on billiards but "... an exposition of the theory of red ball play ..." Again, according to Nelson, the pioneer of this style of play was Harry Gray, George's father, but Nelson feels that young George has taken red ball play to another level. Red ball play was considered the backbone of amateur play as top-of-the-table play was considered to require far too much touch, experience and skill for the amateur.

The book starts with the basics of billiards (the stance, bridge etc.) moves onto 'Practice Strokes' (each shot illustrated by a full-page drawing), and concludes with Gray illustrating a 102 break. The final two chapters consist of a list of some of Gray's big breaks and a section entitled 'George Gray on Himself'.

'Red Ball Play' was published by Cassell & Co. and has stiff card covers with a colour picture[18] of Gray at the table on the front. There are plenty of contemporary adverts spread over 15 glossy pages at the front and back of the volume, most of which are for E. J. Riley. The most unusual of the adverts is for 'Sozodont Powder' – "for Cleansing and Beautifying the Teeth". A copy, with some foxing and a worn spine, fetched £72 on eBay in January 2007; and an earlier copy realised £52.

Value £50 - £70

6.74 **Top of-the-Table Play, Pique and Masse Strokes, Single and Double Baulks, Safety Play, and C. (Volume IX of Billiards : the Strokes of the Game)**

R. Levi
[1912]   R. Levi, Manchester
Paperback   pp657-793, ill., 22 x 16cm

The last volume of Levi's series has a black & white cover and its contents include – 'Top-of-the-Table Play', 'Pique & Masse Strokes', 'Single Baulks & Double Baulks', 'Safety Play', 'Some Little-Known Strokes', 'Transmitted Side & Cushion –Imparted Side'.

Value £130 - £150

6.75 **Billiards for Everybody Volume II**

Charles Roberts ('Vivid')
[1913]   The Charles Roberts, Billiards Supply Co., Leigh [Essex]
Hardback   96pp, ill., plates, 1 port., 18 x 12cm
Notes   This edition has 'Part II' on the cover

Volume II of Charles Roberts' 'Billiards for Everybody' is a separate publication from the other titles listed above (see entry 6.40) and has different contents. These include chapters headed 'How Miss Ruby Roberts Learnt the Top of the Table Game', 'Showing the Run of the Balls on a 23 Break', and 'Some Cannons : Roberts on Billiards, 1864'. The tome is amply illustrated and has stiff, white card covers with blue typography and a picture of Roberts.

Value £40 - £50

---

18 The same picture of Gray features in a b & w postcard on p. 50 of Roger Lee's 'Billiards & Snooker : a Postcard Album '- see entry 7.89

~ 1915 – 1945 ~

6.76   Billiards

Tom Reece / W. G. Clifford
1915   A. & C. Black, London
Hardback   viii, 312pp, ill., plates, 20 x 14cm
Notes   Includes Index

This heavy volume has dark green boards with a lovely gilt picture of a player's arm and cue on the cover. There are two variant dustjackets, the first is white with a b & w photo; and the second is pale orange with the same picture of the player's arm, described above, on it. This edition also included a loose-leaf 4 page publisher's catalogue advertising books on golf, fishing, shooting, bowling, curling and billiards.

There is an enlightening discussion in the first 50 or so pages featuring the origins of the game, billiards in literature ("Almost every other author seems to drag in billiards when he wishes to dwell upon some aspect of human weakness or depravity") and the state of billiards at the time of publication. What follows is an in-depth manual on all facets of the game fully illustrated with 84 b & w photos. There is even a section on choosing a table, lighting a billiard room and brushing the cloth. Rather interestingly, the British Library copy has an article from The Times dated June 24th 1926 stuck onto the rear paste-down endpaper stating that Tom Reece had lost over £8,000 at Manchester Races in one week and been declared bankrupt.

Value   £40 - £60

6.77   Roberts' Billiards for Amateurs

Charles Roberts
[1915]   T. Werner Laurie, London
Hardback   102pp, ill., 18 x 12cm

[1922]   Charles Roberts, London
Paperback   94pp, ill., 19 x 13cm
Notes   2nd edition

There is no date of publication in this book and I'm not sure how the British Library has estimated 1915 as there are few clues in the book itself. The latest date mentioned in the text appears to be 1912 so there is a chance the book may have been published before 1915. This small sized, rather plain volume is bound in dark red cloth and is fully illustrated throughout. The book contains some amusing 'Dont's' [sic] – "Don't throw your cue against walls", and "Don't rush into billiard rooms slamming doors and generally conducting yourself as if you own the universe"! After this Roberts goes on to describe various aspects of play and there are also some contributions by W. Cook. The back of the volume has a catalogue of Laurie's publications and the 2nd edition has pictorial card wrappers.

Value £80 - £120

6.78 Billiards at Home

Charles Roberts
[1918] Robert Scott, London
Hardback x, 110pp, ill., plates, ports., 19 x 13cm
Notes Foreword by Edmund Hudgell

Another book that has no date on the title page, this work has white boards with green typography and a photo of a player making a bridge in the middle of the front cover. This book is rather curious in that it is specifically written for amateurs who play on a 6ft billiard table at home and there is an interesting idea put forward in the General Introduction that a second-class Championship should be established for players who have never competed for the amateur Championship and to be played on a standard 6ft table. The usual topics are covered in the book e.g. 'Winning Hazards', 'Angles' and 'A Learner's Break'. There are a few contemporary adverts at the rear of the book plus a catalogue of Robert Scott publications.

Value £80 - £120

6.79 The Beginner at Billiards

Cut-Cavendish (pseud. of Edwyn Anthony)
[1919] T. Werner Laurie, London
Hardback 110pp, ill., 19 x 13cm
Notes Includes fold out 'Handicap Table for Amateurs'

[1919] T. Werner Laurie, London
Paperback 110pp, ill., 19 x 13cm
Notes As above

There is no date of publication on the title page but the British Library date of 1919 ties in with an advert in the book for 'How to Win at Royal Auction Bridge', by Anthony, which was also published in 1919. The book has decorative green boards with the title being flanked by two tall lamps and underneath the title are two crossed cues and a set of billiard balls. Areas covered include 'Short and Long Losers', 'Screw', 'Side and Drag', and 'Some Don'ts' – "Don't lose your temper. A bad loser is as great a nuisance as a bad winner". The book also includes 'The Rules of Billiards' and a fold-out 'Handicap Table for Amateurs' (drawn up by the Billiards

Control Club) – a complicated looking table whereby a player can fill out the card, send it off to the BCC and obtain a certificate of their handicap. There is also a list of titles in Laurie's Popular Library plus two adverts – 'Chats on Photography' and the aforementioned auction bridge publication.

Value   £80 - £120

6.80   **A Billiard Player in the Making**

S. A. Mussabini ('Ivor')
[1920]   E. Hulton & Co., London
Paperback   115pp, ill., 14 x 21cm

'A Billiard Player in the Making' has thin green cloth covers, with the title in a darker green box angled across the front. The rear cover houses a full-page advertisement for E. J. Riley and pictures one of their tables in the centre. Mussabini's book is very similar in size to the pre-2006 modern day 'Snooker' ('Know the Game' series – see entry 4.38) and has some terrific line drawings of players demonstrating the stance, the bridge hand, using the rest etc. Specific shots are also illustrated right the way through, sometimes with full-page diagrams but very often two to a page. Aside from the instructional sections there are also chapters on 'Care of the Table' and 'Requirements in a Cue, and How to Tip it'. Scipio Africanus Mussabini (1867-1927) was an athletics coach and author who was born in London. In collaboration with Sydenham Dixon he founded a monthly journal on billiards in 1900[19] and later went on to become the proprietor and owner of the journal. When he found himself in financial difficulty during the First World War he became a fee-earning billiards referee.

Value   £140 - £160

6.81   **Billiards for the Million : Volume I**

Riso Levi
[1920]   Riso Levi, Manchester
Hardback   viii, 248pp, ill., 1 plate, 22 x 14cm

There is no date given on the title page of Levi's book, however the Preface mentions articles the author wrote in 1920 and one advert at the rear includes a date of 1920. The book is bound in dark blue cloth with the title and author in gilt at the top of the cover and a gilt billiard table in the bottom right hand corner, and has a blue-green dustjacket. The volume also includes a great colour advert at the rear showing Burroughes Hall and testimonies for Burroughes & Watts' products, plus adverts for Thos. Padmore & Sons, Geo. Wright & Co., E. J. Riley, and Thurston & Co.

---

19   'The World of Billiards' which ran from 14th November 1900 until 4th September 1907 and continued as 'New World of Billiards', 2nd October 1907 to 12th January 1910.

In the Preface the author states that this volume is almost entirely a reprint of articles that appeared in papers between 1919–1920. The book opens with a history chapter (purposely omitted from Levi's 'Billiards : the Strokes of the Game') and moves onto 'Knowledge of the Game', 'True Cueing', and so forth. There are a few illustrations included but the inclination of the book is more towards discussion.

A copy described as worn at head and foot and with a faded spine, and signed by Willie Smith, sold for £50 at the Dominic Winter summer sale of 2006.

Value   £40 - £60

6.82   Billiards : How to Improve Your Game

Frank M. Carruthers
1921   Country Life & George Newnes, London
Paperback   iii, 32pp, 19 x 13cm
Notes   One of the 'Country Life' Booklets

Sections in this book include the basics such as 'How to Make a Bridge', 'The Correct Grip', and 'Swing of the Cue and Sighting' through to the use of side, where the author warns – "never use it unless the shot is one that cannot be made without its application". The final two sections feature brief passages on snooker and pyramids, and pool and cork pool. As with many contemporary books this one features adverts for Riley's, Burroughes & Watts, and an advert for 'Victor' cloth manufactured by A. Fremont & Co. of Hackney, London. Carruthers was Amateur Champion in 1921 and there is a b & w photo of him at the table on the white cover.

Value   £80 - £120

6.83   Billiards for Amateurs

Sidney H. Fry
[1922]   Hodder & Stoughton, London
Hardback   xi, 233pp, ill., plates, 1 port., 23 x 16cm
Notes   Foreword by Bernard Darwin; G. W. Beldam (photog.);
                        includes contributions by Tom Newman, W. J. Peall,
                        Melbourne Inman, Tom Reece, Willie Smith and Claude
                        Falkiner

There are a couple of interesting early chapters in this book entitled 'The Fascination of Billiards' and 'Has the Game Become Too Easy'? These chapters discuss the difficulty of billiards in relation to other ball games, the disparity between the professional and the amateur, the notion that billiards was a game for the 'masses', plus the author also makes some suggestions as to how the game could be made more difficult. Several chapters are written by the players listed above and the whole book is heavily illustrated and, at 233 pages, very detailed. There is no date of publication on the title page but the Foreword is dated June 1922.

A copy of Fry's book, described as tight with a little foxing, achieved a price of £30 on eBay in May 2007; and a further copy with the front board loose, stained to front cover, slightly foxed and corners of the spine bumped, made £31 in October 2007.

Value   £30 - £50

6.84   **Billiards and Games of Pool**

Rolf M. Danery (pseud. of Edward Castillian Randolph & Alfred Emery)
1922   The Bazaar, Exchange & Mart Office, London
Paperback   96pp, ill., 19 x 13cm
Notes   The colourful cover of this book has the title as 'Billiards and Pool Games'; includes Index

As the title makes clear this book is split into two sections, the first being Billiards, and the second shorter section, Games of Pool. There is a brief run through concerning the origin of billiards, the table and accessories before the familiar advice on half-ball shots, screw, side, and cushion strokes begins in earnest. The second part covers ordinary (or common) pool, black pool, single pool, and finally pyramids and snooker. In this second part a chapter is also devoted to games of pool (e.g. Russian pool, selling pool, cork pool, skittle pool etc.) The billiard table pictured on the cover is manufactured by Jelks & Sons who also have an advert at the rear of the book. Other advertisers include the billiard table manufacturers Burroughes & Watts, Orme & Sons and George Edward Ltd., as well as The Bazaar, Exchange and Mart. The book has a white cover with the title and abovementioned table pictured in green, black and white.

Value   £80 - £120

6.85   **Billiards in Lighter Vein**

Riso Levi
[1922]   Riso Levi, Manchester
Hardback   248pp, ill., 19 x 13cm

As was common with Levi's books there is no date of publication in this volume but the British Library have given it a probable date of publication of 1923. However, this is somewhat surprising given that their copy is inscribed by the author to F. L. Billington Greig and dated October 11th 1922! In light of this, and the fact Bob Ledger also dates the book 1922, I have recorded a probable publication date of 1922.

Levi had covered the practical and instructional sides of the game in previous publications and here takes a look at the game with the aid of stories, sketches

145

and anecdotes. Unusual chapter headings include 'Billiards Through A Woman's Eyes', 'A Billiards Cat', and 'How I Nearly Lost £1,000'. There are several billiards related adverts at the back of the book including ones for Levi's previous books and another offering his services as a tutor.

The book is bound in dark blue cloth with the author and title set in the same typeface as Levi's previous publications. The dustjacket is mainly white with a picture of a player at the table and a black cat keeping a very close eye on proceedings. Copies of this volume with the dustjacket are exceptionally scarce and may double the value given below. Copies recently have fetched from a bargain £25 to £77 on eBay; and a copy sold at Dominic Winter's sale of July 2006 realised £70. However, most copies generally sell for between £25 and £35.

Value £25 - £35

6.86 **Billiards : with Description of a Hundred Break Illustrated with Diagrams by J. P. Mannock and Biographies and Portraits of Leading Players**

Harry Young
[1923] Athletic Publications, London
Paperback x, 66pp, [10]pp, ill., ports., 19 x 12cm
Notes J.P. Mannock (ill.); includes a table–'the Champions of 1922' and 'Record Breaks of the Professionals'

"Mr J. P. Mannock ... whom I believe I can fairly describe as the best-known tutor ever associated with the game", so the author states of the illustrator in his introduction. However, this turns out not to be the usual instructional billiards book but a fascinating volume detailing the origin of the game and biographies of leading players. Billiards in literature is mentioned (e.g. Shakespeare's reference to the game in 'Anthony & Cleopatra') as is the verse in Gilbert and Sullivan's opera 'The Mikado'. Mention is also made of Charles Cotton's 'Compleat Gamester' of 1674 ("the first writer on the game to be of any value to the present-day historian") as well as authors such as G. F. Pardon (aka Capt. Crawley) and E. Russell Mardon. There are fourteen portraits in the book to accompany the concisely written biographies and after the last numbered page there are 10 pages of illustrations showing the reader how to make a 100 break. After this there is a 2 page catalogue detailing a selection of Athletic Publications books, an advert for Riley, one for Kays Cue Cement (for sticking on cue tips), and finally Bonzoline and Crystalate billiard balls. I assume the author is the same Harry Young who was the billiards correspondent of the Daily Mail and Evening News who frequently reported on matches played at Thurston's in Leicester Square.

Value £50 - £80

6.87   **How to Play Billiards**

Tom Newman
1923   Methuen & Co., London
Hardback   vii, 219pp, ill., plates, 20 x 13cm
Notes   Includes Index

1926   Methuen & Co., London
Hardback   vii, 219pp, ill., plates, 1 port., 20 x 13cm
Notes   2nd edition; includes Index

1935   Methuen & Co., London
Hardback   vii, 219pp, 19 x 13cm
Notes   3rd edition; includes Index

This very detailed book, from the six times World Professional Billiards Champion Tom Newman, includes four b & w plates but it is not until the second half of the book that it becomes copiously illustrated. These illustrations coincide with the chapters entitled 'You And I Play Billiards', 'Our Game Continued' and 'We Finish Our Game' where Newman talks the reader through a typical game of billiards. The expected chapters include 'Side, Top & Screw', 'Top-of-the-Table Billiards', 'Plain Ball Striking' and so forth. The dark green boards have the title and author's name blocked onto the front and gilt lettering adorns the spine. As was usual practise at this time, Methuen has an 8 page catalogue of its books at the rear of the volume. The 3rd edition has a b & w dustjacket containing a formal portrait of Newman, but as with most billiard books the jacket is scarce.

Value   £40 - £50

6.88   **Advanced Billiards**

Tom Newman / W. G. Clifford
1924   John Long, London
Hardback   312pp, ill., plates, ports., 23 x 15cm
Notes   Includes Index

Although Tom Newman's name appears on the title page of this volume it states in the Acknowledgement that the book was actually written by W. G. Clifford who made notes whilst Newman played the game and talked Clifford through what he was doing. At 312 pages this is an even heftier tome than Newman's 1923 work and obviously goes into the game in some detail. The frontispiece has a formal portrait of Newman taken by Hay Wrightson of New Bond St. There are plenty of b & w plates picturing Newman demonstrating various aspects of play and the book is bound in green cloth and has a buff coloured jacket containing a blurb for the book. Sadly, as with so many pre Second World War billiards book, very few copies have the jacket intact.

Value   £80 - £100

6.89   **Billiards Do's and Dont's** [sic]

Tom Newman
1924   Methuen & Co., London
Hardback   v, 57pp, 8pp, ill., 17 x 11cm
Notes   Includes Index; includes a numbered 8 page catalogue of
                Methuen's books

1932   Methuen & Co., London
Hardback   v, 57pp, ill., 17 x 11cm
Notes   2nd edition; includes Index

This slim, hardback book has dark green boards with a decorative red, black and white picture in the middle depicting three billiard balls, a cue and a piece of chalk. The picture has been pasted onto the board and this technique was a common occurrence before the rise of the dustjacket. There were several 'Do's and Dont's' [sic] books published, including golf, tennis, mah jong, and auction bridge. The title of Tom Newman's book is self-explanatory and all sorts of advice is given over the 57 pages. A few of the more noteworthy examples include "when you fluke, don't apologise" and "don't try to play and dispute the score at the same time". Copies of Newman's work have sold for between £27 and £31 on eBay recently.

Value   £25 - £30

6.90   **Billiards : How to Play and Win**

Melbourne Inman
[1924]   W. Foulsham & Co., London
Hardback   126pp, ill., 1 plate, 15 x 10cm
Notes   Introduction by S. A. Mussabini; part of Foulsham's cloth-
                bound Pocket Library series

[n.d.]   W. Foulsham & Co., London
Hardback   117pp, ill., 1 plate, 15 x 10cm

[n.d.]   W. Foulsham & Co., London
Hardback   128pp, ill., 1 plate, 15 x 10cm

[n.d.]   W. Foulsham & Co., London
Paperback   108pp, ill., 1 plate, 16 x 11cm
Notes   Cost 3/-

148

[n.d.]	W. Foulsham & Co., London
Hardback	108pp, ill., 1 plate, 15 x 10cm
Notes	Wartime reprint costing 2/-

Inman's billiards book went through several reprints with boards of either red, green or blue and 'Billiards' written in black at the top. A dustjacket was also issued – green, white and brown in colour with a table diagram representing the predominant image. The extra pages of the 1st edition are explained by the fact that the pages carrying adverts were numbered in that edition whereas in later editions they remained un-numbered. The paperback edition has a jacket identical to the hardback and turquoise card covers.

Mussabini says of Inman in his Introduction that "doggedness, self-reliance, will-power, and concentration, a combination of match-winning characteristics which may never be excelled in any one man, assisted him to achieve his high ambitions". Inman, affectionately known as the 'Twickenham Terrier', takes the reader through various aspects of billiards and concludes with a chapter called 'Some Past Champions', where he discusses H. W. Stevenson, E. Diggle, Charles Dawson et al. This book is an eBay staple and is easily found on Abe or in secondhand bookshops. However, collectors should make sure they search for copies with the jacket and to ensure a 1st edition check the book has 126 numbered pages.

Value £10 - £15

6.91 Billiards for the Million : Volume II

R. Levi	
[1924]	R. Levi, Manchester
Hardback	248pp, ill., 22 x 14cm

Volume II of 'Billiards for the Million' is bound in dark blue cloth and has the title and author in gilt in the top left corner and a billiard table in gilt in the bottom right hand corner and has a blue-green jacket. The contents include 'Cue tips & ferrules', 'How to Increase the Speed of a Table', 'What Causes a Ball to Kick', etc. This last chapter is interesting because, over 80 years later, players, commentators and amateur scientists are still trying to puzzle out this most vexing of billiards and snooker questions.

Value £40 - £60

6.92 First Steps to Billiards

Willie Smith	
1924	Mills & Boon, London
Hardback	95pp, ill., 1 port., 19 x 13cm
Notes	Part of the 'First Steps' Series

149

Mills & Boon published a number of 'First Steps' titles, covering tennis, golf, fly-fishing, football etc. This effort from the former player Willie Smith has olive green boards with a white jacket and complements his 'Match-Winning Billiards' published in the same year (see entry below). There are no chapter headings present and very few diagrams so the novice may not have found it the best book to learn from.

Value £40 - £50

6.93 Match-Winning Billiards

Willie Smith
1924 Mills & Boon, London
Hardback vii, 215pp, ill., plates, 1 port., 23 x 15cm
Notes Includes Index

Willie Smith's second billiards book, also published by Mills & Boon, is bound in dark blue cloth and has bright gilt lettering on the cover. There are plenty of photographic plates and diagrams to illustrate the text as Smith, a former linotype operator at a newspaper, leads the reader through various aspects of play. Some quirkier chapters include 'Concerning the Scientific Side of the Game and Especially Side' and 'Some Billiard Rights and Wrongs'.

Value £40 - £50

6.94 Plain Talks to Billiard Players

Tom Aiken
[1924] W. & R. Chambers, Edinburgh
Hardback 120pp, ill., 1 port., 19 x 13cm
Notes With a Short History of the Game in Scotland by 'Winning Hazard' (pseud. of Albert de Vere)

Tom Aiken was Scottish Champion in 1902, 1907 and 1909 and says in his Introduction that his book is for the average 'hundred upper' and that he is endeavouring to make his appeal as wide as possible. What follows is a detailed study of the sport accompanied by mainly full-page table illustrations. The first 30 pages are largely biographical and describe various matches that Aiken played at both home and abroad. The contents from chapter five onwards had originally appeared in serial form in the Edinburgh Evening News. Incidentally, Riso Levi described Aiken's book as "a useful little book" and described the man himself as "undoubtedly the finest cueman which she [Scotland] has yet produced". The book has green boards, with a blue title, and originally sold for 2/6 and a few contemporary advertisements are included at the rear of the volume.

A signed copy of this book, with slight foxing to early pages, fetched £36 on eBay in November 2006; whilst a further copy, in very good condition with a facsimile dustjacket, realised £40 in March 2007.

Value   £30 - £40

6.95   **Roberts' Billiards Guide and Rules of Games**

Charles Roberts
1924   Charles Roberts, London
Paperback   48pp, ill., 18 x 13cm

This self-published book by Charles Roberts originally cost 1/- and, unusually, has pink card covers with a photo of Roberts at play on the front. The book contains b & w table illustrations and covers subjects such as advice on accessories, winning hazards, red ball play and so forth. The last 7 pages cover the rules of Snooker Pool, Billiards, and Billiard Golf. The latter is a game where a red is placed on the 'blue' spot and the player who takes the least number of shots to pot it into all 6 pockets wins the game. A copy of this book sold at the Dominic Winter October 2005 sale for £140 against an estimate of £50-£80.

Value   £120 - £160

6.96   **All About Billiards : How to Improve Your Game**

Arthur F. Peall
1925   Ward, Lock & Co., London & Melbourne
Hardback   252pp, ill., plates, 19 x 13cm
Notes   Includes Index

This extensive and detailed study covers all aspects of billiards including common faults and their cures, screw and side, positional cannon play, several sections on technique and so on. The book is illustrated throughout with line drawings and photographic plates. The Preface says the author is a coach at Thurston's and is "... the finest billiard teacher in the country to-day". The book has light olive coloured boards with the title in black and contains plenty of adverts and details of other Ward Lock publications.

Value   £60 - £75

6.97   **Billiards for the Million : Volume III**

R. Levi
[1925]   R. Levi, Manchester
Hardback   xix, 280pp, ill., 22 x 14cm

Volume III of 'Billiards for the Million' is bound in dark blue cloth and has the title and author in gilt in the top left corner and a billiard table in gilt in the bottom right hand corner. All three volumes have a blue-green dustjacket that is incredibly scarce, copies coming up for sale very rarely having the dustjacket intact. The contents include – 'Great Players : Past & Present', 'Crooked Cues', 'Luck at Billiards', 'the Legality of Fine Strokes', and so on. Each volume of 'Billiards for the Million' seems to fetch around £50 when coming up for sale. A good example is the £153 realised on eBay in July 2007 for all three volumes in generally very good condition.

Value £40 - £60

6.98   Billiards Simplified

Unknown author
[1925]   Cassell & Co., London
Paperback   xi, pp13-69, ill., 22 x 14cm
Notes   Cover title is 'Billiards'; part of Cassell's 'Handy' Series (no. 7)

This book contains no date of publication but clues in the book point to a publication date of 1925. These include adverts for a "just published" book, 'Motoring for the Owner-Driver', that the British Library catalogue as being published in 1925; plus an advert for the journal, 'The Amateur Mechanic', that ran from 1924-1926 and was also published by Cassell. 'Billiards Simplified' originally retailed at 6d. and is not particularly well illustrated but it does cover the game of billiards in some detail and was "... intended for the moderate player and the beginner..." 11 pages are devoted to Snooker Pool ("the game... is entirely one of potting...") and there are brief sections on Cork Pool and Billiard Table Tricks. The colourful cover features the often used motif of a player about to play a stroke.

Value £50 - £80

6.99   Dainty Billiards : How to Play the Close-Cannon Game

Tom Reece
1925   C. Arthur Pearson, London
Hardback   108pp, ill., 19 x 13cm

Close in feel and size to 'The Game of Billiards & How to Play It' by John Roberts Junior, 1905 (see entry 6.52), this book was also published by Pearson. The volume is bound in green cloth with the title and an illustration of a player stamped in black on the cover. As the title suggests this book is all about cannon and close play and is divided into ten chapters and is illustrated throughout. There is also an unusual chapter on 'Masse Strokes'. As was normal with billiard books at the time, there are contemporary adverts at the front and back. The dustjacket (which most copies do not have) is chiefly orange and depicts a player, unsurprisingly, executing a close cannon.

In November 2006 a very good copy of this book sold for £51 on eBay although a copy offered for sale in January 2007, priced rather optimistically at £80, failed to sell. However, a signed copy described as very good with a torn and creased dustjacket realised £77 on eBay in December 2007.

Value   **£50 - £60**

6.100   Everybody's Billiards Book

A. D. Macmillan
1925   W. Collins Sons & Co., London
Hardback   230pp, ill., 19 x 13cm

In his Introduction, Albert Duncan Macmillan states that he feels it is more important to lay down the general principles that regulate the movements of the balls than to illustrate how certain shots are played using diagrams. Hence there are relatively few illustrations in this general run-through of half-ball strokes, cannons, top-of-the-table play etc. The book has dark green boards and a 2 page publisher's catalogue at the rear.

Value   **£25 - £35**

6.101   Billiard Table Games : for Tables of all Sizes

W. G. Clifford
[1927]   W. Foulsham & Co., London
Paperback   62pp, ill., 19 x 13cm

[1944]   W. Foulsham & Co., London
Paperback   64pp, ill., plates, 19 x 13cm
Notes   Revised edition; one of Foulsham's 'New' Popular Handbooks

[n.d.]   W. Foulsham & Co., London
Paperback   64pp, ill., 20 x 13cm
Notes   As above

[n.d.]   New Era Press, London
Paperback   62pp, ill., 18 x 13cm
Notes   No. 18 in a series of 23

W. G. Clifford wrote several billiards and snooker books and this work is one of those general volumes that covers billiards, snooker pool, live pool, pyramids, Russian pool etc. The first few pages cover selecting a cue, the bridge, the stance and so forth. The book then moves onto more specific areas of play but is not so well illustrated as some other instructional books. The 1st edition has decorative orange covers, a vibrant black, yellow and green dustjacket and is one of the

153

cheaper books of the pre-war era for the collector to acquire. The undated edition by Foulsham listed above does not have a jacket but has pictorial card covers rather than the orange covers of the other Foulsham editions. The New Era Press edition has simple green card covers with black writing.

Value £10 - £15

6.102   Miniature Billiards : and how it is Played

Joe Davis
[1927]   Sykes, Horbury [Yorkshire] & London
Paperback   16pp, ill., 1 plate, 21 x 13cm

This is one of the scarcest of Davis' books and, according to Bob Ledger, the scarcity is due to the slim paperback book being given away free with a small table. To back up Ledger's claim it does state in the book that "you can have your game of snooker on the 'Joe Davis' miniature table". Davis says on page 1 of the volume "billiards gives you amusement, thrills, exercise, and co-ordination of mind and muscle". He then goes on to demonstrate how you can enjoy some of the above with a short instructional guide that also includes other games played on a billiard table, such as golf, plate pool and cork pool. This book rarely appears for sale but most copies that surface on Abe are normally priced around the £50 mark and are snapped up very quickly.

Value £50+

6.103   Billiards Up-To-Date

Joe Davis
[1929]   John Long, London
Hardback   ix, 222pp, ill., plates, 1 port., 21 x 13cm

This was Joe Davis' only full-scale billiards book and is a rather plain affair with dark red boards and no title on the cover, only the spine. The volume has a white dustjacket with a blurb for the book on it but, as with so many billiards book, is rarely present. In this book Davis focuses more on the technical side of the game – bridge, stance, cue power, using the rest – rather than the different billiards strokes and games. To keep the reader engaged there are plenty of illustrations and a few photos of Davis demonstrating aspects of the text. There is a discrepancy with the date of publication of this book, the reverse of the title page stating 1929 yet the note at the bottom of page 222 stating 1928.

Value £80 - £100

6.104 Billiards

Walter Lindrum

1930	Methuen & Co., London
Hardback	vii, 149pp, ill., plates, 20 x 13cm
Notes	Includes Index

1932	Methuen & Co., London
Hardback	vii, 149pp, ill., plates, 20 x 13cm
Notes	2nd and cheaper edition; includes Index

1934	Methuen & Co., London
Hardback	vii, 149pp, ill., plates, 20 x 13cm
Notes	3rd edition; includes Index

1938	Methuen & Co., London
Hardback	vii, 149pp, ill., plates, 20 x 13cm
Notes	4th edition; includes Index

1948	Methuen & Co., London
Hardback	vii, 149pp, ill., plates, 19 x 13cm
Notes	5th edition; includes Index

1952	Methuen & Co., London
Hardback	vii, 149pp, ill., plates, 19 x 13cm
Notes	Reprint; includes Index

1976	Hicks Smith & Sons, Sydney (Australia)
ISBN	0454000235
Paperback	147pp, ill., plates, 19 x 12cm
Notes	Facsimile reprint of the 1930 edition; includes Index

In his autobiography, 'The Breaks Came My Way', Joe Davis described Walter Lindrum[20] as "the greatest billiards player that ever lived" and few would disagree with him. This offering from the billiards genius arrived in 1930 and was published by Methuen complete with a jacket picturing Lindrum playing a masse shot. Issued with the almost standard green cloth, this 149 page book is fairly well illustrated with photos and diagrams to help the reader follow the text. The lessons cover the bridge hand and how to hit a ball, right through to cannon play. There is a pertinent quote on the back cover of the 1976 edition, namely, "a good billiard player needs the hand and eye of a cricketer and the brain of a chess-player".

---

[20] For a full account of Lindrum's life see 'Walter Lindrum : Billiards Phenomenon' by Andrew Ricketts published by Brian Clouston, Canberra, Australia, 1982.

Various editions have sold on eBay recently with a 2nd edition, complete with the dustjacket, fetching £46 in June 2007; and an earlier auction realising £31 for the 1st edition.

Value   £30 - £40

6.105   **Billiard Tips**

George Steele-Perkins
1930   Arts Club, London
[Hardback]   14pp, 1 port., 21 x 13cm

'Billiard Tips' was printed for private circulation in December 1930 and was compiled from books written by Joe Davis, Tom Newman and Willie Smith – namely, 'Billiards-up-to Date', 'How to Play Billiards', and 'Match-Winning Billiards'. The author in his Foreword confesses that he knows "nothing about Billiards" but still confidently asserts that he is "going to tell you how to play the game, so that you can all beat your opponents". The advice that follows is all well and good but becomes rather tongue-in-cheek as the book progresses. For example, on page 11 when the author is talking of 'Jenny' shots he muses "some prefer long Jennys, some short Jennys, some like them fat, some like them thin . . ."; and on the final page under the heading 'Billiard Etiquette' he says "always walk about and talk when your opponent is playing" and "it is advantageous to cultivate a sneeze which becomes impossible to withhold just as your opponent is about to strike his ball". [description based on a photocopy].

Value   £100 - £200

6.106   **Billiards in the 20th Century**

Riso Levi
[1931]   Riso Levi, Manchester
Hardback   viii, 268pp, viii, ill., plates, 22 x 14cm

[2006]   [Obscure Press][21], [Alcester]
ISBN   9781406799262[22]
Paperback   viii, 268pp, viii, ill., plates, 22 x 14cm

In this still highly readable volume Levi, in his usual combative manner, corrects several players on various points. For example, in his [1924] book 'Plain Talks to Billiard Players' (see entry 6.94) Tom Aiken stated that he had never seen 'drag'

---

21   See www.obscurepress.com for details of Levi's book and other titles Obscure Press have brought back into print.
22   See www.isbn-international.org/en/revision.html for an explanation of 13 digit ISBNs.

mentioned in a book before. Levi rather tartly points Aiken in the direction of his 'Billiards : the Strokes of the Game' and states after reading that book "he [Aiken] will then recognise that he is not the first billiards writer to draw attention of players to this important point".

Frustratingly, as with nearly all Levi's books, there is no date of publication given but on pages 51 and 80 Levi uses the word 'to-day' and follows this with 1931 in brackets. He also frequently talks about the 1930-31 billiards season throughout the book. Perhaps the real value of this volume lies in the 75 page chapter called 'Great Players I Have Watched' where Levi discusses 23 players he has seen play in his lifetime and which reads like a billiards 'who's who' (the piece on George Gray is particularly good). There are various subjects covered in the book - 'A Hundred in Four Minutes', 'Composition Balls' (a surprisingly entertaining discourse of the benefits of composition balls over ivories), 'The Value of One's Own Cue' etc., all contained between dark green boards with the title and author in gilt and Levi's familiar billiard table motif also in gilt to the bottom right corner. The 2006 reprint is a print-on-demand publication that has puce coloured card covers.

Copies of this book normally command around £35-£45 on eBay but an impressive £80 was achieved at the July 2006 Dominic Winter sale for a bright, clean copy signed and inscribed by Levi to 'A.H.Adams' and dated 28th April 1932.

Value £35 - £45 (hb)
in print £13.45 - £16.95 (pb)

6.107 **Joyce Gardner (Women's Champion) Shows Correct Stance and Screw Loser and Cannon – Willie Smith Shows the "Postman's Knock"**

Burroughes & Watts (Corp.)
[1931]   Burroughes & Watts, London
Paperback   [100]pp, plates, 8 x 6cm
Notes   A 'flicker' book

6.108 **Joyce Gardner (Women's Champion) and Willie Smith Cannon and Screw Loser and "Postman's Knock"**

Burroughes & Watts (Corp.)
[1931]   Burroughes & Watts, London
Paperback   [102]pp, plates, 8 x 6cm
Notes   Billiards 'Flicker' no. 19; no advert on back cover

6.109 **Sidney Smith : Masse Stroke and Close Cannon**

Burroughes & Watts (Corp.)
[1931]   Burroughes & Watts, London
Paperback   [102]pp, plates, 8 x 6cm
Notes   Billiards 'Flicker' no. 18; no advert on back cover

6.110 Sidney Smith Shows Masse Stroke and the Close Cannon

Burroughes & Watts (Corp.)
[1931]   Burroughes & Watts, London
Paperback   [100]pp, plates, 8 x 6cm
Notes   A 'flicker' book; contains advert on back cover

6.111 Willie Smith : Cue Grip and Bridge

Burroughes & Watts (Corp.)
[1931]   Burroughes & Watts, London
Paperback   [102]pp, plates, 8 x 6cm
Notes   Billiards 'Flicker' no. 17

6.112 Willie Smith Shows His Cue-Grip and Bridge

Burroughes & Watts (Corp.)
[1931]   Burroughes & Watts, London
Paperback   [100]pp, plates, 8 x 6cm
Notes   A 'flicker' book

Burroughes & Watts produced a series of 'flicker' books in the early 1930s covering sports as diverse as cricket, tennis, golf and greyhound racing. The billiards publications are bound in pale green card covers and, when flicked, demonstrate the shots and techniques featured in each title via cine-photos. These series of flicker books are extremely scarce and rarely surface on the market. A copy, together with a series of 50 cigarette cards featuring shots by Newman Mond (see footnote no. 7), sold at the Dominic Winter July 2006 sale for a combined total of £75.

Value   £40 - £60 each

6.113 Billiards in Easy Stages

Willie Smith
1935   Sir Isaac Pitman & Sons, London
Hardback   vii, 92pp, ill., plates, 19 x 13cm
Notes   Reprinted 1935; includes Index

1939   Sir Isaac Pitman & Sons, London
Hardback   vii, 92pp, ill., plates, 19 x 13cm
Notes   2nd edition; includes Index

1946   Sir Isaac Pitman & Sons, London
Hardback   vii, 92pp, ill., plates, 19 x 13cm
Notes   Reprint

Willie Smith won the World Professional Billiards Championship in 1920 and 1923 and this volume takes the learner through the game in stages – from holding the cue and how to stand, right through to cannon play and strokes against the nap. The various points of the game are illustrated via 7 photos and 25 diagrams. A couple of sections not necessarily found in every billiards book are 'How to use the Rest' and 'The Art of Cue Tipping' - "It is also very exasperating if one's tip falls off during the course of an important game, and this may cause the player to lose the game". A final chapter is entitled 'Care of the Table' where Smith states "heat will cause the woodwork on the table to warp ..." The book is printed on good quality glossy paper and has a black, green and white photographic cover with the jacket repeating the same details. Collectors wishing to obtain a 1st edition should check the reverse of the title page as the reprint has "Reprinted March, 1935" somewhat sneakily tucked away in very small lettering.

Value £15 - £25

6.114 Billiards for the Beginner

W. G. Clifford
[1937] W. Foulsham & Co., London
Paperback 60pp, ill., 19 x 13cm
Notes There was also a Wartime reprint published, costing 2/-

Another book that contains no publication date and there are no clues within the book either. This is a small pocket-sized book featuring a picture of a Riley 'Viceroy' table on the dustjacket and is relatively concise at 60 pages. Over the nine chapters the familiar areas of side, cannon play and safety play are covered. Collectors will want to make sure that they obtain copies with the predominantly white dustjacket. Rather surprisingly, a signed copy with a torn dustjacket made £52 on eBay in December 2007. The signature obviously bumping up the price to a level well above what a standard copy normally sells for.

Value £15 - £20

6.115 Billiards : Complete Guide to Successful Play

Sydney Lee
[1938] Link House Publications, London
Paperback 46pp, ill., 19 x 12cm
Notes Cover title is 'Billiards : Complete Guide *for* Successful Play'

[1943] Link House Publications, London
Paperback 40pp, ill., 19 x 13cm
Notes 2nd edition

This is a paperback book with a b & w photo of the author on the cover and green blocks containing the title and publisher details. There are plenty of full-page table diagrams to illustrate this slim volume and all the expected areas are analysed plus there is also a 'Rules of Billiards' chapter. The book also features an advert for tuition from Lee where those interested could apply to Burroughs' Hall, Soho Square, the 'Home of Billiards'. Perhaps the former British Empire Amateur Champion, Sydney Lee, is best remembered as the referee on the TV show 'Pot Black' where he officiated up until 1980 when illness forced him to retire.

Value £30 - £40

6.116 **All About Billiards and How to Pot**

Arthur F. Peall
[1939]   Ward, Lock & Co., London & Melbourne
Hardback   252pp, ill., plates, 19 x 13cm
Notes   Includes Index

[2006]   [Obscure Press], [Alcester]
ISBN   9781406793970
Paperback   252pp, ill., plates, 22 x 14cm
Notes   As above

This volume is an updated version of Peall's earlier book 'All About Billiards : How to Improve Your Game' published in 1925 (see entry 6.96). The only significant differences being some of the photos appear on different pages in the later work and chapter eight has the new title of 'How to Pot, and Snooker' rather than 'Winning Hazards'. At the time of publication Arthur Peall was a coach at Thurston's and was said to be "... the finest billiard teacher in the country today ...". At 252 pages this is a very detailed study of the game complete with b & w photos and amply illustrated with line drawings. The rather plain looking book is bound in olive green cloth with title, author and three billiard balls in black on the cover.

Value £15 - £20 (hb)
in print £13.45 - £16.99 (pb)

~ Post 1945 ~

6.117 **The 100-Break Target**

Victor Anton
1947   Southern Editorial Syndicate, London
Hardback   96pp, ill., plates, 19 x 13cm
Notes   'Ray' (ill.)

In his Introduction, Anton directs the beginner to the final chapter of his book ('Beginners This Way, Please') where there is a short glossary of the terms used in the sport. After digesting the contents the reader can turn to the first two sections of the book. These deal with the usual billiards topics and are accompanied by some amusingly drawn cartoons from the well-known cartoonist of the time, 'Ray'. Anton is certainly not shy in stating his opinions and this makes for a lively read. The British Library copy is bound in orange cloth and the title sits neatly in a rectangle toward the top of the cover. However, the British Library copy may well have been re-bound because other copies exist that are bound in red cloth and have the title in black lettering.

Value £120 - £150

6.118   Billiards Solitaire

Chris Hudson
1983   [Chris Hudson], no place of publication given
ISBN   None given
Paperback   [12]pp, ill., 15 x 11cm

"Billiards Solitaire is a method the billiards enthusiast can employ to improve his game by practicing certain key strokes". So says Chris Hudson on the first page of his self-published booklet. The key strokes number eight in total, are fully illustrated and cover shots such as 'The ¾ Ball Run Through', 'Top-of-the-Table' and 'The Drop Cannon'. The copy I have seen has been inserted into a dark brown card cover but this may not have been a feature of all copies.

Value £5 - £10

1897 and 1905 editions of John Roberts' work on billiards. The 1897 edition is worth £120-£150 whereas the 1905 edition fetches a far more modest £25-£35. See entries 6.36 and 6.52.

Early 20th century billiards books often had decorative designs block stamped onto the boards and many featured contemporary adverts. 'The Game of Billiards and How to Play It' features an advert for 'Crystalate' billiard balls on the rear board.

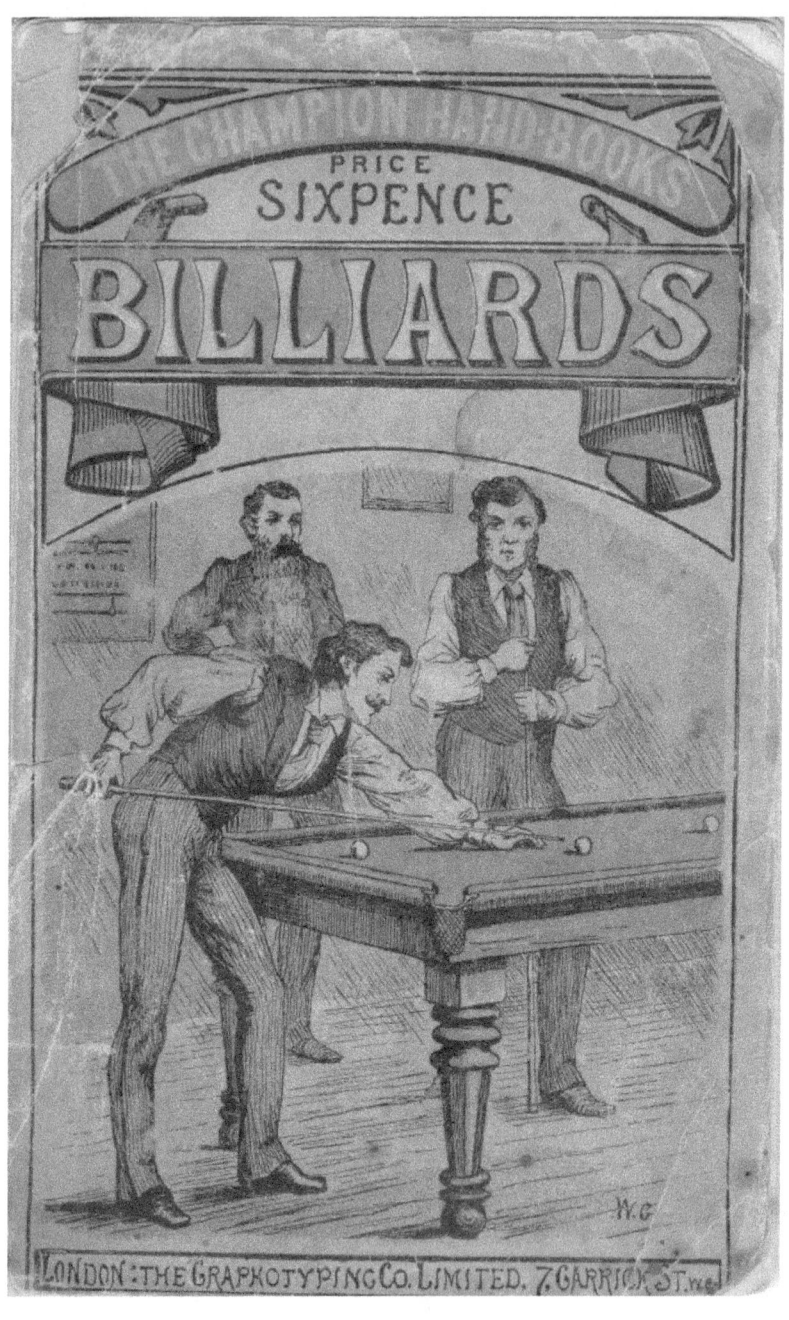

1873 edition of 'Billiards for Beginners' by Captain Rawdon Crawley. The 1st edition of 1868 sells for £250-£350 in very good condition. See entry 6.19.

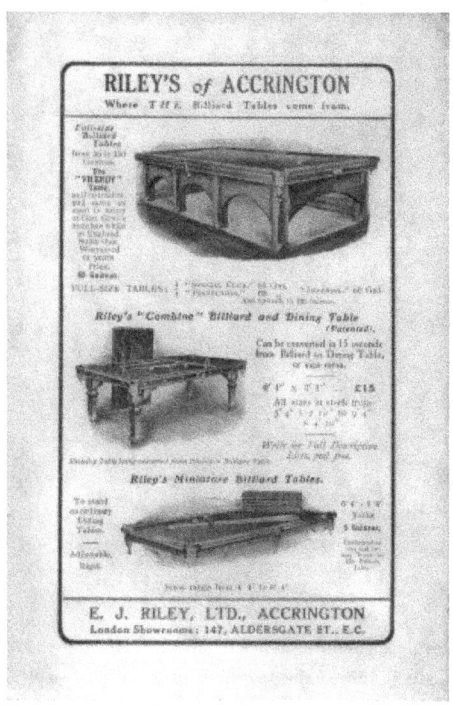

Front and back covers of George Gray's 'Red Ball Play' published in 1911 in paperback format. The book is worth £50-£70 in very good condition. See entry 6.73.

Pictured are a selection of billiards books published between 1862 and 1897. The most valuable is the book shown at bottom left which would expect to fetch £300-£500. See entry 6.15.

Pictured are a selection of billiards books published between 1907 and 1937. The most valuable is probably the volume shown at bottom right which is worth £120-£160. See entry 6.95.

Rolf Danery was a pseudonym for the authors Edward Castillian Randolph and Alfred Emery and their one work on billiards now sells for £80-£120. See entry 6.84. Willie Smith's book is worth £15-£25. See entry 6.113.

1st and 2nd edition covers of Sydney's Lee's work on billiards issued by Link House Publications. The 1st edition now commands £30-£40 in very good condition. See entry 6.115.

~ Miscellaneous ~

7.0   Billiard Stories and Anecdotes

Unknown author
[1824]   F. Welstead & Sons, London
Paperback   75pp, 18 x 12cm

There are eleven chapters in this volume, all covering anecdotes that it says in the Preface "have been published before" but unfortunately not stating where. The first is called 'The Head of my Profession' and details a young gentleman's adventures in the city of Bath, playing and watching some of the better players of that city. Other chapters include 'The Marker', 'Billiards & Busking' and 'Billiards at Clatherduffie'. The cover is an interesting one, depicting two swordsmen clashing swords on top of a billiard table. [description based on a photocopy].

Value   £500 - £800

7.1   Games of Pool : Describing the Various English and American Pool Games, and Giving the Rules in Full

C. Compton Moore
[1890]   L. Upcott Gill, London
Paperback   96pp, ill., 19 x 13cm
Notes   Includes a numbered 12 page catalogue of Gill's books

In the Preface to this work Moore says that "we have done here that which, so far as we know, has never been attempted before – to collect within the covers of a handy book particulars of all known modern Games of Pool, and the rules that govern them". There then follows details of 15 games of pool, examples of which include Pin Pool, Fifteen-Ball Pool, Losing Pyramids, and Penny Pot – "for the invention of this game "Captain Crawley" and many modern players have claimed credit . . . it is really almost too worthless to be mentioned . . .". The contents list of the book is rather unique in that all the games are listed alphabetically but do not run from page 1 – so Ordinary or Common Pool is 7th on the contents list but begins from page 1. The title page rather optimistically states the volume is 'illustrated' but in truth there are only a handful of illustrations scattered throughout. The book has a lovely colourful cover and there are a few contemporary advertisements included. This is another of those books that is incredibly scarce and rarely appears for sale.

Value   £100 - £200

7.2   **Pyramids and Pool Games with a Chapter on Winning Hazards**

J. P. Buchanan
1896   George Routledge & Sons, London
Hardback   83pp, ill., 19 x 13cm
Notes   Part of the 'Oval' Series of Games publications

1896   George Routledge & Sons, London
Paperback   83pp, ill., 18 x 12cm
Notes   As above; includes Appendix–'The Rules of Pyramids, Shell Out, Pool, Single Pool, Black Pool, Snooker Pool, Skittle Pool and Cork Pool'

Buchanan's book is bound in attractive deep red boards with a picture of two players at the table stamped onto the cover. The paperback has a thin green cloth covering with the title etc. in black on the front cover and an extraordinary advert for Brooke's 'Monkey Brand' Soap on the rear cover. A few contemporary adverts are also included as well as an extensive catalogue of Routledges' books. The 'Oval' Series of Games books featured topics such as football, swimming, baseball and athletics. In this volume J. P. Buchanan takes the reader through the various games of pyramids and pool, all illustrated with full-page diagrams. In the Introduction the author, in answer to critics who say that pool games are only designed for promoting gambling, states that "true it certainly is that no one of these games can very well be played for *love*".

Value   £150 - £200

7.3   **The Game Beautiful**

'An Expert'
[1905]   [Burroughes & Watts], London
Paperback   31pp, ill., plates, 19 x 13cm
Notes   Includes 5 samples of billiard cloth (with prices) fixed to the reverse of the rear cover

This book is principally an advertising vehicle for Burroughes & Watts products and, indeed, there is a 14 page 'Price List of Billiard Tables & Accessories' at the rear. The first 17 pages cover subjects as diverse as a brief history of the game, billiards at home, and an argument for billiards in terms of light exercise – "of all indoor sports Billiards is the most healthy and exhilarating". The volume is wrapped in buff coloured card covers and has an eye-catching front cover illustration of a billiard table with fancy lighting, whereas the rear cover features a silhouette-type portrait of a player.

Value   £40 - £60

7.4   The Possibilities of Nuku Billiards : Together with Rules for Billiards, Snooker, and Russian Pool

J. P. Mannock
[1911]   No publisher details given, [Exeter?]
Paperback   15pp, ill., 21 x 10cm

'Nuku' Billiards was a game played with a small spring-cue on a miniature table and was designed for "excellent practice, immensely improving the game of an average player on a full-sized table". The hints and guidance are illustrated with three diagrams and the rear of the book covers the rules mentioned in the title over 4 pages. The book has fawn coloured card wrappers and the rear of the cover states that the game of 'Nuku' was available from John Webber & Sons of Exeter.

Value   £30 - £50

7.5   "Rileys" of Accrington : Where the Billiard Tables Come From"

E. J. Riley Ltd.
[1911]   [E. J. Riley], [Accrington]
Paperback   23pp, 11 x 8cm
Notes   Title taken from cover

This book has buff coloured card covers and includes sections entitled 'Rules for Billiards', 'Size of Rooms' and 'Care of the Table'. There is also a 1 page article called 'How to Select a Cue' by G. Nelson, ex-Yorkshire Champion – "the cue should lie well on the bridge band, a Cue that does not do so is badly balanced"; plus a piece named 'How to Tip a Billiard Cue' by S. A. Mussabini.

Value   £50 - £100

7.6   50 Years of Billiards in Grimsby

Bob Lincoln
[1915]   [Bob Lincoln], [Grimsby]
Hardback   116pp, plates, ports., 22 x 14cm

In Lincoln's address to the reader he says it is not "my intention to pose as an expert or yet critic on the game but simply to chronicle the rise of it in the Fisheries". He certainly achieves that aim with the help of match results, statistics and informed insight into some of the main players and characters in the local leagues. The book is bound in green cloth and has a russet coloured leather spine.

Value   £340 - £360

7.7 **The Billiards Association and Control Council : Constitution and Regulations**

Billiards Association & Control Council
[1919] B.A. & C.C. / [The Cricket Press], London
Paperback 20pp, 21 x 14cm

This slim book is wrapped in dark green card covers and discusses the B.A. & C.C. Constitution, specific points regarding the Association rules and has a list of regulations. The only date mentioned in the book is 1919 but it may well have been published after this.

Value £50 - £70

7.8 **The Billiards Annual and Year-Book : the Official Handbook of the Billiards Association and Control Council 1927**

W. G. Clifford (Ed.)
1927 Sporting Handbooks, London
Hardback 141pp, ports., 17 x 10cm
Notes Foreword by the Earl of Lonsdale

This pocket-sized book has dark green, thick card covers with a picture of a player at the table on the cover and originally sold for 2/-, and the text is interspersed with adverts and photographs of the leading players of the day. The book is packed with facts and figures including the B.A. & C.C. Constitution, details of affiliated associations, rules, the origin and development of English billiards (by W. G. Clifford), some modern 'Playing Tendencies' (by Tom Newman), and 'S. Africa Reports Progress'. There are also plenty of tournament results for district, professional and amateur championships. The book has thick glossy paper and is very scarce, rarely coming up for sale.

Value £100 - £200

7.9 **National Billiards Halls Association : Rules**

National Billiards Halls Association
[1934] [N.B.H.A.], [London]
Paperback 16pp, 13 x 9cm

The National Billiards Halls Association was founded on 30th November 1933 and the Association was presided over by T. W. Clark of Temperance Billiards Halls Ltd. This small book, with red card covers and black typography, contains the Rules of the Association. These are split into 23 segments and encompass topics such as subscriptions, resignations, the Annual Meeting and so on.

Value £30 - £50

7.10   National Billiards Halls Association : Rules

National Billiards Halls Association
[1935]   [N.B.H.A.], [London]
Paperback   16pp, 13 x 9cm

The 1935 N.B.H.A. Rules has the same red card covers as the 1934 edition and covers the same subject matter. The President was still T. W. Clark and the Council included representatives from Nottingham, the Home Counties and Scotland.

Value   £30 - £50

7.11   Billiards and Snooker Teasers Explained – And a Guide to Wise Spending

Burroughes & Watts (Corp.)
[1936]   Burroughes & Watts, London
Paperback   24pp, ill., plates, 22 x 14cm
Notes   No title page–title taken from cover

7.12   Billiards and Snooker Teasers Explained

Burroughes & Watts (Corp.)
[1937]   Burroughes & Watts, London
Paperback   28pp, ill., plates, 22 x 14cm
Notes   As above

7.13   Billiards and Snooker Teasers : Fifth Edition

Burroughes & Watts (Corp.)
[1938]   Burroughes & Watts, London
Paperback   31pp, ill., plates, 22 x 14cm
Notes   Includes Index

7.14   Billiards and Snooker Teasers : Sixth Edition – September, 1939

Burroughes & Watts (Corp.)
[1939]   Burroughes & Watts, London
Paperback   32pp, ill., plates, 22 x 14cm
Notes   Includes Index

7.15   Billiards and Snooker Teasers : Seventh Edition – October, 1949

Burroughes & Watts (Corp.)
[1949]   Burroughes & Watts, London
Paperback   32pp, ill., plates, 22 x 14cm
Notes   Includes Index

7.16   **Billiards and Snooker Teasers : Eighth Edition – September, 1950**

        Burroughes & Watts (Corp.)
        [1950]   Burroughes & Watts, London
        Paperback   32pp, ill., plates, 22 x 14cm
        Notes   Includes Erratum strip and Index

7.17   **Billiards and Snooker Teasers : Ninth Edition – September, 1951**

        Burroughes & Watts (Corp.)
        [1951]   Burroughes & Watts, London
        Paperback   32pp, ill., plates, ports., 22 x 14cm
        Notes   Includes Index

7.18   **Billiards and Snooker Teasers : Tenth Edition – September, 1952**

        Burroughes & Watts (Corp.)
        [1952]   Burroughes & Watts, London
        Paperback   31pp, ill., plates, 22 x 14cm
        Notes   Includes Index

7.19   **Billiards and Snooker Teasers : Eleventh Edition 1953 - 1954**

        Burroughes & Watts (Corp.)
        [1953]   Burroughes & Watts, London
        Paperback   31pp, ill., plates, 22 x 14cm
        Notes   Includes Index

7.20   **Billiards and Snooker Teasers : Twelfth Edition 1954 - 1955**

        Burroughes & Watts (Corp.)
        [1954]   Burroughes & Watts, London
        Paperback   31pp, ill., plates, 22 x 14cm
        Notes   Includes Index

7.21   **Billiards and Snooker Teasers : Thirteenth Edition 1955-1956**

        Burroughes & Watts (Corp.)
        [1955]   Burroughes & Watts, London
        Paperback   31pp, ill., plates, 22 x 14cm
        Notes   Includes Errata strip attached to page 1 amending the contact details of the Hull representative; includes Index

7.22   **Billiards and Snooker Teasers : Fourteenth Edition 1956-1957**

        Burroughes & Watts (Corp.)
        [1956]   Burroughes & Watts, London

Paperback 31pp, ill., plates, 22 x 14cm
Notes Includes Index

7.23   Billiards and Snooker Teasers Explained : Fifteenth Edition 1957-1958

Burroughes & Watts (Corp.)
[1957] Burroughes & Watts, London
Paperback 31pp, ill., 1 port., plates, 22 x 14cm
Notes Includes Index

7.24   Billiards and Snooker Teasers Explained : Sixteenth Edition 1958-1959

Burroughes & Watts (Corp.)
[1958] Burroughes & Watts, London
Paperback 31pp, ill. (some col.), plates, 22 x 14cm
Notes Includes Index

7.25   Billiards and Snooker Teasers : Seventeenth Edition 1959-1960

Burroughes & Watts (Corp.)
[1959] Burroughes & Watts, London
Paperback 31pp, ill., plates, 22 x 14cm
Notes Includes Index

7.26   Billiards and Snooker Teasers Explained : Eighteenth Edition 1960-1961

Burroughes & Watts (Corp.)
[1960] Burroughes & Watts, London
Paperback 31pp, ill., plates, 22 x 14cm
Notes Includes Index

7.27   Billiards and Snooker Teasers Explained : Nineteenth Edition 1961-1962

Burroughes & Watts (Corp.)
[1961] Burroughes & Watts, London
Paperback 31pp, ill. (some col.), plates, 22 x 14cm
Notes Includes Index

7.28   Billiards and Snooker Teasers Explained : Twentieth Edition 1962-1963

Burroughes & Watts (Corp.)
[1962] Burroughes & Watts, London
Paperback 29pp, ill. (some col.), plates, 22 x 14cm
Notes Includes Index

7.29   **Billiards and Snooker Teasers : Twenty First Edition 1963-1964**

Burroughes & Watts (Corp.)
[1963]   Burroughes & Watts, London
Paperback   31pp, ill. (some col.), plates, 22 x 14cm
Notes   Includes Index

7.30   **Billiards and Snooker Teasers : Twenty-Second Edition 1964–1965**

Burroughes & Watts (Corp.)
[1964]   Burroughes & Watts, London
Paperback   31pp, ill. (some col.), plates, 22 x 14cm
Notes   Includes Index

7.31   **Billiards and Snooker Teasers : Twenty-Third Edition 1965-1966**
Burroughes & Watts (Corp.)
[1965]   Burroughes & Watts, London
Paperback   31pp, ill. (some col.), plates, 22 x 14cm
Notes   Includes Index

'Billiards & Snooker Teasers' (very often called 'Billiards & Snooker Teasers Explained') were a series of 21 booklets, published by the manufacturer Burroughes & Watts, which were principally product catalogues but which in addition explained the rules of the game via scores of 'teasers' spread throughout the pages. As the 1960–1961 edition states "you will appreciate this book. It has been planned to fill a need. It contains explanations of knotty points in the interpretations of the Rules of Billiards and Snooker". The teasers covered questions such as 'What is a Snooker?', 'Fouls & Penalties', 'The Referee & his duties' etc. As well as the teasers there were plenty of tips such as 'Looking After Your Billiard Table', which includes short lists entitled 'Tip Your Cues This Way' and 'Brushing & Ironing'. There were also plenty of advertisements for traditional snooker equipment such as cues, as well as more unusual products such as the "Hoover" Dustette, advertised as – "the most modern and efficient way to "brush" your Billiard Table".

These highly desirable booklets also contained some fascinating articles and features that are invaluable to anyone who is interested in the history of the two sports. For example, the 1953–1954 edition featured a nice centre spread entitled 'Billiard Table Makers Through Seven Reigns' that pictured photos of 6 tables made by Burroughes & Watts "in six of the seven reigns from William IV to Elizabeth II"; and the 1952 edition had a centre spread entitled 'From Mace to Billiard Cue' covering the development of the cue.

All the books have a hole punched in the top left corner and string inserted in the hole so that the books could be hung up in the billiard room. They also have very attractive covers – for example, the 1961–1962 edition has the red ball dressed as a schoolmaster with the two white balls dressed as schoolboys.

'Billiards & Snooker Teasers' sell for extraordinary sums considering their fairly modest contents. For example, a very good copy of the 1938–1939 edition, with pages browned and rear cover soiled, fetched £82 on eBay in March 2007; and very good copies of the 1961–1962 and 1955–1956 editions commanded £62 (April 2007) and £63 (March 2007) respectively. Various copies have sold on eBay for between £14 and £82 over the past few years but any edition very rarely sells for less than £25.

Value   £25 - £85 each

7.32 Notes on the Game of Snooker

[Sidney Gillett]
[194?]   Thurston & Co., London
Paperback   12pp, ill., 21 x 13cm

[194?]   Thurston & Co., London
Paperback   12pp, ill., 19 x 12cm

It is difficult to date this publication but the cover says the address of Thurston's is "33 Cheyne Walk[23], late of Leicester Square", so it must have been published sometime after 1940 when the Leicester Square premises were blitzed and the company moved its administrative functions to the factory at Chelsea. The larger book has attractive card covers in black, white and turquoise and the contents include discussion of some of the rules plus hints on tipping cues, and tips on brushing and ironing billiard tables where the reader is warned "do not iron the cushion cloths". The smaller format book has a b & w striped cover with the title details in red typography sitting in a rectangle tilted at an angle across the cover.

Value   £30 - £50

7.33 Notes on the Game of Snooker and why Thurston's are at Chelsea

[Sidney Gillett]
[194?]   [Thurston & Co.], London
Paperback   24pp, ill., plates, 19 x 12cm

Wrapped in pale yellow card wrappers this book is printed on glossy paper and was originally issued for customers of the House of Thurston. The first section is basically the same as the two books detailed above but the second part deals with the bombing of Thurston's former Leicester Square premises in October 1940. The

---

23 Cheyne Walk (pronounced 'Chainy') has had several notable residents, most recently Mick Jagger and Keith Richards of the 'Rolling Stones'. It has often attracted artists and writers and Elizabeth Gaskell, Henry James, Dante Gabriel Rossetti and the artist, J.M. W. Turner, all lived there.

company moved to Chelsea after this catastrophic event, an area of London on page 18 described thus "... that part facing the river was a fashionable rendezvous and frequently called Hyde Park of the Thames".

Value £30 - £50

7.34 **Snooker Guide : to Improved Play, Rule Problems, Table Upkeep, Etc.**

W. A. Camkin / Birmingham Billiards Ltd.
[194?/195?]   W. A. Camkin / Birmingham Billiards Ltd.
Paperback   12pp, plates, 21 x 13cm

This publication is essentially an advertising vehicle for W. A. Camkin & Birmingham Billiards but has few actual adverts in the book. The 12 pages are bound in bright orange card covers and contents include 'Snooker Problems Simplified', a 2 page spread penned by Joe Davis called 'How to Improve Your Snooker Play', 'The Care & Maintenance of a Billiard Table', and 'More Problems Explained'. Bill Camkin, described by Clive Everton as "a lively Birmingham billiard trader", was, along with Joe Davis, the instigator of the World Professional Snooker Championship. Indeed, Camkin actually refereed the first final, won by Joe Davis.

Value £50 - £100

7.35 **Catalogue of the Exhibition of Billiards Antiquities : with a History of Billiards by Sir John Squire and an Addendum on the Development of the Implements used in the Game by Sidney Gillett**

Sir John Squire / Sidney Gillett
1940   The Billiards Association & Control Council, [London]
Paperback   29pp, ill., plates, ports., 19 x 12cm

The proceeds of this exhibition were donated to the Lord Mayor's Red Cross and St. John War Organisation Appeal and a bright red cross features on the pale orange card covers, along with details of the exhibition. After a piece entitled 'The History of Billiards' by Sir John Squire – "he who tries to trace the origin of a game usually finds himself in an ancient mist" – there follows a detailed list of the 65 items in the exhibition itself. Some of the antiquities on show included a copy of Mingaud's 1839 book on billiards, a cube of white chalk used prior to 1845 and the "heaviest cue ever made, weighs 41 ozs." Finally there is a section on the Game of English Billiards by Gillett, the former managing director of Thurston's.

Value £30 - £50

7.36   **Handbook and Constitution of the Women's Billiards Association**

Bessie Munro Wright (Ed.)
[1946]   [Women's Billiards Association], [London]
Paperback   47pp, plates, ports., 19 x 13cm
Notes   Cover title is 'Illustrated Handbook of the Women's Billiards Association'

The cover of this booklet has a photo of a pensive looking Valerie Hobson[24], screen star of 'Great Expectations' and 'Blanche Fury', and President of the Women's Billiards Association. Inside the glossy card covers there is a quiz, a blank page for autographs, a written Constitution, a glossary of technical terms, plus tips from the leading female players of the day.

Value   £40 - £60

7.37   **Billiards – Snooker Sports Annual 1947**

Bessie Munro Wright (Comp. & Ed.)
1947   Billiards Association & Control Council, London
Paperback   112pp, ill., plates, ports., 29 x 22cm

This 1947 annual contained contributions from Stanley Newman, Walter Donaldson, Riso Levi and J. P. Priestley (his famous piece entitled 'Thurston's' is reproduced from the Saturday Review of 20th April 1929) and encompassed subjects as varied as Snooker Psychology, Women Wield the Cue, and details of the Welsh Billiards Association. There are some fabulous cartoons and plates in the book and plenty of contemporary adverts to hold the interest of social historians of the sport. The book has a very pale orange cover with green and black typography and has cartoons of Sid Field, Horace Lindrum, Joe Davis and Bobby Howes on the front cover.

Value   £40 - £60

7.38   **1948 Handbook and Constitution of the Women's Billiards Association**

Bessie Munro Wright
[1947]   [Women's Billiards Association], [London]
Paperback   32pp, ill., plates, ports., 19 x 13cm

As with the previous years' publication an exotic looking Valerie Hobson is pictured on the yellow cover of this slender publication. Inside is an article by Horace Lindrum called 'Billiards and Snooker for Amateurs', and to keep the

---

24   For further information on Valerie Hobson see en.wikipedia.org/wiki/Valerie_Hobson

reader entertained there is also a snooker quiz and a piece entitled Women's Billiards in India.

Value   £40 - £60

7.39   **Snooker Digest**

Walter Donaldson
[1947]   No details given
Paperback   31pp, ill., plates, ports., 25 x 19cm

[1948]   No details given
Paperback   25pp, ill., plates, 19 x 13cm

This slim booklet was reproduced with permission of the Glasgow Noon Record and the vibrantly coloured cover shows that it cost 1/-. Inside is a biographical sketch of Donaldson followed by a few pages of tips on play. There are a small number of cartoons and b & w photos throughout (including some of Donaldson in the army) and details of how Donaldson could be contacted for exhibitions. The 1947 version had more pages because it also briefly covered sports such as cricket, rugby, golf and tennis.

Value   £50 - £80

7.40   **Snooker Guide : to Improved Play, Rule Problems, Maintenance, etc.**

Joe Davis
[1948]   Joe Davis Billiards Supplies Ltd., London & Paignton
Paperback   [16]pp, 1 plate, 21 x 13cm

The bright card wrappers of this booklet feature a b & w photo of Davis and an illustration of a billiard table set against a vivid yellow and green background. The publication is chiefly an advertising vehicle for Davis' billiard supply company but does have some miscellaneous sections scattered throughout, principally 'Rule Problems Explained'. The last date mentioned in the book is 1948, although there is a possibility it may have been published in the early 1950s.

Value   £50 - £80

7.41   **The Billiards Association and Control Council : Rules and Regulations**

[Billiards Association and Control Council]
[1966]   [B. A. & C. C.], London
Paperback   11pp, 21 x 14cm
Notes   Amended in 1969

181

This book is wrapped in pale green card covers and despite the cover mentioning the date 24th November 1965, must have been published in 1966 as it says on page 2 "at a meeting held on June 8th 1966". The book includes a rather dry rules and regulations section spread over the 11 numbered pages and was amended in 1969, with a sticker containing a few paragraphs being placed on the inside of the rear cover.

Value £15 - £25

7.42 The Park Drive Official Snooker and Billiards Year Book

Clive Everton (Ed. & Comp.) / John Silverton (written contributions)
[1973]   [London]
ISBN   None given
Paperback   92pp., ill., plates (some col.), ports. (some col.), 21 x 14cm
Notes   Sponsored by Gallaher Ltd.

There is no date of publication in this slender paperback but tournament details up to and including 1972 are listed so the British Library estimate of 1973 would seem accurate. The information contained between the colourful card covers is a real mixture – 'Men at the Top' (player profiles), 'On the Circuit', 'Top Amateurs' and 'The Maximum Men'. Aside from this there is a snooker quiz, a feats chapter, and over 20 pages of tournament results and statistics. This book is rather an anomaly for collectors in that it doesn't appear for sale very often but doesn't necessarily command high prices; although a copy signed by John Spencer, but only in good condition and with the book having come away from the cover, fetched £10 on eBay in December 2007.

Value £3 - £5

7.43 Pot Black

Reg Perrin (Comp.)
1975   British Broadcasting Corporation (BBC), London
ISBN   0563124717
Paperback   96pp, ill., plates, ports., 20 x 13cm

7.44 Pot Black

1975   BBC, London
ISBN   0563170611
Paperback   96pp, ill., plates, ports., 20 x 13cm
Notes   New edition; there appear to be two versions of this edition with one having 'BBC–Television One' printed at the bottom of the front cover and on the spine

7.45 Pot Black

1977	BBC, London
ISBN	0563172711
Paperback	96pp, ill., plates, ports., 20 x 13cm
Notes	New revised edition

7.46 Pot Black

1979	BBC, London
ISBN	0563176326
Paperback	111pp, ill., plates, ports., 20 x 13cm
Notes	As above

7.47 Pot Black

1980	BBC, London
ISBN	0563177896
Paperback	136pp, ill., plates, ports., 19 x 13cm
Notes	As above

7.48 Pot Black

1981	BBC, London
ISBN	0563179015
Paperback	159pp, ill., plates, ports., 20 x 13cm
Notes	As above; Foreword by Brian Wenham

7.49 Pot Black

1982	BBC, London
ISBN	0563179945
Paperback	176pp, ill., plates, ports., 20 x 13cm
Notes	As above

7.50 Pot Black

1983	BBC, London
ISBN	0563201320
Paperback	183pp, ill., plates, ports., 20 x 13cm
Notes	As above

7.51 Pot Black

1984	Treasure Press, London
ISBN	0907812732
Hardback	176pp, ill., plates, ports., 20 x 13cm
Notes	1984 printing of the 1982 revised edition; Foreword by Brian Wenham

7.52   **Pot Black**

        1984   BBC, London
        ISBN   0563202939
        Paperback   176pp, ill., plates, ports., 20 x 13cm
        Notes   New revised edition; cover has 'New 1985 edition' at the top; Foreword by Reg Perrin

When the TV programme 'Pot Black' was launched in 1969 from a studio converted from a cinema I'm sure nobody had any idea of the impact it would have on the sport. Indeed, people had to be press-ganged into joining the audience and even the canteen staff were cajoled into filling the empty seats. The compiler of the books, Reg Perrin, went on to become the show's producer and kicks off the first book with a piece called 'Pot Black : the Game'. In this piece he discusses the origins of the sport, the table, table maintenance and accessories. After this follows an instructional guide from Joe Davis called 'How to Pot', based on his book 'Complete Snooker for the Amateur' (see entry 4.11), plus Rules of Snooker, player profiles, trick shots and so on. The books increased in length as the series progressed mainly because new players, such as Tony Meo, Tony Knowles and Silvino Francisco, were invited to the tournament and details of these players were added to the player profiles. The cost of the books also rose, the first selling for a mere 65p and later editions costing over £3. Right through the series there are numerous essays by players and commentators concerning all aspects of the game and plenty of b & w photographs. All editions, but especially the later ones, come up regularly for sale on eBay and are frequently found in secondhand bookshops and charity shops. Collector's should note that the 1975 and 1977 editions both have the same cover, so check the publication date on the reverse of the title page to avoid confusion.

        Value   £2 - £4 each

7.53   **The Ladbroke Snooker International Handbook**

        Clive Everton (Ed. & Comp.)
        [1976]   [Ladbrokes Leisure], [London]
        ISBN   0905606000
        Paperback   96pp, ill., plates, ports., 21 x 15cm
        Notes   Bert Hackett (ill.); Neil Wigley (photog.); Janice Hale (researcher)

The Ladbroke International Series was a tournament between England and the Rest of the World broadcast by Thames TV that first aired in 1975. This handbook accompanies the second series that was recorded at the Holiday Inn, Swiss Cottage. This series was notable for the surprise at the completion of one session when Eamonn Andrews stepped forward and uttered the words "this is your life" to Ray

Reardon[25]. The book features profiles of the participating players, the basic rules of billiards, snooker and pool (accompanied by some humorous cartoons from the pen of Bert Hackett), followed by a 27 page statistics section. The 'How to Play' section includes b & w photos of a very young Mike Hallett, billed as 'Boys' Champion 1975 (Hallett was British Under 16 Champion at the time).

Value £3 - £5

7.54   **How to Beat Your Dad at Snooker**

Brian Halter
1979   [Brian Halter], Bristol
ISBN   None given
Paperback   19pp, ill., 21 x 15cm

Brian Halter
1986   Barton Publications, Bath
ISBN   None given
Paperback   63pp, [15]pp, ill., 21 x 15cm
Notes   Revised title of '**How to Beat Your Dad at Snooker : Including : Thoughts on Pool**'

[1993]   [Brian Halter], Chepstow
ISBN   None given
Paperback   19pp, ill., 22 x 15cm

[199-]   [Brian Halter], [Chepstow]
ISBN   None given
Paperback   63pp, ill., ports., 22 x 15cm

Halter's series of self-published books began with a 19 page publication in 1979 and expanded to the 63 page book published sometime in the 1990s. The 1993 edition begins with a reprint of a newspaper article concerning the author's campaign to allow women to play snooker in working men's clubs and private clubs (many of whom discriminate against women). There then follows a series of snippets on instructional play, a few 'ask the ref' scenarios , 6 illustrated hints on play, and finally 2 snooker poems. The expanded version of 63 pages has a richly coloured cover showing 2 children whacking their poor old Dad with snooker cues as he miscues and rips the cloth of the table! This edition includes plenty of diagrams and a couple of cartoons all with the intention of aiding the reader in their quest to fulfil the book's title. These publications are offbeat self-published snooker books that are extremely hard to track down.

Value £10 - £20

---

[25]   A subject covered briefly on pages 116-117 of Reardon's 1982 autobiography – see entry 1.9

7.55 Championship Snooker

Terry Griffiths / Clive Everton
1981   Queen Anne Press, London
ISBN   0362005435
Hardback   135pp, ill., plates, ports., 22 x 15cm
Notes   Bert Hackett (ill.) / Jack Fitzmaurice (ill.)

The dustjacket of this volume published by Queen Anne Press displays Griffiths' style of play wonderfully. His head is way above the cue and the trademark bridge hand with the four fingers placed on the table as two pairs close together, rather than all four spread evenly, is very distinctive. This is one of those books that doesn't fit neatly into any single category as the first 40 or so pages are instructional, another section is biographical, a further portion deals with Griffiths' remarkable fortnight at the Crucible in 1979 and the final part details Griffiths' time on the 1979-1980 snooker circuit as reigning world champion. The book has black boards with silver lettering to the spine and shouldn't prove too difficult to track down.

Value   £3 - £5

7.56 World Snooker with Jack Karnehm

Jack Karnehm / John Carty
1981   Pelham Books, London
ISBN   0720713285
Paperback   126pp, plates (some col.), ports. (some col.), 30 x 21cm
Notes   Includes list of County Association secretaries

There are some unusual chapters in this book; the ones on health & fitness, referees, and snooker craftsmen spring to mind. The rest is a mixture of player biographies, maximum men, snooker at The Crucible and so on. The book also predicts the ascendancy of Steve Davis and the increasing flow of money into the sport. Karnehm won the world amateur billiards championship in 1969 and went on to forge a successful career as a national coach and television commentator.

Value   £3 - £5

7.57 Pot Black Diary [1983]

Reg Perrin (Comp.)
1982   Collins Glasgow, [Glasgow]
ISBN   None given
Paperback   64pp, [74]pp, ill., plates, ports., 16 x 9cm
Notes   Published in association with BBC TV; Dave Muscroft and BBC (photogs.)

The 'Pot Black Diary' for 1983 included miscellaneous information plus the official rules of snooker and was issued with a dustjacket.

Value £2 - £4

7.58   World Snooker with Jack Karnehm No. 2

Jack Karnehm / John Carty
1982   Pelham Books, London
ISBN   0720713986
Paperback   128pp, plates (some col.), ports. (some col.), 30 x 21cm

A second 'World Snooker' book was commissioned by Pelham due to the first book selling so well and the fact that snooker in the early 1980s was such a fast changing sport, with new stars emerging rapidly. Included in this publication are features on Dennis Taylor, the Welsh professionals, referees, and the cloth used on snooker tables.

Value £3 - £5

7.59   The Cruel Game : the Inside Story of Snooker

Jean Rafferty
1983   Elm Tree Books/Hamish Hamilton, London
ISBN   0241109507
Hardback   192pp, plates, ports., 24 x 16cm
Notes   Mary Rafferty (photog.); includes Index

1983   Elm Tree Books/Hamish Hamilton, London
ISBN   0241109515
Paperback   192pp, plates, ports., 23 x 16cm
Notes   As above

This book is a vivid portrayal of one year on the snooker circuit penned by the freelance journalist Jean Rafferty, from the Jameson International in September 1981 through to the Pontin's Professional & Open Championships in May 1982. Interspersed with chapters describing the tournaments are sections on players such as Tony Meo, Alex Higgins and Terry Griffiths. The author also takes the reader behind the scenes, talking to sponsors, managers and players. 'The Cruel Game' is bound in green cloth and has a colourful jacket.

Value £4 - £8

7.60   **Pot Black Diary [1984]**

Reg Perrin (Comp.)
1983   Collins Glasgow, [Glasgow]
ISBN   None given
Paperback   64pp, [74]pp, ill., plates, ports., 16 x 9cm
Notes   Published in association with BBC TV; Eric Whitehead and BBC (photogs.)

Includes the official rules of snooker and was issued with a dustjacket.

Value   £2 - £4

7.61   **Snooker**

Janice Hale
1983   Independent Television Books, London
ISBN   0907965237
Paperback   48pp, ill. (some col.), ports. (some col.), 30 x 21cm
Notes   TV Times Special

Janice Hale is currently associate editor of the magazine Snooker Scene and was editor of the 'Rothmans Snooker Yearbooks' (see entries 8.18-8.24). This TV Times Special covers the 1982-1983 season and the bulk of the publication features tournament details and player profiles. A small 5 page section at the back includes details on 'Pot Black', women's snooker, and the ITV and BBC commentary teams. The inside of the back cover lists the draw for the Jameson International due to be played in September 1983. This is another of those snooker publications that is not especially valuable but can be hard to track down, appearing only intermittently on eBay, Abe and Amazon and rarely found in secondhand bookshops.

Value   £3 - £5

7.62   **Sportsviewers Guide : Snooker**

Peter Bills
1983   David & Charles, Newton Abbot
ISBN   0715385062
Hardback   64pp, ill. (some col.), plates (some col.), ports. (some col.), 22 x 16cm
Notes   Foreword by Ray Reardon; part of the 'Sportsviewers Guides' Series

The British Library has catalogued this book as 'snooker history', but in truth it is a real mixture of the different facets of the game. Chapter headings include 'History & Development', 'The Stars', 'Venues', 'Equipment', and so forth. This book can be picked up fairly cheaply from Amazon or Abe and is often to be found in charity shops and appears regularly on eBay.

Value £2 - £3

7.63 **Pot Black Diary [1985]**

Reg Perrin (Comp.)
1984 Collins Glasgow, [Glasgow]
ISBN None given
Paperback 64pp, [74]pp, ill., plates, ports., 16 x 9cm
Notes Published in association with BBC TV; Dave Muscroft and BBC (photogs.)

This 1985 Pot Black Diary was issued with a colourful dustjacket and includes pieces entitled 'The Joe Davis Story', 'The Pot Black Story', 'Practice Makes Perfect'!, plus the official rules of snooker.

Value £2 - £4

7.64 **Snooker**

Peter Arnold
1984 Deans International Publishing, London
ISBN 0603036147
Hardback 96pp, plates (some col.), ports. (some col.), 29 x 22cm
Notes Produced exclusively for W H Smith

Peter Arnold wrote three snooker books and this, his first, is an all encompassing work with laminated pictorial boards, produced for W H Smith. There are only five chapters, the first two covering the development and growth of snooker, the next snooker around the world, and the fourth called 'The Modern Stars'. The final chapter is an instructional one called, predictably, 'How to Play Snooker' where Arnold states - "snooker is a game of touch. It is no good being able to play the shot if at the important moments anxiety, a failure of nerve, a loss of concentration, or a rush of excitement leads to an inability to execute a shot that would be child's play in practice".

Value £3 - £5

7.65 **Snooker Kings**

Unknown author
1984 Quadriga Ltd., London
ISBN 0900608293

Paperback	[16]pp, col. plates, 30 x 22cm
Notes	Introduction by Clive Everton

'Snooker Kings' was a sticker book, along the lines of the well-known Panini[26] football sticker albums, that was published some time after Steve Davis' 1984 World Championship triumph 18–16 over Jimmy White. In total there were 126 stickers to collect mainly featuring pictures of players, match officials and commentators at the World Championships held at Sheffield's Crucible Theatre. Surprisingly few copies of the album itself seem to have survived as they rarely surface for sale. However, the stickers themselves are generally more common but it is rare for all 126 to be offered for sale together; normally the stickers appear in piecemeal lots on eBay. The book has yellow card covers with pictures of Steve Davis, Alex Higgins, John Parrott and Ray Reardon on the front.

Value £15 - £20 (complete with all stickers)

7.66 Enjoying Snooker with Ray Reardon : A Personal Guide to the Game

Ray Reardon / John Hennessey

1985	Orbis Publishing, London
ISBN	0856139092
Paperback	128pp, col. ill., plates (mostly col.), ports. (mostly col.), 22 x 28 cm
Notes	Includes Glossary and Index

1986	Orbis Publishing (for Marks & Spencer), London
ISBN	None given
Paperback	192pp, col. ill., plates (mostly col.) ports. (mostly col.), 28 x 22cm
Notes	Revised and extended edition; includes Glossary and Index

Snooker was so popular in the 1980s that even Marks & Spencer got in on the act, Orbis publishing Reardon's book on their behalf. This is another of those all-encompassing books, packed full of photos, and covering topics including the snooker circuit, men in power, profiles of some of the games top players, plus a small instructional section. The 1st edition is a rather awkward oblong shape but the dimensions of the revised edition were altered and it sits more easily on the bookshelf.

Value £4 - £8

---

26 For more information on Panini see en.wikipedia.org/wiki/Panini_%28stickers%29 or www.paninionline.com/collectibles/institutional/bt/uk/

7.67   **Pot Black Diary [1986]**

Reg Perrin (Comp.)
1985   Collins Glasgow, [Glasgow]
ISBN   None given
Paperback   64pp, [82]pp, ill., plates, ports., 16 x 9cm
Notes   Published in association with BBC TV; Dave Muscroft and BBC (photogs.)

The attractive dustjacket of this diary has a referee's gloved hand spotting the black ball and the Pot Black tournament trophy in gilt in the bottom left hand corner. The contents are comprised of details of snooker around the globe, the World Professional Snooker Championship, profiles of 19 players, a snooker quiz, a statistics section, plus the official rules of snooker.

Value   £2 - £4

7.68   **Minute Book of the Billiards Association 31st January, 1885 to 21st January, 1892**

Billiards & Snooker Control Council
1986   B. & S. C. C., [Leeds]
ISBN   None given
Hardback   271pp, facsims., 23 x 20cm
Notes   First printing limited to 15 copies

This volume was published to mark the occasion of the Council's centenary, 1885–1985 and is a heavy book bound in plain green cloth. The contents include facsimiles of original hand-written minutes (some of which are decidedly difficult to decipher) of committee meetings of the Billiard Association, plus some facsimiles of typed minutes. Also included is a copy of the Rules of the Billiard Association of Great Britain and Ireland, India and the Colonies.

Value   £50 - £70

7.69   **Monitoring Tobacco-Sponsored Snooker on BBC TV 1985-86**

John L. Roberts
1986   Health Education Council, London
ISBN   None given
Paperback   20pp, plates, 30 x 21cm
Notes   Report produced by the North West Regional Health Authority

This report focuses on TV coverage of tobacco-sponsored snooker on BBC TV before and after controls were introduced by the BBC in April 1986. The report states that "coverage of snooker following the new controls still amounts to the BBC giving the tobacco sponsors two to three 30 second commercial advertisements per hour for 199 hours a year". Accompanying the text are an abundance of photos depicting players smoking in front of tobacco company advertising boards and the author argues that the firms also decked out the arenas in their own brand colours, although rather strangely the photos don't fully illustrate this as they are all in b & w. There are four Appendices at the back reprinting various letters to The Times and Sheffield Star, plus an extract from Broadcast journal. It is debatable whether this report is specifically about snooker but I feel there is enough discussion of the game to warrant its inclusion and I imagine this scarce item would be highly coveted by collectors.

Value £20 - £30

7.70   **Pocket Money : Bad-Boys, Business-Heads and Boom-time Snooker**

Gordon Burn
1986   William Heinemann, London
ISBN   0434098280
Hardback   211pp, 23 x 14cm
Notes   Reprinted 1986

1987   Pan Books, London
ISBN   0330300830
Paperback   222pp, ports., 20 x 13cm
Notes   Revised edition; ports. by David Bailey

1992   Mandarin Paperbacks, London
ISBN   0749313331
Paperback   221pp, ports., 20 x 13cm
Notes   Revised edition; ports. by David Bailey

With a rather extravagant title, this book was one of several written in the mid '80s when the popularity of snooker soared. To realise just how popular the sport had become, examine the rear of the 1st edition dustjacket and study the number of *front* page headlines the players were creating at that time. Following the snooker circus, the book focuses on Barry Hearn and his Matchroom team and the 'bad-boys' of the title – Alex Higgins, Jimmy White and Kirk Stevens. The author uses a quote originally aimed at legendary baseball star Babe Ruth when describing Alex Higgins – "he may not have been an utter social boor, but he was something less than tactful, something less than gracious, something very much less than sensitive". The book culminates in Joe Johnson's famous victory over Steve Davis in the 1986 World Championship final. This book is not especially valuable but the 1st edition can be difficult to track down (the reprint being much more common) and the 1987 Pan Books edition doesn't appear for sale often either. Unusually, all three editions have different covers and the revised editions included a new chapter called 'Twelve Months On'.

Value £4 - £8

7.71 Snooker Diary [1987]

Reg Perrin (Comp.)
1986   Collins Glasgow, [Glasgow]
ISBN   None given
Paperback   64pp, [82]pp, ill., plates, ports., 16 x 9cm
Notes   Eric Whitehead (photog.)

Includes the official rules of snooker and was issued with a dustjacket.

Value   £2 - £4

7.72 Snookered

Donald Trelford
1986   Faber & Faber, London
ISBN   0571136400
Paperback   200pp, plates, ports., 22 x 14cm
Notes   Foreword by Dennis Taylor; includes Bibliography

Yet another snooker book published in the mid '80s when the snooker boom was at its peak. Snooker is not a sport you would expect the highbrow publisher Faber & Faber to get involved with, but the fact this book was written by a former editor of The Observer may have swayed them. Donald Trelford embarked on his snooker adventure in early 1984 and the resultant book is part history and part anecdotal. Trelford's time on the snooker circuit ended, luckily for him, with the famous Taylor v Davis 1985 World Championship final and both players are featured in colour line drawings on the front cover of the book. This book occasionally appears on eBay and can also be found in secondhand bookshops and charity shops for a modest sum.

Value   £3 - £5

7.73 Snooker Diary [1988]

Reg Perrin (Comp.)
1987   Collins Glasgow, [Glasgow]
ISBN   None given
Paperback   64pp, [82]pp, ill., plates, ports., 16 x 9cm
Notes   Eric Whitehead (photog.)

Includes the official rules of snooker and the diary was issued with a dustjacket.

Value   £2 - £4

7.74 Snooker, Pool and Billiards

Peter Arnold
1987 Kingfisher Books, London
ISBN 0862722934
Hardback 80pp, ill. (mostly col.), plates (mostly col.), 19 x 12cm
Notes Reprinted 1988; a Kingfisher Factbook; text editing Angela Royston; Rhoda and Robert Burns, Peter Stevenson (ills.); includes Index

1987 Pan Books, London
ISBN 0330299344
Paperback 80pp, ill. (mostly col.), plates (mostly col.), 18 x 12cm
Notes Part of the 'Pocket Library'; text editing Angela Royston; Rhoda and Robert Burns, Peter Stevenson (ills.); includes Index

This small hardback book is aimed at the younger reader and covers a wide range of subjects, including a few pages on both pool and billiards. The book is chiefly instructional but in addition covers the story of snooker and great players. Kingfisher published over two dozen 'Factbooks' ranging from aircraft to birds, music to trains. The book is not especially valuable but the collector may have to be patient when searching for a copy.

Value £2 - £3

7.75 Snooker Today

Peter Arnold
1987 Hamlyn Publishing, Twickenham
ISBN 0600552357
Hardback 96pp, plates (mostly col.), ports. (mostly col.), 31 x 24cm
Notes Produced exclusively for W H Smith; David Muscroft (photog.); includes Index

This book by Peter Arnold draws on his earlier work 'Snooker' (see entry 7.64), although it must be added they are not the same book. It is a general overview of snooker with chapters entitled 'The Growth of the Game', 'The Professional Game Today', 'The Base of the Pyramid', 'The Professional Circuit', 'Today's Leading Players', and 'Behind the Scenes'. The book has laminated pictorial boards that replicate the photos on the dustjacket.

Value £3 - £5

7.76 Billiards and Snooker Control Council Diary [1989]

Unknown author
[1988] Calendars & Diaries, Bristol
ISBN None given
Paperback 56pp, ill., 18 x 10cm

The majority of this publication is a standard diary but there are 4 pages detailing the Billiards and Snooker Control Council plus a list of County Secretaries as at 19th October 1988.

Value £2 - £4

7.77 Snooker Diary [1989]

Reg Perrin (Comp.)
1988 Collins Glasgow, [Glasgow]
ISBN None given
Paperback 64pp, [82]pp, ill., plates, ports., 16 x 9cm
Notes Eric Whitehead (photog.)

The 'Snooker Diary' for 1989 included details of snooker around the globe, the World Professional Snooker Championship, profiles of 19 players, a snooker quiz, a statistics section, plus the official rules of snooker. The diary was issued with a richly coloured dustjacket showing a pack of reds being hit by the cue ball.

Value £2 - £4

7.78 Snooker Games : Games of the Snooker Table

Mike Stooke
1988 Poolman Publications, Salisbury
ISBN 0951297708
Paperback 20pp, ill., 21 x 15cm

Subtitled 'Five of Today's Most Popular Alternative Games', the five games covered in this book are 'Chase the Green', 'Crash', 'Cricket', 'Golf' and 'Russian Pool'. The precise rules are provided for each game and there are three illustrations to aid the reader in understanding the different games. Rather bizarrely, there is a cartoon of a cricketer holding a snooker cue on the contents page of the book. This is a thin book with a colourful red, black and white cover that originally sold for £2.95.

Value £3 - £5

7.79   The Snooker Handbook

Unknown author
1988   Ward Lock, [London]
ISBN   None given
Paperback   31pp, ill., plates (mostly col.), ports. (mostly col.), 15 x 11cm
Notes   Produced by Ward Lock for Younger's Tartan Special

This pocked-sized paperback book is divided into seven chapters – 'History of Snooker', 'Snooker's Greats', 'Snooker Quiz', 'Snooker's Principal Venues', 'Great Snooker Achievements', 'Snooker Champions', and 'Answers'. The 'Principal Venues' segment covers the Crucible, Wembley Conference Centre, the Guildhall, and the Hexagon Theatre. There are an abundance of photos and numerous facts and statistics throughout.

Value   £3 - £5

7.80   The Official 1990 Matchroom Snooker Special

Ian Morrison
1989   Hamlyn, London
ISBN   0600566005
Hardback   61pp, plates (mostly col.), ports. (mostly col.), 27 x 20cm
Notes   Introduction by Steve Davis

Hamlyn published a number of snooker books and this effort is an annual-sized hardback featuring the 8 players signed to Barry Hearn's Matchroom stable in the late '80s. The book includes a run-down of the 1988-89 season, profiles the Matchroom players and also profiles some of their rivals. Proving that the Matchroom players were not always goody-two-shoes we learn on page 60 that "on the eve of the 1988 Tennents UK Championship the W. P. B. S. A announced fines totalling £34,000 on the Matchroom team for failing to give press interviews during the Rothmans Grand Prix". The book is not especially valuable and regularly appears on eBay and is a charity shop regular.

Value   £2 - £3

7.81   Scottish Billiards and Snooker Association : Calendar 1989/90

Scottish Billiards & Snooker Association
[1989]   S.B. & S.A., Dunfermline
ISBN   None given
Paperback   96pp, 15 x 11cm
Notes   Sponsored by Benson and Hedges

This publication has orange card covers, a colour that is synonymous with the book's sponsors, Benson & Hedges. Included over the 96 pages are Scottish tournament details, an August 1989–June 1990 calendar, plus a plethora of adverts including 18 pages devoted to Scottish snooker clubs. Interestingly, there is a 6 page section dedicated to doping in sport and drug testing – remember, an official must be with the person providing a sample to ensure that samples are not switched!

Value £3 - £5

7.82 **Snooker Diary [1990]**

Reg Perrin (Comp.)
1989 Collins Glasgow, [Glasgow]
ISBN None given
Paperback 64pp, [82]pp, ill., plates, ports., 16 x 9cm
Notes Eric Whitehead (photog.)

Issued with a dustjacket and includes the official rules of snooker.

Value £2 - £4

7.83 **Snooker – the Players , the Shots, the Matches**

Terry Smith
1989 Macdonald (for Marks & Spencer), London
ISBN None given
Paperback 192pp, col. ill., plates (mostly col.), ports. (mostly col.), facsims., 30 x 22cm
Notes Includes Index

1990 Queen Anne Press, London
ISBN 0356195074
Paperback 192pp, ill. (mostly col.), plates (mostly col.), ports. (mostly col.), 30 x 22cm
Notes As above

A further offering published on behalf of Marks & Spencer, this book has eight chapters entitled 'The History of the Game', 'Great Games', 'Profile of the Pros', 'Snooker Today', 'The Amateur Game', 'Rules of the Game of Snooker', 'Results', and 'World Rankings'. The first chapter is especially informative and details the origins and history of billiards and snooker and contains some evocative b & w photos. The 1990 edition had a Macdonald-Queen Anne Press sticker placed over the St. Michael logo on page 3 and the bibliographic details on another sticker on page 4. Interestingly, at the top of the title page it still states "this edition published for Marks & Spencer plc in 1989 by Macdonald & Co. (Publishers) Ltd.", and it would appear that Queen Anne Press took the leftover copies of the 1989 edition and assigned it an ISBN and attempted to promote it without the Marks & Spencer association.

Value £3 - £5

7.84   **Take Up Snooker**

Philip Yates (principal contributor) / Noel Whittall & Philip Gardner (Eds.)
1989   Springfield Books, Huddersfield
ISBN   0947655611
Paperback   48pp, ill., plates, 21 x 10cm
Notes   Chris Oxlade (ill.); John Hipkiss (photog.)

'Take Up Snooker' was part of a series of pocket guides introducing popular indoor and outdoor sports. This effort, from the snooker journalist Phil Yates, outlines the basic techniques using diagrams and photos[27], whilst the most important rules are explained in full. The final page has a list of Useful Addresses, including overseas contacts. This book is extremely difficult to find and collectors may have to be patient when searching for a copy.

Value £5 - £10

7.85   **Pot Black Cue Sports Diary 1990-1991**

Terry Smith
[1990]   Eagle Sports Publications, London
ISBN   094835111X
Paperback   [192]pp, plates, ports., 15 x 10cm
Notes   Eric Whitehead (photog.)

By 1990 'Pot Black' had taken on sponsorship of the snooker diary and it states on page 2 that the book has been "compiled with exciting excerpts from past issues of Pot Black, the world's No. 1 Cue Sports magazine". The diary also includes statistics from the snooker season, fixtures for the 1990–1991 season and information and profiles of the world's top 32 players.

Value £2 - £4

7.86   **The History and Rules of Snooker**

The Word Factory
1991   Virgin Games, London

---

[27] Mostly featuring Roger Bales, a professional between 1984-1993, whose highest World Ranking was 58.

ISBN	None given
Paperback	121pp, ill., plates, ports., facsims., 15 x 21cm

This is rather an unusual snooker book, encompassing as it does the history of snooker, the rules of snooker, and a profile of Jimmy White (the book is subtitled on the cover 'And the Jimmy White Story'). The text itself is only 31 pages in length and is then repeated in French, German and Italian. I assume the book was given away with the console game 'Jimmy White's Whirlwind Snooker' that was released by Virgin Games in the same year, as the book has no price on the covers or an ISBN which is unusual for a book published in 1991.

Value   £3 - £5

7.87 The Book of Snooker and Billiards Quotations

Eugene Weber / Clive Everton	
1993	Stanley Paul & Co., London
ISBN	0091776201
Paperback	159pp, ill., ports., 22 x 14cm
Notes	Includes Index

Clive Everton needs no introduction but Eugene Weber was chief librarian of the Press Association when this book was published. There are forty one short chapters included in the book, with titles such as '147', 'Drugs', 'Hustling', 'Luck' and 'Self-Image'. The chapters are arranged alphabetically by title and some quotes include – "I think it's a great idea to talk during sex, as long as it's about snooker" (Steve Davis); "The first time I met the Hurricane, I took an instant dislike to him. The second time I beat him up" (Cliff Thorburn); "There's too much money. All the fun's gone out of it. We're in the world of agents and managers now" (Ray Reardon). There are some cartoons scattered throughout the book illustrating the various quotes and the colourful cover (drawn by Robin Bouttell) features cartoons of ten of the better known players.

Value   £3 - £5

7.88 The Complete History of Border Snooker

Rob Shiel	
[1995]	Rob Shiel, [Scotland]
ISBN	None given
Paperback	44pp, plates, ports., 21 x 15cm
Notes	Foreword by Ian Doyle; includes the rules of the Border Billiards & Snooker Association

With a self-explanatory title, Shiel takes the reader through Border snooker history with the aid of league tables and lists of various tournament and cup winners. To

199

add some local flavour many of the winning teams and individuals are featured in b & w photos scattered throughout the publication. As well as Shiel, there are also contributions from others connected with the Scottish snooker scene. The book has red card covers with a silhouette of a snooker table spread over the front and back. Originally costing £2.50, this book has only appeared for sale once recently and fetched £18 on eBay.

Value £15 - £20

7.89 **Billiards and Snooker : a Postcard Album**

Roger Lee
1996   Reflections of a Bygone Age, Nottingham
ISBN   1900138166
Paperback   [64]pp, plates. (some col.), ports., 21 x 15cm
Notes   ISBN is incorrectly printed on reverse of front cover;
                'Postcard Album' series no. 1

Compiled by one of the world's foremost billiards and snooker collectors, Roger Lee, this is a delightful book showcasing a selection of the author's collection of, what was at the time, over 2,000 postcards. Including billiard and snooker tables in royal palaces, country houses and schools; comic postcards; pictures of billiard halls; manufacturers; and players – a varied assortment has been chosen to illustrate how well both games are represented in postcard form. The publisher's specialise in books featuring picture postcards in a vast array of subjects.

Value in print £5.95

7.90 **A Guide to World Snooker**

Unknown author
[1998]   Imperial Tobacco, Bristol
ISBN   None given
Paperback   [40]pp, col. ill., col. plates, col. ports., 15 x 11cm

This pocket-sized guide was available by sending two 20s or four 10s cigarette pack fronts from any Embassy cigarettes to Imperial Tobacco and the contents include short articles and pieces on who is the greatest player, a snooker quiz, facts and figures, the women's game etc. This book regularly appears on eBay, copies normally being in excellent condition, and should only cost the collector a few pounds.

Value £2 - £3

7.91 Snooker Legends

Dean P. Hayes
2004 — Sutton Publishing, Stroud
ISBN — 0750932333
Paperback — viii, 134pp, plates, ports., 25 x 18cm
Notes — Reprinted 2005; Foreword by Terry Griffiths; includes list of World Professional Snooker Champions 1927–2003

This book consists of over 30 biographies of some of the greats of the game such as Joe and Steve Davis, Ray Reardon, Stephen Hendry et al, plus a few of the quirkier players to have graced the green baize, namely Tony Drago and Cliff Wilson. Each piece is about 3 pages in length and includes a list of career highlights (although it must be noted that some reviewers on Amazon feel this information is not entirely accurate). The title of the book on the cover is 'Snooker Legends and where are They Now'? and this is the name most collectors will know the book by.

Value — in print £12.99

7.92 The Snooker Quiz Book

John D. T. White (Comp.)
2004 — Apex Publishing, Clacton on Sea
ISBN — 190444427X
Paperback — vii, 203pp, 21 x 15cm
Notes — Foreword by Dennis Taylor

The compiler of 'The Snooker Quiz Book' has written it as a fan and included 1,500 questions to test other fans and experts on the game. As the blurb on the back cover states the book covers "the whole gamut of UK and international tournaments, current players and past masters, nationalities, rankings, venues, top earners, maximum breaks and nicknames". Particularly appealing are the 'Who Am I?' quizzes. There are no illustrations in the book and if you get stuck all the answers are listed at the back.

Value — in print £7.99

7.93 Masters of the Baize : Cue Legends, Bad Boys and Forgotten Men in Search of Snooker's Ultimate Prize

Luke Williams / Paul Gadsby
2005 — Mainstream Publishing, Edinburgh
ISBN — 1840188723
Hardback — 256pp, plates (some col.), ports. (some col.), 25 x 16cm
Notes — Includes Appendix detailing World Snooker Championship finals 1927–2004; Notes; Bibliography; and Index

2006	Mainstream Publishing, Edinburgh
ISBN	1840188723
Hardback	272pp, plates (some col.), ports. (some col.), 25 x 16cm
Notes	Revised and updated edition; includes Appendix detailing World Snooker Championship finals 1927–2006; Notes; Bibliography; and Index

Another snooker book with the ubiquitous green boards and predominantly red and green dustjacket, this is a fine recent addition to the relatively sparse literature devoted to snooker. Published by the well-known sports publishers, Mainstream, the authors detail the careers of the 20 World Champions, plus Jimmy White. These portraits have been extensively researched and include a horde of information. Disappointingly, there are only 8 pages of photos but there is an excellent Bibliography and a chapter at the end entitled 'Who is the Greatest?' where Williams and Gadsby rank their top ten players. The 2006 edition has been updated and includes chapters on the 2005 and 2006 World Champions, Shaun Murphy and Graeme Dott.

Value   **in print £15.99**

7.94 Black Farce and Cue Ball Wizards : the Inside Story of the Snooker World

	Clive Everton
2007	Mainstream Publishing, Edinburgh
ISBN	9781845961992
Hardback	399pp, ill., plates (some col.), ports. (some col.), 25 x 16cm
Notes	Includes Index

It has often been said never to judge a book by its cover. However, the absolutely stunning dustjacket photography is easily matched by the gripping tale told over the 399 pages of Clive Everton's superlative book. If snooker politics is your thing, and it's a subject surprisingly alluring and captivating, then 'Black Farce' will be your nirvana. The author begins the book by sketching his early career in journalism, the beginnings of the professional game (including a couple of deadpan lines on the womanising ways of John Pulman) and the setting up of his news agency and 'Snooker Scene' magazine. However, the majority of the tome is spent savaging snooker's world governing body in general, and Geoff Foulds and Rex Williams in particular. As early as page 13 Everton says "snooker's underlying problem clearly was – as it was to remain – an inept governing body", and to demonstrate that ineptitude scores of examples of mismanagement, poor decision making and decidedly spurious expense claims litter the book. As Everton says at the start of chapter twenty seven - "in 20 years, the game's situation had degenerated from one of glittering promise to a bleak battle for survival. In some Orwellian fashion, the forces of honesty and progress had been demonised by the inept, the inert and the incompetent. The battle for power had been won by those who had no idea how to use it to the game's benefit". Although snooker fans who care about the game will weep with frustration whilst reading this book, it is an engrossing read and a grand addition to the snooker canon.

Value **in print £17.99**

7.95 **Greatest Moments of Snooker**

Ian Welch
2007   Green Umbrella Publishing, Swindon
ISBN   9781906229429
Hardback   93pp, plates (mostly col.), ports. (mostly col.), 16 x 16cm
Notes   Part of the 'Greatest Moments of' series

'Greatest Moments of Snooker' has the dark cover of so many 21st century snooker books; this one a laminated one featuring pictures of Fred and Joe Davis, Steve Davis, Dennis Taylor and Ronnie O'Sullivan. There are 22 'Greatest Moments', beginning with 'Legendary Joe Davis Beats Brother Fred 1940' and ending with 'Graeme Dott and Peter Ebdon, Longest Frame 2006'. Scattered in between are Terry Griffiths becoming the first qualifier to become world champion, Cliff Thorburn's historic 147 at the Crucible, Stephen Hendry becoming the youngest ever world champion and so on. The book contains plenty of colour and b & w photos and is part of a series featuring sports such as boxing, football, grand prix and rugby. Incidentally, the book has a RRP of £6.99 on the rear cover but it appears that it is only available as part of a book and DVD ('History of Snooker') combination set priced at £15 (although I imagine this is the sort of product that will end up in remainder shops or be heavily discounted to shift any remaining copies).

Value **in print (including DVD) £15**

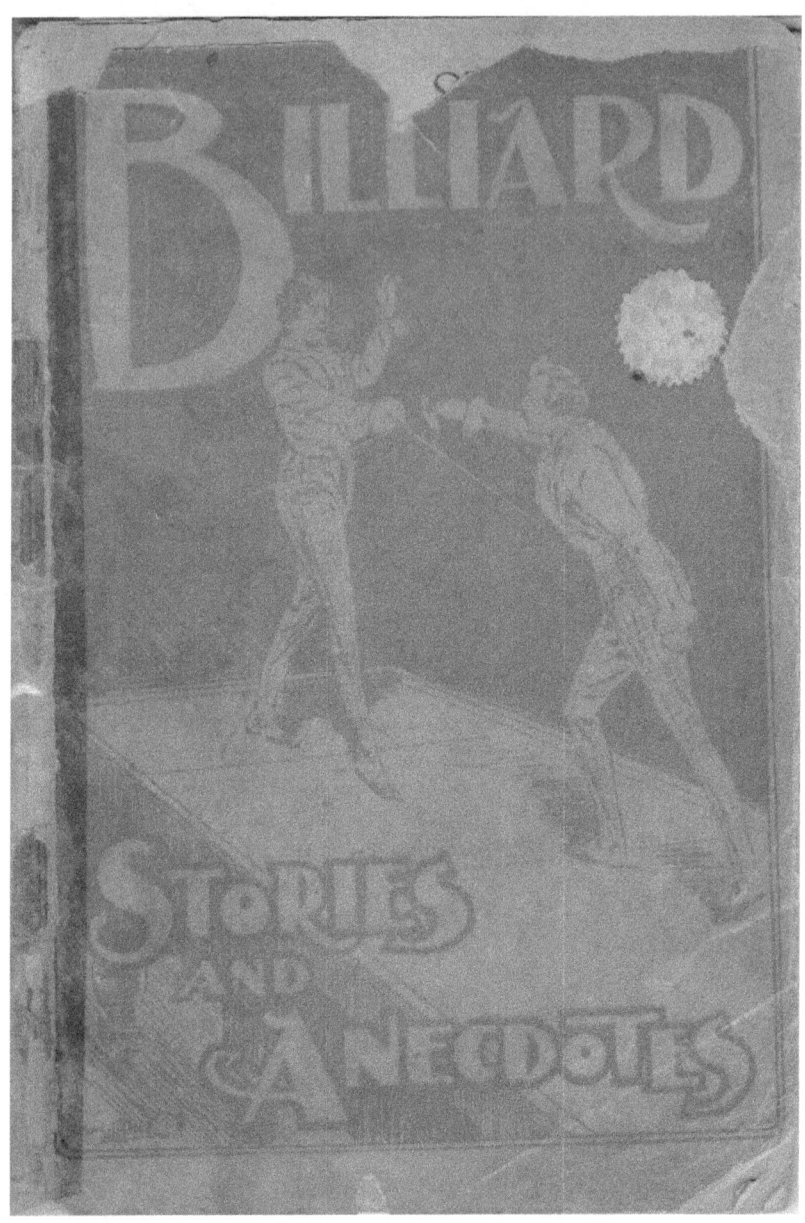

'Billiard Stories and Anecdotes' was published by F. Welstead & Sons of London in 1824. The book is understandably scarce and would probably command £500-£800 if it appeared for sale today. See entry 7.0.

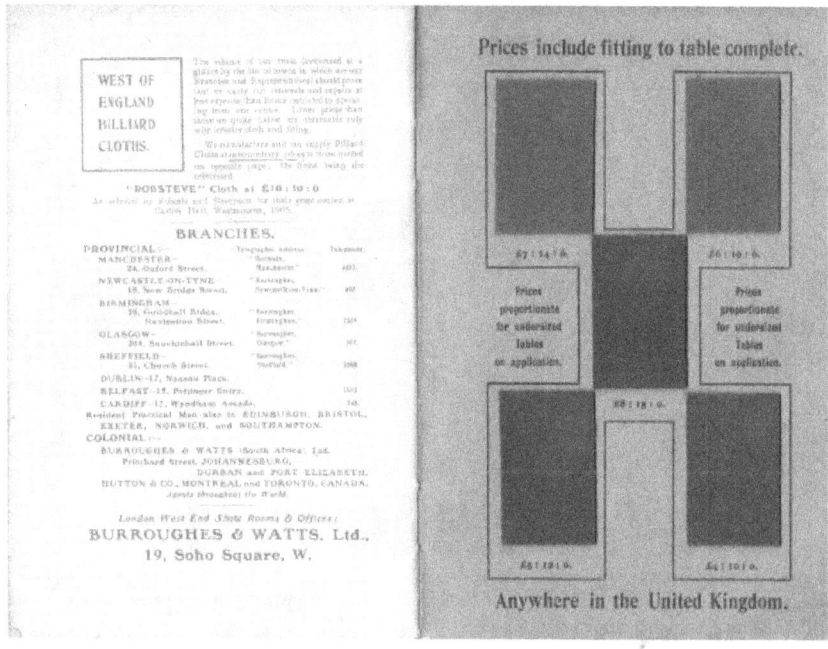

Front and reverse of rear cover of 'The Game Beautiful' a 1905 Burroughes & Watts publication valued at £40-£60. The reverse of the back cover features 5 samples of billiard cloth with prices. See entry 7.3.

'Masters of the Baize' was first published in 2005 and is a superb work on the players that have won the World Snooker Championship. See entry 7.93.

'Billiards and Snooker Teasers Explained' are highly desirable books published by Burroughes & Watts between the 1930s and 1960s. The copy pictured here is the 1961-1962 edition which has a superb decorative cover. Copies regularly appear on eBay and normally command an absolute minimum of £25. See entries 7.11 – 7.31.

Front and back covers of Roger Lee's 'Billiards and Snooker Postcard Album'. The front cover features a formal portrait of Joe Davis, whereas the back cover demonstrates how billiards was used in a romantic sense on postcards. See entry 7.89.

~ REFERENCE BOOKS ~

8.0 **The Billiard Annual for 1902**

W. H. Robbins (Ed.)
[1902]   Simpkin, Marshall, Hamilton, Kent & Co., London
Paperback   102pp, 140pp, 1 plate, 1 port., 19 x 13cm

The British Library has catalogued this annual as being published in 1901. However, this is incorrect as the annual mentions 'Modern Billiards' by John Roberts (see entry 6.43) which was published in 1902. It has dark green card covers with the title etc. in black lettering and a drawing of a player at the table in the centre. It seems there was a hardback edition of this annual because on the cover it states a paper cover edition was 1/- whereas the cloth bound version cost 2/6 but I have been unable to trace a copy of the cloth bound edition.

1902 was the first publication of 'The Billiard Annual' because the Preface says the 'Annual' "now makes its first appearance", and the frontispiece of the book has a great photographic plate of John Roberts playing a massé shot. The annual is divided into two sections, the first containing a useful bibliography (describing the books listed in some detail), rules, essays on equipment and accessories plus an unusual 3 page list of principal hotels in London that had billiard rooms. Section two contains an extensive and detailed 'Diary' of the most important games played from 1st October 1900 to 30th September 1901. Unusually, both sections have separately numbered pages so that section two begins again at page 1 rather than continuing from page 102.

Value £100 - £200

8.1 **The Billiard Annual for 1909-1910**

W. H. Robbins (Ed.)
[1909]   No publisher details, London
Paperback   128pp, ill., 19 x 13cm

In the Preface of the 'Billiard Annual' it states that the publication is making a re-appearance, which presumably is from the 1902 edition (see entry above). Wrapped in pale green, glossy card covers the volume has a fantastic period drawing of a small boy struggling to reach up to the table on the front plus plenty more superb drawings and cartoons throughout. This book is a real miscellany containing as it does the first rules reprinted from the 'Compleat Gamester' of c.1640, and various updated and revised rules from 1775 to 1900. Also included are tables detailing championship matches and professional matches for the 1908-1909 season, player profiles ('The Professional Experts'), plus details of specific matches and hints on play.

Value £100 - £200

8.2 The Billiard Year-Book for 1910

Herbert S. Oakley / W. Wilson Ruttle (Eds.)
1909   Adam & Charles Black, London
Hardback   viii, 120pp, ill., plates, ports., 19 x 13cm
Notes   Includes Index

An advert for this book in 'The New World of Billiards' of November 3rd 1909 boasts that it is the first official reference book ever issued. There is certainly an awful lot of information packed between the decorative covers including 'Billiards & Music', 'Billiards & the Law : Absurd Legislation which needs Amending', plus plenty of tables of match statistics. Oakley and Ruttle's book originally cost 1/- and has an extensive Index.

Value £100 - £200

8.3 John Roberts' Billiards Annual, 1909 : The Billiard Year Book for 1910

John Roberts Junior
[1909]   Simpkin, Marshall, Hamilton, Kent & Co., London
Paperback   144pp, 1 port., 19 x 13cm
Notes   Includes contributions by 'Critique', 'Observer' and Hamilton Pritchard; includes Bibliography

There is no date of publication in this book but the title doesn't make it difficult to assume it was almost certainly published in 1909. Further clues are the tournament details of the 1908-'09 season included in the book and the British Library copy containing a British Museum stamp dated 1909.

This paperback annual has a striking dark green, decorative cover featuring a billiard table in each corner advertising 'Schweppes' and the title in black in the centre. The most important aspect for the collector, however, is that the book contains a 4 page Bibliography that lists well over 100 books either exclusively devoted to billiards or works containing chapters on the game. The earliest work listed in the Bibliography is a French title of 1642 and the earliest English titles (exclusively concerned with billiards) date from the 1770s.

There is a real miscellany of subjects in the book, including 'New Patents applied for and Sealed', 'Billiards as an Aid to Health' and 'Billiards for Ladies'. Another fascinating section for historians of the game is 'Billiard Biographies' where such luminaries as James Barber, Jack Carr, Charles Hughes and John Roberts Senior and Junior are discussed.

Value £100 - £200

8.4 **John Roberts' Billiards Annual, 1910 : the Billiard Year Book for 1910-11**

John Roberts
1910 Adam & Charles Black, [London]
Hardback 164pp, 19 x 12cm
Notes 2nd year of issue; includes contributions by F. D. Bone, Edgar Wallace, 'Observer', George Reid, and Charles Vidal Diehl

This annual has thick white card covers with green lettering and a portrait of Roberts in an oval cartouche in the centre. Some unusual chapter headings include 'Billiards in the Army', 'Billiards in India and Australia', and 'Snooker Pool – Points About the Rules'.

Value £100 - £200

8.5 **The Billiard Annual : Fixtures, Rules of Billiards, Snooker, Bagatelle, etc. etc. : Season 1925-26**

Charles Roberts (Ed.)
[1925] The Sydenham Press, London
[Paperback] 16pp, 14 x 11cm

This pocket-sized book has dark green covers and is a handy reference book featuring a rules section, billiard fixtures, a record of the Billiard Champions of England, 1825–1925, and a brief piece called 'Snooker Questions Answered'. [description based on a photocopy].

Value £100 - £200

8.6 **News of the World Snooker Annual 1984/85**

Julian Worthington (Ed.)
1984 Invincible Press, London
ISBN 0855430486
Paperback 128pp, plates., ports., 17 x 13cm
Notes Foreword by Fred Burcombe

8.7 **News of the World Snooker Annual 1985/86**

1985 Invincible Press, London
ISBN 0855430524
Paperback 127pp, plates, ports., 18 x 13cm

8.8   Snooker Annual 1986/87

1986	Invincible Press, London
ISBN	085543080X
Paperback	128pp, ports., 17 x 12cm
Notes	The ISBN for this edition is the same as the 1987/88 edition; only the cover has 'News of the World', not the title page

8.9   Snooker Annual 1987/88

1987	Invincible Press, London
ISBN	085543080X
Paperback	96pp, 17 x 13cm
Notes	The ISBN for this edition is the same as the 1986/87 edition; only the cover has 'News of the World', not the title page

8.10   News of the World Snooker Annual 1988/89

[1988]	Invincible Press, London
ISBN	0855431520
Paperback	96pp, 1 port., 17 x 13cm

8.11   News of the World Snooker Annual 1989/90

[1989]	Invincible Press, London
ISBN	0855431822
Paperback	96pp, plates, ports., 17 x 13cm
Notes	Terry Smith (photog.)

8.12   News of the World Snooker Annual 1990/91

1990	Invincible Press, London
ISBN	0855432128
Paperback	128pp, plates, ports., 17 x 13cm
Notes	Terry Smith (photog.)

These pocket-sized, paperback reference books provided details of the previous season's tournaments in the form of a commentary on each tournament backed up with match results and highest break winners. Overseas tournaments, such as the Australian and Canadian Championships are covered, along with the World Billiards Championship, amateur tournaments, U-21 and junior tournaments, and women's competitions. If that isn't enough for you, then check out the prize money table, the world rankings table or the profiles of the world's top players. The annuals often turn up on eBay and in secondhand bookshops and the collector shouldn't have to pay more than a few pounds for each of them.

Value   £2 - £3 each

8.13 **Snooker Year** [see also Benson and Hedges Snooker Year books below]

    Clive Everton (Ed.)
1984	Virgin Books, London
ISBN	0863690513
Paperback	128pp, ill., plates (some col.), ports. (some col.), 27 x 21cm
Notes	Cover title is 'Benson and Hedges Snooker Year'; includes Snooker Glossary

1984	Virgin Books, London
ISBN	086369070X
Paperback	128pp, ill., plates (some col.), ports. (some col.), 27 x 21cm
Notes	Export edition; includes Snooker Glossary

8.14
1985	Virgin Books, London
ISBN	0863691005 (UK and Eire edition) / 0863691048 (Export edition)
Paperback	160pp, ill., plates (some col.), ports. (some col.), 27 x 21cm
Notes	2nd edition; ISBN on back cover is 0863690513 (same as 1984 edition); cover title is 'Benson & Hedges Snooker Year'; includes Snooker Glossary

8.15
1986	Virgin Books, London
ISBN	0863691668
Paperback	160pp, ill., plates (some col.), ports. (some col.), 27 x 21cm
Notes	3rd edition; cover title is 'Benson & Hedges Snooker Year'; includes Snooker Glossary and Billiards Glossary

The blurb on the back cover of this book states that it contains a "comprehensive review of the tournament scene and a series of profiles of the leading players". These tournament statistics and player profiles are accompanied by plenty of b & w and colour photos plus a few b & w cartoons. There is quite an extensive section on the amateur game at the rear of the book and other subjects covered include the British circuit, masters of snooker, past masters, the overseas circuit, and women's snooker. This edition includes contributions from Steve Acteson, Alexander Clyde, John Dee, Michael Gouge, Alan Green, Janice Hale, John Hennessy, Graham Nickless, and Terry Smith. This is the 1st edition of a series of books that will be known to most collectors as the 'Benson & Hedges Snooker Year'.

Value   £3 - £5 each

8.16 **Benson and Hedges Book of Snooker**

    Ian Morrison
1985	Hamlyn Publishing, Twickenham
ISBN	None given

Hardback	176pp, ill. (some col.), plates (some col.), ports. (some col.), facsims, 29 x 22cm
Notes	First published in 1985 as 'The Hamlyn Encyclopedia of Snooker' [see below]; Introduction by Dennis Taylor; David Muscroft (photog.)

Value	£4 - £8

8.17 The Hamlyn Encyclopedia of Snooker

Ian Morrison

1985	Hamlyn Publishing, Twickenham
ISBN	0600501922
Hardback	176pp, ill. (some col.), plates (some col.), ports. (some col.), facsims., 29 x 22cm
Notes	2nd impression 1986; 3rd impression 1986; Introduction by Dennis Taylor; David Muscroft (photog.)

1987	Hamlyn Publishing, Twickenham
ISBN	0600556042
Hardback	176pp, ill. (some col.), plates (some col.), ports. (some col.), facsims., 29 x 22cm
Notes	Revised and updated edition

As the blurb on the colourful dustjacket states this book is "an A-Z reference book giving results, scores, biographies, dates and general information on technique, dress and the rules of the game". Open the vibrant cover of this encyclopedia and inside you will find pages crammed full of photos, illustrations, player profiles, statistics, snooker venues, referee profiles, snooker terms, equipment, manufacturers and so on and so forth. The information is arranged alphabetically, the first entry being 'Amateur' and the last 'Zimbabwe' – where we learn that the first National Championships were held in that country in 1967.

Value	£4 - £8

8.18 Rothmans Snooker Yearbook 1985-86

Janice Hale (Ed.)

1985	Queen Anne Press, London
ISBN	0356120228
Hardback	255pp, plates, ports., 22 x 16cm
Notes	Forewords by Rothmans Publications and David Vine; written with the assistance of Clive Everton and Julie Kane

1985	Queen Anne Press, London

	ISBN	0356120236
	Paperback	255pp, plates, ports., 21 x 15cm
	Notes	As above

8.19   Rothmans Snooker Yearbook 1986-87

	Janice Hale (Ed.)	
	1986	Queen Anne Press, London
	ISBN	0356123626
	Hardback	287pp, plates, ports., 22 x 16cm
	Notes	As above

	1986	Queen Anne Press, London
	ISBN	0356123634
	Paperback	287pp, plates, ports., 21 x 15cm
	Notes	As above

8.20   Rothmans Snooker Yearbook 1987-88

	Janice Hale (Ed.)	
	1987	Queen Anne Press, London
	ISBN	0356146901
	Paperback	319pp, plates, ports., 21 x 15cm
	Notes	Foreword by Rothmans Publications; written with the assistance of Clive Everton and Julie Kane

8.21   Rothmans Snooker Yearbook 1988-89

	Janice Hale (Ed.)	
	1988	Queen Anne Press, London
	ISBN	0356158853
	Paperback	317pp, plates, ports., 21 x 15cm
	Notes	As above

8.22   Rothmans Snooker Yearbook 1989-90

	Janice Hale (Ed.)	
	1989	Queen Anne Press, London
	ISBN	0356179222
	Paperback	334pp, plates, ports., 21 x 15cm
	Notes	As above; incorrect ISBN of 0356179227 given on title page

8.23   Rothmans Snooker Yearbook 1990-91

	Janice Hale (Ed.)	
	1990	Queen Anne Press, London
	ISBN	0356191028

Paperback	383pp, plates, ports., 21 x 15cm
Notes	Written with the assistance of Clive Everton and Julie Kane

8.24 Rothmans Snooker Yearbook 1991-92

Janice Hale (Ed.)	
1991	Queen Anne Press, London
ISBN	0356197476
Paperback	381pp, plates, ports., 21 x 15cm
Notes	As above

The series of 'Rothmans Snooker Yearbooks' were packed full of statistics, tournament results, player records and profiles, ranking tables, and prize money lists, as well as details on the amateur game, professional billiards and the women's game. They also included an 'Editor's Review of the Season' plus short articles such as 'A Year in Snooker Politics' by Clive Everton and 'How a Tournament Happens' written by Janice Hale. The books have a distinctive dark blue colour, a colour associated with the Rothmans brand, and the first two editions were issued in both paperback and hardback, the latter being much scarcer than the former.

Value £3 - £5 each

8.25 Snooker : the Records

Clive Everton	
1985	Guinness Superlatives, Enfield
ISBN	0851124488
Paperback	160pp, ill., plates (some col.), ports. (some col.), 26 x 19cm
Notes	Includes Index

Despite its title, 'Snooker : the Records' looks back at the whole history of snooker *and* billiards but with an emphasis on modern players and tournaments. After an introductory essay, 'Snooker in the television age', the book moves onto record earnings, tournament statistics and player profiles. There is an extensive section on billiards and after this follows a chapter called 'Round the World', where billiards and snooker in various countries (e.g. Australia, New Zealand, Malta and India) is noted and discussed. There is a lot of information packed into this book and, with Everton being the author, the reader knows the information is of some authority. The cover features a colour photo of Dennis Taylor and there are plenty of colour photos throughout.

Value £3 - £5

8.26 **Benson and Hedges Snooker Year**

Terry Smith (Ed.) / Dennis Taylor (Associate Ed.)
1987   Pelham Books, London
ISBN   0720717973
Paperback   158pp, plates (some col.), ports. (some col.), 25 x 19cm
Notes   4th edition

8.27 **Benson and Hedges Snooker Year**

Terry Smith (Ed.) / Dennis Taylor (Associate Ed.)
1988   Pelham Books, London
ISBN   0720718961
Hardback   191pp, plates (some col.), ports. (some col.), 26 x 20cm
Notes   5th edition

8.28 **Benson and Hedges Snooker Year**

Terry Smith (Ed.) / Dennis Taylor (Associate Ed.)
1988   Pelham Books, London
ISBN   0720718309
Paperback   191pp, plates (some col.), ports. (some col.), 25 x 19cm
Notes   5th edition

8.29 **Benson and Hedges Snooker Year**

Terry Smith (Ed.) / Terry Griffiths (Associate Ed.)
1989   Pelham Books, London
ISBN   0720719445
Hardback   160pp, plates (some col.), ports. (some col.), 25 x 19cm
Notes   6th edition

8.30 **Benson and Hedges Snooker Year**

Terry Smith (Ed.) / Terry Griffiths (Associate Ed.)
1989   Pelham Books, London
ISBN   0720719100
Paperback   160pp, plates (some col.), ports. (some col.), 25 x 19cm
Notes   6th edition

8.31 **Benson and Hedges Snooker Year**

Terry Smith (Ed.) / Stephen Hendry (Associate Ed.)
1990   Pelham Books, London
ISBN   0720719550
Paperback   160pp, plates (some col.), ports. (some col.), 25 x 19cm
Notes   7th edition

8.32   Benson and Hedges Snooker Year

Terry Smith (Ed.) / Stephen Hendry (Associate Ed.)
1991   Pelham Books, London
ISBN   0720719836
Paperback   160pp, plates (mostly col.), ports. (mostly col.), 25 x 19cm
Notes   8th edition

The 'Benson and Hedges Snooker Year' series of books were a string of reference books that contained a bewildering amount of information and statistics. There were also some excellent photographs throughout the series, particularly those taken of the players relaxing away from the table. The books also contained stand-alone articles on such people as John Parris, the legendary cue maker and cue doctor, and 'Whispering' Ted Lowe, the man behind the microphone. All editions turn up regularly for sale on eBay and shouldn't prove too difficult to track down in charity shops and secondhand bookshops.

Value   £3 - £5 each

8.33   Official W.P.B.S.A. Diary Yearbook 1987-1988

Terry Smith
[1987]   Eagle Sports Publications, Hove
ISBN   094835111X
Paperback   [208]pp, plates, ports., 15 x 9cm
Notes   Eric Whitehead (photog.)

The diary section of this Yearbook runs from September 1987–December 1988 and the remainder of the volume features player profiles, tournament statistics and contemporary advertisements.

Value   £2 - £4

8.34   Official W.P.B.S.A. Diary Yearbook 1988-1989

Terry Smith
[1988]   Eagle Sports Publications, Hove
ISBN   094835111X
Paperback   [224]pp, plates, ports., 15 x 10cm
Notes   Eric Whitehead (photog.)

The World Professional Billiards & Snooker Association was formed in 1968 and this, their second diary yearbook, was published 20 years after their formation. As well as player profiles and tournament statistics the publication also includes the rules of snooker and billiards. There are plenty of adverts right through the book, many of them offering the services of players for exhibitions and promotional purposes. The review of the 1987-1988 season shows that the 1987 Tennents UK Championship was an eventful one – Joe Johnson missing the final pink when set for a 147 and also suffering chest pains during the quarter final ("those pains were frightening – I thought I was a goner"). Then two hours before the start of play on the second day of the final it was discovered that water had been thrown onto the table and it had to be re-clothed – the job was finished with only five minutes to spare. The colourful cover features Steve Davis with the World Championship trophy and the diary part of the book runs from September 1988 to December 1989.

Value £2 - £4

8.35 Snooker at the Crucible

Ian Morrison
1988 Ian Morrison Sports Services, Runcorn
ISBN None given
Paperback 25pp, 21 x 15cm
Notes Includes Index

At the time of publication, Ian Morrison was a freelance sports author and statistician who had penned a few snooker books, most notably "The Hamlyn Encyclopedia of Snooker" in 1985 (see entry 8.17). As the title makes clear this slim booklet is a record of snooker at Sheffield's Crucible Theatre beginning with details of the Crucible's eleven finals at the time of publication, and ending with 'Crucible Titbits'. The book is packed full of statistics in tabular format and is wrapped in b & w card covers. Once again, this is one of those modern books that rarely surfaces for sale presumably because of a small print run.

Value £10 - £20

8.36 Who's Who in Snooker

Ian Morrison
1988 Hamlyn, London
ISBN 0600557138
Paperback 128pp, plates (some col.), ports. (some col.), 27 x 20cm
Notes David Muscroft and Trevor Smith (photogs.)

This is a paperback book that includes profiles of over 70 players, referees and managers, accompanied by both colour and b & w photos. Some of the gems hidden within the pages include the fact that Nigel Gilbert wore a glove on his bridge hand because he perspired a lot, and that Stephen Hendry had purchased an £18,000 Mercedes with some of his prize money. Perhaps the real appeal of this work is to read about the lesser known snooker players and speculate on what they are doing now. Good examples include the aforementioned Gilbert, Mark Bennett,

Roger Bales, Steve Duggan, and Dene O'Kane. There is a good quote from Joe O'Boye – "I don't regret anything – you're only young once and you can't buy youth", presumably when asked why he never really fulfilled his early potential.

Value £3 - £5

8.37   **Official W.P.B.S.A. Diary Yearbook 1989-1990**

       Terry Smith
       [1989]   Eagle Sports Publications, London
       ISBN   094835111X
       Paperback   [208]pp, plates, ports., 15 x 10cm
       Notes   Eric Whitehead (photog.)

This volume features player profiles, tournament statistics and contemporary advertisements, as well as a diary section.

Value £2 - £4

8.38   **Snooker : Records · Facts and Champions**

       Ian Morrison
       1989   Guinness Publishing, Enfield
       ISBN   0851123643
       Paperback   160pp, plates (some col.), ports. (some col.), 26 x 19cm
       Notes   Includes Index

This 160 page paperback book is crammed so full of information and statistics it is difficult to know where to begin describing it. All the World Championship results since 1927 are given and a match report is featured for every final between 1977–1989. Other sections include the W. P. B. S. A, maximum men, Mike Watterson, classic matches, great rivalries, world rankings, the non-professional game and so on. Some facts include - "the first official total clearance was by Sidney Smith in compiling a break of 133 in the 1936-7 Daily Mail Gold Cup" and that "the first woman to referee a championship match in Britain was Rae Craven . . . on 24 February 1963". Incidentally, the photo of Stephen Hendry on the cover is almost identical to the one on the front of the 1988-89 'Rothmans Yearbook' (see entry 8.21).

Value £3 - £5

8.39   **The World Snooker Almanac : the Top 100 Players in Photographs**

Eric Whitehead
1993   Eric Dobby Publishing, Orpington
ISBN   185882009X
Hardback   xix, 117pp, [8]pp, col. plates, col. ports., 18 x 10cm

Roughly the same dimensions as a pocket diary, inside this book the well-known snooker photographer, Eric Whitehead, profiles the top 100 players in the game in the early '90s. Each entry gives information on the player, tournaments won, ranking tournament results in 1992/93, highest ranking etc. The book also includes a 5 page 'History of Snooker' by the journalist Phil Yates, a few pages devoted to the women's game, and a section for fans to collect those all important autographs. The book was issued without a jacket, has pictorial laminated boards and is an eBay stalwart.

Value   £2 - £3

8.40   **The CueSport Book of Professional Snooker : the Complete Record and History**

Eric Hayton / [John Dee]
2004   Rose Villa Publications, Lowestoft
ISBN   095485490X
Paperback   viii, 1056pp, plates, ports., 22 x 15cm

There is a staggering amount of information in this statistical book and it is no surprise to learn that the volume took three years to compile. The first twenty nine chapters cover 140 pages and detail the story of snooker primarily from the 1920s right up to the 2003/04 snooker season. After this come full results of over 60,000 matches! Proving that statistics do not lie (at least in sport), on page 125 it says that Marcu Fu is a player to watch (he reached the semi-finals of the 2006 World Championships) and that Graeme Dott has shown marked improvement over the past year – he won the 2006 World Championship. Anyone who has played snooker at a reasonable standard will know of someone who has turned pro at some stage and checking their stats is the real fascination of this book. The three players from Suffolk that this author played against in younger days had varying success on the pro circuit. John Disney didn't win a single match during his one season as a professional in 1992-1993; Phil Mumford gained a top world ranking spot of 427 and won 45.65% of his matches; whilst Chris Barnett fared the best, reaching 306 in the world rankings and winning 47.62% of his pro matches.

Value   in print £20

'The Billiard Annual for 1909-1910' has a superb period drawing on the cover and would sell for £100-£200 in today's market. See entry 8.1.

~ HANDBOOKS & RULE BOOKS ~

~ Billiards Rule Books ~

9.0   **Rules of Billiards**

Gamages
[n.d.]   Gamages, London
Paperback   8pp, 14 x 11cm

Gamages were based in Holborn and also had a City branch at 107 Cheapside. This brief rule book was essentially published as an advertising tool in the hope that customers would follow the message on the reverse of the front cover and "write (or 'phone) for our special lists of Billiards and Table Tennis".

Value   £60 - £80

9.1   **The Rules of Billiards**

[Billiards Control Club]
1909   [BCC Publications], [London]
Paperback   16pp, 13 x 9cm
Notes   Authorised by the Billiards Control Club

Value   £20 - £40

9.2   **The Rules of Billiards**

Billiards Control Club
1912   [BCC Publications], [London]
Paperback   16pp, 12 x 9cm
Notes   Includes a 1 page 'Alterations and Additions to Rules' dated January 1912 attached to the title page; authorised by the Billiards Control Club

Value   £20 - £40

9.3   **The Rules of the Game of English Billiards**

The Billiards Association & Control Council (B.A. & C.C.)
1935   B.A. & C.C., London
Paperback   24pp, 13 x 9cm

Notes   Reprint of the 1919 1st edition; authorised by the B.A. & C.C.

Value   £20 - £40

9.4   The Rules of the Game of English Billiards

B.A. & C.C.
1937   B.A. & C.C., London
Paperback   26pp, 13 x 8cm
Notes   Reprint of the 1919 1st edition; includes 3 pages of Amendment slips entitled 'Amendments to the Rules of English Billiards'; authorised by the B.A. & C.C.

Value   £20 - £40

9.5   Rules of the Game of English Billiards

B.A. & C.C.
1942   B.A. & C.C., London
Paperback   31pp, 12 x 9cm
Notes   Reprint of the new revised edition of 1939; authorised by the B.A. & C.C.; includes Index

Value   £15 - £30

9.6   Rules of the Game of English Billiards

B.A. & C.C.
1943   B.A. & C.C., London
Paperback   31pp, 12 x 9cm
Notes   Reprint of the 1939 New Revised edition; authorised by the B.A. & C.C.; includes Index

Value   £15 - £30

9.7   Rules of the Game of English Billiards
B.A. & C.C.
[1944]   B.A. & C.C., London
Paperback   31pp, 12 x 9cm
Notes   Authorised by the B.A. & C.C.; includes Index

This book has green card covers and originally sold for 1 shilling and threepence.

Value   £15 - £30

9.8   Rules of the Game of English Billiards

B.A. & C.C.
1946   B.A. & C.C., London
Paperback   31pp, 12 x 9cm
Notes   Reprint of the 1939 New Revised edition; authorised by the
                B.A. & C.C.; includes Index

The 1946 'Rules of the Game of English Billiards' cost 1/3 and has green and white marbled card covers. The rear cover carries an advert for Crystalate, Bonzoline and Vitalite, Billiard and Snooker balls.

Value   £15 - £30

9.9   Rules of the Game of English Billiards

B.A. & C.C.
1952   B.A. & C.C., London
Paperback   31pp, 13 x 9cm
Notes   Authorised by the B.A. & C.C.; includes Index

Value   £15 - £30

9.10   Rules of the Game of English Billiards

B. & S.C.C.
[197-]   B. & S.C.C., [Huddersfield]
Paperback   26pp, 12 x 9cm
Notes   35th edition; authorised by the B. & S.C.C.; includes Index

Value   £5 - £10

9.11   Rules of the Game of English Billiards

B. & S.C.C.
[197-]   B. & S.C.C., [Huddersfield]
Paperback   31pp, 13 x 9cm
Notes   Authorised by the B. & S.C.C.; includes Index

Value   £5 - £10

~ Snooker Rule Books ~

9.12   **The Rules of the Game of Snooker**

B. A. & C.C.
1933   B. A. & C.C., London
Paperback   21pp, 13 x 9cm
Notes   Reprint of the 1926 edition; authorised by the B. A. & C.C.;
              includes Index

Value   £20 - £40

9.13   **The Rules of the Game of Snooker**

B.A. & C.C.
1934   B.A. & C.C., London
Paperback   21pp, 13 x 8cm
Notes   Reprint of the 1926 edition; authorised by the B.A. & C.C.;
              includes Index

The 1934 rule book has dark green card covers, sold for 1-/ and the rear cover carries an advert for Bonzoline, Crystalate, Vitalite Billiard and Snooker balls; a similar advert to which was still being used 12 years later on the 'Rules of the Game of English Billiards'.

Value   £20 - £40

9.14   **The Rules of the Game of Snooker**

B.A. & C.C.
1936   B.A. & C.C., London
Paperback   22pp, 13 x 9cm
Notes   Reprint of the 1926 edition; authorised by the B.A. & C.C.;
              includes Index

The 1936 rule book also has dark green card covers, sold for 1/- and includes an 'Amendment to Rule 4 of the Rules of Snooker' and 'Amendment to Rule 5 of the Rules of Volunteer Snooker'.

Value   £20 - £40

9.15   **The Rules of the Game of Snooker**

B.A. & C.C.
[1938]   B.A. & C.C., London

Paperback	25pp, 13 x 9cm
Notes	January 1938 reprint of the 1926 1st edition; authorised by the B.A. & C.C.; includes Index

The 1938 snooker rule book was originally priced at 1/- and bound in green card wrappers. It contains three adverts for the 'Billiard Player' stating "thousands of eager-to-buy Folk read the up-to-date Billiard Player". The book includes the embossed symbol of the B.A. & C.C (two world globes with a Union Jack flag stuck into one of them) on the first page of the book. Regarding this symbol, in the 1965 'Handbook' it states "the Official Seal of the Billiards Association & Control Council is embossed upon all authorised publications of the B.A. & C.C.".

Value £20 - £40

9.16 Rules of the Game of Snooker

B.A. & C.C.	
1940	B.A. & C.C., London
Paperback	34pp, 13 x 9cm
Notes	Reprint of the 1939 New Revised edition; authorised by the B.A. & C.C.; includes Index

Value £15 - £30

9.17 Rules of the Game of Snooker

B.A. & C.C.	
1943	B.A. & C.C., London
Paperback	34pp, 12 x 9cm
Notes	December 1943 reprint of the 1939 New Revised edition; cover has date of 1944; authorised by the B.A. & C.C.; includes Index

Value £15 - £30

9.18 Rules of the Game of Snooker

B.A. & C.C.	
1946	B.A. & C.C., London
Paperback	34pp, 13 x 9cm
Notes	Reprint of the 1939 New Revised edition; cover has date of 1946-7; authorised by the B.A. & C.C.; includes Index

Value £15 - £30

9.19   Rules of the Game of Snooker

B.A. & C.C.
1948   B.A. & C.C., London
Paperback   34pp, 12 x 9cm
Notes   Reprint of the New Revised edition of January 1939;
                 authorised by the B.A. & C.C.; includes Index

Value   £15 - £30

9.20   Rules of the Game of Snooker

B.A. & C.C.
[1949]   B.A. & C.C., London
Paperback   34pp, 13 x 9cm
Notes   Reprint of the New Revised edition of January 1939;
                 authorised by the B.A. & C.C.; includes Index

By the time this edition was published in 1949, the rules book had gone through three revised editions and had been reprinted 22 times. Interestingly, the back cover still holds an advert for 'Crystalate Balls' stating that Joe Davis made the world's record snooker break of 138 using them. This rule book originally sold for 1 shilling and threepence and has green card wrappers.

Value   £15 - £30

9.21   Rules of the Game of Snooker

B. A. & C.C.
[n.d.]   B. A. & C.C., London
Paperback   34pp, 13 x 9cm
Notes   31st edition; authorised by the B. A. & C.C.; includes Index

Value   £15 - £30

9.22   Rules of the Game of English Snooker

B. A. & C.C.
[n.d.]   B. A. & C.C., London
Paperback   31pp, 13 x 9cm
Notes   37th edition; authorised by the B. A. & C.C.; includes a 1 page
                 'Alterations to Rules' pasted to inside of rear cover; includes
                 Index

Value   £15 - £30

9.23 **Rules of the Game of Snooker**

B. A. & C.C.	
[196-]	B. A. & C.C., London
Paperback	30pp, 13 x 9cm
Notes	40th edition; authorised by the B. A. & C.C.; includes Index

Value £10 - £20

9.24 **Rules of the Game of Snooker**

B. A. & C.C.	
[196-]	B. A. & C.C., London
Paperback	31pp, 13 x 9cm
Notes	41st edition; authorised by the B. A. & C.C.; includes Index

Value £10 - £20

9.25 **Rules of the Game of Snooker**

B. & S.C.C.	
[197-]	B. & S.C.C., [Huddersfield]
ISBN	None given
Paperback	31pp, 13 x 9cm
Notes	43rd edition; authorised by the B. & S.C.C.; includes Index

Value £5 - £10

9.26 **Rules of the Game of Snooker**

B. & S.C.C.	
[1978]	B. & S.C.C., [Huddersfield]
ISBN	None given
Paperback	31pp, 12 x 9cm
Notes	Authorised by the B. & S.C.C.; includes Index

This small book has yellow card covers with the title in black typography in the centre. Below this is a drawing of a hand and cue about to strike a white ball onto a red, the snooker balls depicted as globes of the world. The first section is entitled 'General Rules' and the second 'Rules of the Game of Snooker'.

Value £5 - £10

229

9.27 Rules of the Game of Snooker

World Professional Billiards and Snooker Association
1993　　　　　　　W.P.B.S.A., Bristol
ISBN　　　　　　　None given
Paperback　　　　　28pp, 15 x 11cm

This rule book originally cost £1.95 and has pale green card covers that carry an advert for 'Riley' on the back. Sprinkled throughout the rules are colour adverts for companies associated with snooker such as the snooker cloth manufacturers Strachan and Hainsworth, as well as Embassy and Benson & Hedges.

Value　　　　　　　　　　　　　　　　　　　　　　　　　　　　　　£3 - £5

~ Mixed Rule Books ~

9.28 Hennig Bros. Book of Rules of the Games of Billiards, Pool, and Pyramids and Bagatelle

Hennig Brothers
[1880]　　　　　　Hennig Brothers, London
[Hardback]　　　　16pp, ill., 16cm
Notes　　　　　　　Includes publisher's catalogue of billiard tables and products

Hennig Bros. were billiard table makers established in 1862 whose offices were located on New Oxford Street in London. This book originally sold for 3d. and the Hennig Brothers aim when publishing it was that readers may "possess, in a compact form, for ready reference, and at a price within the reach of the most humble, a reliable guide how to play the various games, both on the Billiard and Bagatelle Table, and how to act during their progress". The book includes, amongst others, 'Rules for the English Game', 'American or Four-Ball Game', 'Cramp Game Rules', 'Pyramids', 'Pyramids Pool' and 'Black Pool' ("it is an intricate and not particularly interesting game"). [description based on microfilm copy].

Value　　　　　　　　　　　　　　　　　　　　　　　　　　　　　£60 - £80

9.29 The Rules of the Game of Billiards, authorised by the Billiard Association of Great Britain and Ireland, Revised and Redrafted, March 1898

Billiard Association of Great Britain and Ireland, India, and the Colonies
1898　　　　　　　Billiard Association of Great Britain and Ireland,
　　　　　　　　　India, and the Colonies
Hardback　　　　　71pp, 11 x 9cm

This early rule book has black boards with the cover title, 'Billiard Association Rules of Billiards, Pool, Pyramids, Snooker's Pool, And Russian Pool', neatly placed in the centre. Early rule books such as this are incredibly scarce and hardly ever surface for sale.

Value £20 - £40

9.30 The Rules of Billiards, Pool, Pyramids and C., & C.

[F. H. Ayres]
1904 F. H. Ayres, London
[Hardback] 46pp, ill.

This book includes rules for numerous games including Black Pool, Skittle Pool, Snooker's Pool, Cork Pool, Pyramid Pool, Russian Pool, Mug's Pool, and Italian Skittles. The book tells the reader that Skittle Pool is played with 3 billiard balls and 12 skittles; Mug's Pool with 3 billiard balls, 3 octagonal skittles and 10 marbles; and Italian Skittles with 3 billiard balls, 5 skittles and 16 marbles! Includes adverts for Ayres Table Billiards, Bagatelle Boards and combined Marking Board and Cabinet. [description based on microfilm copy].

Value £60 - £80

9.31 Billiard Association Rules of Billiards, Pool, Pyramids, Snooker's Pool and Russian Pool

Billiard Association of Great Britain & Ireland, India, & the Colonies
[1905] Billiards Association of Great Britain & Ireland, India, & the Colonies, London
Hardback 71pp, 11 x 9cm
Notes Authorised by the Billiard Association of Great Britain & Ireland; rules based on the March 1898 revised and redrafted edition

Originally retailing at 1 shilling and sixpence, this rule book has black boards with gilt lettering. It includes Rules of the Billiard Association of Great Britain & Ireland, India, & the Colonies, plus Rules of the Billiard Championship. There is also a 3 page Appendix where a clue to the date of publication is given because it states "at a meeting of the Committee held on November 28th 1905".

Value £20 - £40

9.32   **The Rules of the Game of Billiards, authorised by the Billiard Association of Great Britain and Ireland, Revised and Redrafted September 1907**

Billiard Association of Great Britain & Ireland, India, & the Colonies
1907   Billiards Association of Great Britain & Ireland, India, & the Colonies, London
Hardback   74pp, 11 x 9cm
Notes   Revised and redrafted edition; authorised by the Billiard Association of Great Britain & Ireland

This hardback rule book has black boards with the title etc. blocked in gilt in the centre. Apart from the rules of the games also included are the Rules of the Billiard Association of Great Britain & Ireland, India, & the Colonies, plus an Appendix on pages 73 and 74. This Appendix states, amongst other things "that no Amateur be allowed to play in any public match at which a charge is made for admission, without previously obtaining a permit from the Association". A copy of this rule book, in generally good condition, fetched £55 on eBay in October 2007.

Value   £20 - £40

9.33   **The Rules of the Game of Billiards, authorised by the Billiard Association of Great Britain and Ireland, Revised January 1909**

Billiard Association of Great Britain & Ireland, India, & the Colonies
1909   Billiards Association of Great Britain & Ireland, India, & the Colonies, London
Hardback   78pp, 11 x 9cm
Notes   January 1909 revised edition; authorised by the Billiard Association of Great Britain & Ireland

With the same black boards and gilt lettering as the 1907 edition, this rule book also includes a section called Rules of the Billiard Championship where in less enlightened times it stated – "all matches shall be played with ivory balls".

Value   £20 - £40

9.34   **The Rules of Billiards, Pool, Pyramids and C., and C.**

[F. H. Ayres]
1910   F. H. Ayres, London
Paperback   50pp, ill., 14 x 11cm

This paperback rule book published by F. H. Ayres has lovely deep red card covers and originally cost 1/-. The book includes games such as 'Black Pool', 'Cork Pool', 'Mug's Pool' and 'Skittle Pool', as well as billiards. There are 6 un-numbered pages of contemporary adverts at the rear promoting such Ayres products as Shuttlecocks,

Table Billiards and Bagatelle Boards.

Value £60 - £80

9.35 **The Rules of Billiards, Pool, Pyramids and C., and C.**

[F. H. Ayres]
1913 F. H. Ayres, London
Paperback 50pp, ill., 14 x 11cm

This rule book has dark green covers and features the same eleven games that were detailed in Ayres' 1910 rule book. Like the 1910 publication, the back of the book has 6 un-numbered pages advertising various Ayres products. Incidentally, F. H. Ayres were a manufacturer of billiard tables, bagatelle boards etc. who were based at 111 Aldersgate Street, London and part of the purpose of publishing rule books would have been to promote their own products.

Value £60 - £80

9.36 **The Rules of Billiards, Pool, Pyramids, Snooker Pool, Indian Pool, Volunteer Snooker and Penalty Pool**

Billiards Control Club
1913 [BCC Publications], London
Hardback 54pp, 13 x 9cm
Notes Approved by the Council of the Billiards Control Club

Originally costing 1/-, this rule book has red boards with gilt lettering and the section headings within the book are printed in red type-face. Areas covered include 'Spotting the Balls', 'Penalties', 'Improper Conduct', and 'Foul Strokes'.

Value £20 - £40

9.37 **The Rules of Billiards, Pool, Pyramids, Snooker Pool, Indian Pool, Volunteer Snooker and Penalty Pool**

Billiards Control Club
1917 [BCC Publications], London
Hardback 54pp, 13 x 8cm
Notes Approved by the Council of the Billiards Control Club

The 1917 Billiards Control Club rule book has stiff, red card covers and originally cost 1/6 and the section headings are printed in red type-face.

Value £20 - £40

9.38   **The Rules of the Games of English Billiards, Pool, Pyramids, Snooker, Volunteer Snooker, and Russian Pool**

B.A. & C.C.
1920   B.A. & C.C., London
Hardback   110pp, 14 x 9cm
Notes   Authorised by the B.A. & C.C.; includes loose-leaf, 4 page 'Amendment to Rules'

The 1920 B.A. & C.C. rule book has dark green boards with gilt lettering, and one rule to note is that "the referee shall be the sole judge of fair or unfair play, and shall be responsible for the proper conduct of the game". The brief section on the game of 'Shell Out' states "a game similar to Pyramids where each player plays for himself against all the others is sometimes played under the name of Shell Out. In this game the white ball is always the cue-ball. A double value is usually given to the last red. Reds, whether pocketed by a lawful or a foul stroke, are not re-spotted or *owed* : points forfeited are added to each of the opposing scores".

Value   £20 - £40

9.39   **The Rules of the Games of English Billiards, Pool, Pyramids, Snooker, Volunteer Snooker, and Russian Pool**

B.A. & C.C.
1922   B.A. & C.C., [London]
Hardback   112pp, 14 x 9cm
Notes   Reprint of the 1920 1st edition; authorised by the B.A. & C.C.

Value   £20 - £40

9.40   **The Rules of the Games of English Billiards, Pool, Pyramids, Snooker, Volunteer Snooker, and Russian Pool**

B.A. & C.C.
1924   B.A. & C.C., London
Hardback   112pp, 14 x 9cm
Notes   Reprint of the 1920 1st edition; authorised by the B.A. & C.C.

A small, pocket-sized rule book bound in dark green cloth with the title in gilt on the front. This is a standard rule book that, apart from the formal rules, also notes the alternative names for the games included e.g. Pyramids aka Pyramids-Pool; Snooker aka Snooker's Pool; and Russian Pool aka Indian Pool, Toad-in-the-Hole or Slosh.

Value   £20 - £40

9.41 **The Rules of the Games of English Billiards, Pool, Pyramids, Snooker, Volunteer Snooker, and Russian Pool**

B.A. & C.C.
1926   B.A. & C.C., [London]
Hardback   118pp, 14 x 9cm
Notes   Authorised by the B.A. & C.C.

Originally selling for 2/-, this pocket-sized book has dark green boards with gilt lettering on the cover. Included are several advertisements at both the back and front with one for 'Gray's Billiard Cue Attachment' – "designed to secure a true delivery of the cue exactly parallel with the bed of the billiard table". The other adverts are principally for billiard and snooker manufacturers such as Camkin Ltd., John Winn, Jelks & Son, John Bennett, and Orme & Sons Ltd. To demonstrate how popular early rule books are with collectors, a copy of this book (described as very good, with minor rubbing to cloth) sold for £23.50 on eBay in March 2007.

Value   £20 - £40

9.42 **The Rules of the Games of English Billiards, Pool, Pyramids, Snooker, Volunteer Snooker, and Russian Pool**

B.A. & C.C.
1928   B.A. & C.C., London
Hardback   118pp, 14 x 9cm
Notes   Authorised by the B.A. & C.C.

Value   £20 - £40

9.43 **The Rules of the Games of English Billiards, Snooker, Volunteer Snooker, Pyramids, Pool, and Russian Pool**

B.A. & C.C.
1929   B.A. & C.C., London
Hardback   117pp, 14 x 9cm
Notes   Authorised by the B.A. & C.C.; includes Index

Value   £20 - £40

9.44 **The Rules of the Games of English Billiards, Snooker, Volunteer Snooker, Pyramids, Pool, and Russian Pool**

B.A. & C.C.
1931   B.A. & C.C., London
Hardback   119pp, 13 x 9cm
Notes   Authorised by the B.A. & C.C.; includes Index

Pre World War Two rule books can achieve impressive sums when appearing for sale and a copy of this edition fetched £33 on eBay in November 2007.

Value £20 - £40

9.45 **The Rules of the Games of English Billiards, Snooker, Volunteer Snooker, Pyramids, Pool, and Russian Pool**

B.A. & C.C.
1932   B.A. & C.C., London
Hardback   117pp, 13 x 9cm
Notes   Authorised by the B.A. & C.C.; includes Index

Value £20 - £40

9.46 **The Rules of the Games of English Billiards, Snooker, Volunteer Snooker, Pyramids, Pool, and Russian Pool**

B.A. & C.C.
1935   B.A. & C.C., London
Hardback   115pp, 13 x 9cm
Notes   Authorised by the B.A. & C.C.; includes Index

By 1935 the B.A. & C.C. rule book cost 2/- and had dark green boards with gilt lettering to the centre of the cover. The rear pastedown endpaper features an advert for 'Bonzoline, Crystalate, Vitalite' Billiard & Snooker balls; whereas the front pastedown carries a list of B.A. & C.C. publications.

Value £20 - £40

9.47 **The Rules of the Games of English Billiards, Snooker, Volunteer Snooker, Pyramids, Pool, and Russian Pool**

B.A. & C.C.
1935   B.A. & C.C., London
Hardback   54pp, 26 x 21cm
Notes   Includes amendment slips; authorised by the B.A. & C.C.; includes Index

This large format rule book has thick, dark green card covers with leather trim. It includes a few amendment slips concerning the rules and several national break competition forms for both billiards and snooker at the back of the volume. It is unclear why two 1935 rule books were published in different sizes (unless the B.A. & C.C. felt the amendments made in the large format edition couldn't wait until

1936) but the larger format book is by far the scarcer and most collectible of the two.

Value £20 - £40

9.48 **The Rules of the Games of English Billiards, Snooker, Volunteer Snooker, Pyramids, Pool, and Russian Pool**

B.A. & C.C.
1936   B.A. & C.C., London
Hardback   115pp, 13 x 9cm
Notes   Authorised by the B.A. & C.C.; includes Index

A copy of this rule book, in very good condition and with an insert detailing amendments to rules, fetched an impressive £51 on eBay in February 2007.

Value £20 - £40

9.49 **Handbook and Rules of English Billiards · Snooker · Volunteer Snooker · Pool · Pyramids · Russian Pool**

B.A. & C.C.
[1937]   B.A. & C.C., London
Paperback   111pp, ill., 17 x 11cm
Notes   Handbook for 1937-1938; authorised by the B.A. & C.C.; includes Index

In his Introduction John Bisset, Chairman of the B.A. & C.C., says "this Handbook appertaining to English Billiards and kindred games will, I believe, satisfy a long-felt want. It contains a variety of information, historical, useful and instructive, never gathered together before in one publication. It should be of the utmost use and value in all billiard rooms, both public and private, where these games are played". As well as the various rules there are sections on 'Brief History of Billiards', 'Certification of Referees', 'Cues and Tips', 'Notable Achievements', 'Championship Results', etc.

Value £20 - £40

9.50 **The Rules of the Games of English Billiards, Snooker, Volunteer Snooker, Pyramids, Pool, and Russian Pool**

B.A. & C.C.
1937   B.A. & C.C., London
Hardback   115pp, 13 x 8cm
Notes   Includes amendment slips; authorised by the B.A. & C.C.; includes Index

This particular edition of the B.A. & C.C. rule book includes some amendment slips (with no page numbers assigned to them), each one being placed at the beginning of the appropriate game to which it applies. Completist collector's will no doubt wish to hunt down copies with the amendment slips but it is doubtful whether many copies exist that still have the slips present.

Value £20 - £40

9.51 **Handbook and Rules of English Billiards · Snooker · Volunteer Snooker · Pool · Pyramids · Russian Pool**

B.A. & C.C.
[1938] B.A. & C.C., London
Paperback 111pp, ill., 17 x 11cm
Notes Handbook for 1938-1939; authorised by the B.A. & C.C.; includes Index

Value £20 - £40

9.52 **Handbook and Rules of English Billiards · Snooker · Volunteer Snooker · Pool · Pyramids · Russian Pool**

B.A. & C.C.
1938 B.A. & C.C., London
Paperback 111pp, ill., 17 x 11cm
Notes Authorised by the B.A. & C.C.; includes Index

The only difference in the main body of text between this publication and the one listed immediately above is that this edition has a few strips pasted over some of the rules where amendments have been made. A copy of this rule book sold for £20 on eBay in November 2007 and a copy sold earlier that year realised £21.

Value £20 - £40

9.53 **Handbook and Rules of English Billiards · Snooker · Volunteer Snooker · Pool · Pyramids · Russian Pool**

B.A. & C.C.
1940 B.A. & C.C., London
Paperback 112pp, ill., 17 x 11cm
Notes Handbook for 1939-1940; authorised by the B.A. & C.C.; includes Index

Value £15 - £30

9.54   **Handbook and Rules of English Billiards · Snooker · Volunteer Snooker · Pool · Pyramids · Russian Pool**

B.A. & C.C.
1944   B.A. & C.C., London
Paperback   112pp, ill., 17 x 11cm
Notes   Authorised by the B.A. & C.C.; includes Index

A copy of this rule book, in very good condition, sold for £16.50 on eBay in November 2006.

Value   £15 - £30

9.55   **Handbook and Rules of English Billiards · Snooker · Volunteer Snooker · Pool · Pyramids · Russian Pool**

B.A. & C.C.
1945   B.A. & C.C., London
Paperback   112pp, ill., plates, ports., 17 x 11cm
Notes   Authorised by the B.A. & C.C.; includes Index

Value   £15 - £30

9.56   **Handbook and Rules of English Billiards · Snooker · Volunteer Snooker · Pool · Pyramids · Russian Pool**

B.A. & C.C.
1946   B.A. & C.C., London
Paperback   113pp, ill., plates, ports., 17 x 11cm
Notes   Authorised by the B.A. & C.C.; includes Index

Value   £15 - £30

9.57   **Handbook and Rules of English Billiards · Snooker · Volunteer Snooker · Pool · Pyramids · Russian Pool**

B.A. & C.C.
1946   B.A. & C.C., London
Paperback   113pp, ill., plates, ports., 17 x 11cm
Notes   New illustrated edition; authorised by the B.A. & C.C.; includes Index

Value   £15 - £30

9.58 **Handbook and Rules of English Billiards · Snooker · Volunteer Snooker · Pool · Pyramids · Russian Pool**

B.A. & C.C.
1947
Paperback
Notes

B.A. & C.C., London
113pp, ill., plates, ports., 17 x 11cm
New illustrated edition; authorised by the B.A. & C.C.; includes Index

Value £15 - £30

9.59 **Handbook and Rules of English Billiards · Snooker · Volunteer Snooker · Pool · Pyramids · Russian Pool**

B.A. & C.C.
1947
Paperback
Notes

B.A. & C.C., London
113pp, ill., plates, ports., 17 x 11cm
New illustrated edition; authorised by the B.A. & C.C.; includes Index

Collectors should note that this edition has 1947-48 on the cover whereas the edition listed immediately above has the date 1947 only. The only other difference would appear to be that this edition has a Questionnaire included at the front which is basically an order form for B.A. & C.C. publications and payment of annual subscription fees.

Value £15 - £30

9.60 **Handbook and Rules of English Billiards · Snooker · Volunteer Snooker · Pool · Pyramids · Russian Pool**

B.A. & C.C.
1949
Paperback
Notes

B.A. & C.C., London
114pp, ill., plates, ports., 18 x 11cm
New illustrated edition; authorised by the B.A. & C.C.; includes Index

Value £15 - £30

9.61 **Handbook and Rules of English Billiards · Snooker · Volunteer Snooker · Pool · Pyramids · Russian Pool**

B.A. & C.C.
1950
Paperback

B.A. & C.C., London
117pp, ill., plates, ports., 18 x 11cm

	Notes	New illustrated edition; authorised by the B.A. & C.C.; includes Index

Value £15 - £30

9.62 Handbook and Rules of English Billiards · Snooker · Volunteer Snooker · Pool · Pyramids · Russian Pool

B.A. & C.C.
1951   B.A. & C.C., London
Paperback   118pp, ill., plates, ports., 18 x 11cm
Notes   New illustrated edition; authorised by the B.A. & C.C.;
                        includes Index

Value £15 - £30

9.63 Handbook and Rules of English Billiards · Snooker · Volunteer Snooker · Russian Pool

B.A. & C.C.
1953   B.A. & C.C., London
Paperback   102pp, ill., plates, ports., 17 x 11cm
Notes   New illustrated edition; authorised by the B.A. & C.C.;
                        includes Index

Value £15 - £30

9.64 Handbook and Rules of English Billiards · Snooker · Volunteer Snooker · Russian Pool

B.A. & C.C.
1954   B.A. & C.C., London
Paperback   105pp, ill., plates, ports., 17 x 11cm
Notes   New illustrated edition; authorised by the B.A. & C.C.;
                        includes Index

Value £15 - £30

9.65 Handbook and Rules of English Billiards · Snooker · Volunteer Snooker · Russian Pool

B.A. & C.C.
1955   B.A. & C.C., London
Paperback   105pp, ill., plates, ports., 18 x 11cm

Notes		New illustrated edition; authorised by the B.A. & C.C.; includes Index
Value		£15 - £30

9.66 Handbook and Rules of English Billiards · Snooker · Volunteer Snooker · Russian Pool

B.A. & C.C.
1957   B.A. & C.C., London
Paperback   106pp, ill., plates, ports., 17 x 11cm
Notes   New illustrated edition; authorised by the B.A. & C.C.; includes Index

Value   £15 - £30

9.67 Handbook and Rules of English Billiards · Snooker · Volunteer Snooker · Russian Pool

B.A. & C.C.
1957   B.A. & C.C., London
Paperback   106pp, ill., plates, ports., 17 x 11cm
Notes   New illustrated edition; authorised by the B.A. & C.C.; includes Index

This particular 1957 edition has a page pasted onto the first page entitled 'Championships' that states "this edition of the Handbook was printed before the 1957-58 Championship results were known. They are given below". The other 1957 edition listed immediately above does not have this information.

Value   £15 - £30

9.68 Handbook and Rules of English Billiards · Snooker · Volunteer Snooker · Russian Pool

B.A. & C.C.
1958   B.A. & C.C., London
Paperback   105pp, ill., plates, ports., 17 x 11cm
Notes   New illustrated edition; authorised by the B.A. & C.C.; includes Index

Value   £15 - £30

9.69 **Handbook and Rules of English Billiards · Snooker · Volunteer Snooker · Russian Pool**

        B.A. & C.C.
        1960   B.A. & C.C., London
        Paperback   106pp, ill., plates, ports., 18 x 11cm
        Notes   New illustrated edition; authorised by the B.A. & C.C.; includes Index

        Value   £10 - £20

9.70 **Handbook and Rules of English Billiards · Snooker · Volunteer Snooker · Russian Pool**

        B.A. & C.C.
        1962   B.A. & C.C., London
        Paperback   106pp, ill., plates, ports., 18 x 12cm
        Notes   Illustrated edition; authorised by the B.A. & C.C.; includes Index

        Value   £10 - £20

9.71 **Handbook and Rules of English Billiards · Snooker · Volunteer Snooker and Snooker Plus**

        B.A. & C.C.
        1965   B.A. & C.C., London
        Paperback   106pp, plates, ports., 18 x 11cm
        Notes   Illustrated edition; authorised by the B.A. & C.C.; includes Index

The 1965 'Handbook' originally sold for 6/- and has dark green card wrappers. Each individual game covered in the volume has its own Index, apart from 'Snooker Plus' – a game played using the same rules as snooker but with two extra colours (orange and purple) where the former ball is worth 8 points and the latter 10. After the rules sections are statistics under the headings 'Notable Achievements' and 'Records and Notable Achievements'.

        Value   £10 - £20

9.72   **Handbook and Rules of English Billiards · Snooker · Volunteer Snooker and Snooker Plus**

B.A. & C.C.
1967   B.A. & C.C., London
Paperback   108pp, plates, ports., 18 x 11cm
Notes   Authorised by the B.A. & C.C.; includes Index

This rule book has pale green, stiff card covers with the title etc. on the cover in a darker green. Despite the title, this volume covers more than just rules and has chapter headings such as 'Cues and Tips', 'History of Billiards', 'Notable Achievements' and 'National Champions'. There are plenty of b & w photos of players scattered throughout the book and a few contemporary adverts.

Value   £10 - £20

9.73   **Handbook and Rules of English Billiards · Snooker · Volunteer Snooker and Snooker Plus**

B.A. & C.C.
1968   B.A. & C.C., London
Paperback   112pp, plates, ports., 18 x 11cm
Notes   Authorised by the B.A. & C.C.; includes Index

Value   £10 - £20

9.74   **Handbook and Rules of English Billiards · Snooker · Volunteer Snooker and Snooker Plus**

B.A. & C.C.
1970   B.A. & C.C., London
Paperback   118pp, plates, ports., 17 x 12cm
Notes   Authorised by the B.A. & C.C.; includes Index

Value   £5 - £10

9.75   **Handbook and Rules of English Billiards · Snooker · Volunteer Snooker and Snooker Plus**

Billiards & Snooker Control Council
1970   B. & S.C. C., Huddersfield
Paperback   118pp, plates, ports., 18 x 12cm
Notes   Illustrated edition; authorised by the B. & S.C. C.; includes Index

By the time the 'Handbook and Rules' was printed for the second time in 1970 (presumably because of decimalisation) the Billiards Association and Control Council had become the Billiards and Snooker Control Council and relocated from London to Huddersfield. The only other difference between this publication and the one listed immediately above appears to be that the cover has 'Price 45p' on whereas the B.A. & C.C. edition has 'Price Nine Shillings (45 New Pence)' and is fractionally larger. Collectors should be aware of this, especially when bidding for unseen copies on eBay.

Value £5 - £10

9.76 **Handbook and Rules of English Billiards · Snooker · Volunteer Snooker and Snooker Plus**

B. & S.C. C.
1973 B. & S.C. C., Huddersfield
Paperback 118pp, plates, ports., 18 x 12cm
Notes Cover has 1973 on it; illustrated edition; authorised by the B. & S.C. C.; includes Index

Value £5 - £10

9.77 **Handbook and Rules of English Billiards · Snooker · Volunteer Snooker and Snooker Plus**

B. & S.C. C.
1973 B. & S.C. C., Huddersfield
Paperback 118pp, plates, ports., 18 x 11cm
Notes Cover has 1974 on it; illustrated edition; authorised by the B. & S.C. C.; includes Index

Value £5 - £10

9.78 **Handbook and Rules of English Billiards · Snooker · Volunteer Snooker and Snooker Plus**

B. & S. C. C.
[1975] B. & S. C. C., Huddersfield
Paperback 136pp, plates, ports., 18 x 12cm
Notes Authorised by the B. & S. C. C.; includes Index

On page 47 of this book it states "a player should not be penalised if, when using the rest, the rest head falls off and touches a ball". The likelihood of that happening is extremely remote but this point usefully illustrates the level of detail contained

245

in the rules of snooker and billiards. The usual statistics sections follow the rules and the book is bound in bright green, almost turquoise, card wrappers.

Value £5 - £10

9.79 **Handbook and Rules of English Billiards · Snooker · Volunteer Snooker**

B. & S. C. C.
1978   B. & S. C. C., Huddersfield
Paperback   144pp, plates, ports., 18 x 12cm
Notes   Includes two Amendment slips; includes Index

Interspersed throughout the 'General Rules', 'Rules of Snooker', and 'Rules of Volunteer Snooker' are a few b & w photos of prominent players as well as advertisements for billiards and snooker related products. In addition to rules there are also lists of National Coaches, County Association Secretaries, and tables of 'Notable Achievements', 'Championship Results' etc. The book has bright yellow, thin cloth covers with the title in black and this edition marked a general move away from rule books that had previously featured green covers. Serious collectors will want to make sure they have copies with the two loose Amendment slips.

Value £3 - £5

9.80 **Handbook and Rules of English Billiards and Snooker**

B. & S. C. C.
1984   B. & S. C. C., Leeds
Paperback   192pp, plates, ports., 15 x 11cm

Value £3 - £5

9.81 **Handbook and Rules**

B. & S. C. C.
1988   B. & S. C. C., Leeds
Paperback   192pp, plates, ports., 15 x 11cm

With a somewhat shortened title, this edition of the 'Handbook and Rules' has an attractive dark green cover with a golden lion holding an English flag and the lion walking across the three billiard balls. As well as rules there are plenty of tables and statistics throughout the book.

Value £3 - £5

9.82   **Rules of the Games of Snooker and English Billiards**

The World Professional Billiards & Snooker Association (W. P. B. S. A) and International Billiards & Snooker Federation (I. B. & S. F.)
1995   W. P. B. S. A and I. B. & S. F., [Bristol]
Paperback   iii, 41pp, 15 x 11cm
Notes   Includes loose-leaf Errata

The pages in this rule book are numbered S1-S23 for snooker and then B25-B41 for billiards. All the rules of both games are included and there are three Notes pages at the back for the player to make any necessary observations.

Value   in print £5

9.83   **The Billiards and Snooker Referees' Handbook**

John Street / Peter Rook
1997   John Street, Exeter
ISBN   095333120X
Paperback   x, 145pp, ill. (some col.), 21 x 15cm
Notes   Includes Errata slip; Foreword by Steve Davis

Some copies of this book have no publisher details listed on page ii, whereas others have a sticker clearly stating the book was published by John Street in Exeter. The book has card covers which are the same shade of green as snooker table cloth and the book was limited to 1,000 copies. John Street has been a referee since 1960 and Peter Rook qualified in 1983, and after a brief introduction to the history of snooker and other similar table games, there follows an in-depth manual on the rules of snooker based on the September 1995 edition of the 'Rule Book'. However, the first part of the book is called 'The Art of Refereeing' and deals with the tools of the referee's trade - "Two pairs of White Gloves (the extra pair in case of accidents) and these *must* be cotton" - pre-match preparation, during the match, and the care of a billiard table. There are a smattering of coloured illustrations throughout the book. A rather battered copy of this publication, and heavily water stained, sold on eBay for £50 in 2007 so I would expect better copies to fetch considerably more. Needless to say, I was absolutely delighted when I picked up my own excellent copy in a charity shop for £1.99!

Value   £50 - £70

9.84 Rules of the Games of Snooker and English Billiards

W. P. B. S. A
[1998]   [W. P. B. S. A], [Bristol]
Paperback   ppS1-S23A, ppB25-B41, [10]pp, 30 x 24cm
Notes   Includes Sussex Referees Association Explanatory Notes

This rule book is an A4 sized publication with the individual pages enclosed in protective plastic wallets and printed on a variety of coloured pages. The rules are accompanied by Sussex Referees Association notes and the final ten, un-numbered, pages deal with such topics as 'The Image' [of the referee] – "the good referee will sport a dark blazer wearing the EASB badge", 'The Purpose & Functions of a Referee', 'Accessories', etc. There are a couple of blank pages at the rear to record frame scores.

Value   **£5 - £10**

A selection of billiards and snooker rule books. Those pictured range from 1967 (top left) to 1998 (bottom right).

~ APPENDIX ~

There follows a list of books which I have not been able to see personally and only have scant information on. These entries have been compiled from library catalogues, bibliographies and other reference works. As I have not been able to check these books there may be inaccuracies in the entries and, indeed, some books listed may not be entirely concerned with billiards or may turn out to be product catalogues. I have not attempted to value these books as that would be immensely difficult.

10.0 **The Acts of the Game of Billiards : Small Size, for the Pocket**

[1772] Bladdon [or Bladen?], [London]

According to Craven this work is cited in the Bibliotheca Britannica which is a bibliography of 50,000 works compiled by Robert Watt and published in four volumes in 1824 in Edinburgh.

10.1 **The Odds of the Game of Billiards**

[1772] Bladdon [or Bladen?], [London]

The English Amateur Billiards Association says this work is the earliest known book in English devoted entirely to the game of billiards and goes on to say that "no examples are known to exist outside the British Library collection". However, this book is not on the British Library catalogue and I have not been able to see a copy. Most sources seem to list the book as being published by Bladdon but no publisher of that name is present on the British Library catalogue either, the most similar company name publishing books at that time being Bladen. There is also a chance that this book and entry 10.0 above are the same work.

10.2 **Billiards : Instructions to Play the Game with Ease and Propriety**

[1801]

10.3 **Mr Hoyle's Treatise on the Game of Billiards : a New Edition, Greatly Improved and Corrected, with the Assistance of Eminent Markers**

Edmond Hoyle / Charles Jackson
1808 T. Davidson, London
[Hardback] 85pp

This publication is listed on the British Library catalogue but, unfortunately, was one of a number of works concerning billiards that was destroyed during the Second World War. It is a shame it didn't survive because that would clear up the confusion because I imagine the work was wrongly catalogued and is almost certainly an edition of 'Hoyle's Games' and not solely concerned with billiards as the title suggests.

10.4   A Poetical Essay on the Game of Billiards

E. White
1808   [London]

This book may well have been confused with E. White's 1807 publication 'A Practical Treatise on the Game of Billiards' (see entry 6.3).

10.5   A Practical Display of Billiards : Comprising the Whole Art and Science of the Game

R. Mulberry
[1820?]   [London?]
Notes   Folio

Yet another publication listed on the British Library catalogue as being destroyed during the Second World War.

10.6   Rules and Regulations to be Observed at the Game of Billiards

Gillow & Co.
1820   W. Minshall, Lancaster
[Hardback]   46pp

10.7   Billiards : How to Play

D., Colonel
[1842]
Notes   Reissued in [1875]

This book may have been confused with Colonel B's 'A Hand Book to the Game of Billiards', although there is some discrepancy with the dates (see entry 6.8).

10.8 The Billiard Player's Handbook : Containing the Rules of all the Fashionable Games, Together with Some Useful Hints to Learners

        1847   S. Y. Collings, London
        [Paperback]   16pp

Craven says of the publication that there were "two issues : one with white paper cover, the other with yellow paper cover; advertisements on back cover differ".

10.9 Billiards : the Proper Attitude in Playing the Game

        [1866]   H. Weede, London
        [Paperback]   20pp
        Notes   A pamphlet of 20 pages

10.10 The Game of Billiards : as Practised by the Most Scientific Players

        [Henry Lea]
        [1866]   [Henry Lea], [London]
        Notes   "A little book, published by Henry Lea, and curious as containing the rules of Fortification Billiards, a game now quite obsolete".

10.11 Morison & Co., Billiard Table Makers, 78 George Street, Edinburgh

        [1874]   [Morison & Co], [Edinburgh]
        [Hardback]   25pp, 17cm

The National Library of Scotland has catalogued this publication using the key words 'billiards rules' and 'pool games rules', although the book may well be a product catalogue with the rules included.

10.12 Billiard Tables, Past and Present : a Paper Read before the Liverpool Polytechnic Society, May 5, 1883

        T. Marsden
        1883   A. Russell, Liverpool
        [Hardback]   104pp [or 93-104pp?], 23cm

Craven lists this work as a 104 page book; however the Library of Congress catalogues the work as being of only 12 pages. The very fact that it was a paper read at a learned Society almost certainly rules out the possibility that it is a book of 104 pages! Therefore, the work is probably contained in a volume featuring other papers that were read at the Liverpool Polytechnic Society on the same day.

10.13 Billiards Simplified : or, How to Make Breaks

[1885?] F. Warne, London
[Hardback] iv, 181pp, ill., 20cm

Craven says that this book "probably predates the first Burroughes and Watts edition". However, that is extremely unlikely as there was an edition in print published by Burroughes & Watts in 1884, and there well may have been earlier editions as the company was founded as early as 1836.

10.14 The New All-Round Game, New Declared All-Round Game, English cannon game [of Billiards], Rules, Directions, Instructions, Diagrams

M. H. Wrigley
[1886] Manchester
[Hardback] 13cm

10.15 Two New Games of Billiards : New Method of Scientific Scoring

[1886] J. Heywood, Manchester
[Hardback] 32pp

10.16 Penalties for Foul Strokes at a Glance – Compiled from the Rules of the Billiard Association of Great Britain & Ireland

Charles Vidal Diehl (Ed.)
1905 London
[Hardback] 15cm

10.17 Billiard Souvenir of the World's Champions – the Eventoscope – being topical souvenirs of current events

W. Smith Herbert (Ed.)
1908 London

10.18 Souvenir of the Foxwold Billiard Circle and the Deeds of its Members to December 1st, 1908, etc.

Peter Henry Emerson
1908 [P. H. Emerson], Southbourne-on-Sea
[Hardback] 73pp

10.19   A Game of Billiards

    Wallace Ritchie
    [1910]   Burroughes & Watts, London

10.20   The Foxwold Billiard Circle : Rules and Regulations for the Various Competitions, Lists of Winners, Record Makers, Breaks and Honours, etc.

    Peter Henry Emerson
    1913   P. H. Emerson, Foxwold
    [Hardback]   20pp

10.21   Clarke's Pool Combine : Rules for a Game

    [1923]   W. J. Lloyd & Co., London

10.22   Constitution and Programme

    Women's Billiards Association
    [1931]   Women's Billiards Association, London
    [Paperback]   13pp

According to London Metropolitan University's library catalogue, this work was a pamphlet almost certainly written by Teresa Billington-Greig (see entry 3.1 for further information on her and her husband).

10.23   Rheolau Snwcer

    B. & S. C. C.
    [1985]   B. & S. C. C., [London]
    [Paperback]   25pp, 12cm

A Welsh language copy of the B. & S. C. C. rule book published in 1985, the details of which were found on the National Library of Wales catalogue. I assume the book was a paperback as most rule books of the last 30 years have been published in this format.

~ Index Of Authors, Editors & Compilers ~

~ A ~

Adamson, F. C.	4.42
Aiken, Tom	6.94
'Amateur, An'	6.1, 6.2, 6.4
Anthony, Edwyn–pseudonym of Cut-Cavendish	6.79
Anton, Victor	6.117
Armistead (Corp.)	6.26
Arnold, Peter	4.28, 7.64, 7.74, 7.75
Atkinson, Geoff	3.15
Ayres, F. H. (Corp.)	9.30, 9.34, 9.35

~ B ~

B., Colonel	6.8
Bennett, Joseph	6.22, 6.23
Billiard Association of Great Britain & Ireland, India, & the Colonies (Corp.)	9.29, 9.31-9.33
Billiards Association & Control Council (Corp.)	5.7, 5.9, 7.7, 7.41, 9.3-9.9, 9.12-9.24, 9.38-9.74
Billiards Control Club (Corp.)	9.1, 9.2, 9.36, 9.37
Billiards & Snooker Control Council (Corp.)	7.68, 9.10-9.11, 9.25-9.26, 9.75-9.81, 10.23
Bills, Peter	7.62
Birmingham Billiards Ltd. (Corp.)	7.34
Borrows, Bill	1.21
Boru, Sean	1.25
'Bos'un', The (psued. of Osworth & Beeson)	4.3
Broadfoot, Major W., R. E.	6.33
Buchanan, J. P.	6.32, 7.2
Buck, Henry	6.20
Burn, Gordon	7.70
Burroughes & Watts (Corp.)	6.28, 6.107-6.112, 7.11-7.31
Butler, Frank	1.11
Buxton, Peter	1.9

~ C ~

Callan, Frank	4.34
Camkin, W. A (Corp.)	7.34
Carruthers, Frank M.	6.82
Carty, John	7.56, 7.58

255

'Cavendish'–pseudonym of Jones, Henry	6.22, 6.23
Charlton, Eddie	3.3, 4.16, 4.21
Clare, Norman	2.8, 2.9
Clifford, W. G.	2.0, 4.7, 4.18, 6.76, 6.88, 6.101, 6.114, 7.8
Cook, William (Jnr.)	6.21, 6.60
Cook, William (Snr.)	6.16, 6.27
Cooper, A. W.	6.34
Copp, Darren	4.41, 4.43
Crawford, the Earl of–see also Lindsay, James Ludovic	6.31
Crawley, Captain Rawdon–pseudonym of Pardon, George Frederick	6.12
Cut-Cavendish–pseudonym of Anthony, Edwyn	6.79

~ D ~

D., Colonel	10.7
Danery, Rolf M.–pseudonym of Randolph, Edward Castillian and Emery, Alfred	6.84
Davis, Fred	1.6, 4.17
Davis, Joe	1.5, 4.4, 4.6, 4.8, 4.9, 4.11, 5.1, 6.102, 6.103, 7.40
Davis, Steve	1.8, 1.10, 3.15, 4.20
Dawson, Charles	6.48
Dee, John	4.34, 8.40
de Vere, Albert–see 'Winning Hazard'	6.24
Dew, John	6.0
Diehl, Charles Vidal	10.16
Dimsdale, C. D.	4.5
Dixon, Sydenham	6.37, 6.57
Docherty, John	1.17
Donaldson, Walter	7.39
Dorkins, Bob	4.23
Drayson, Alfred Wilks	6.29
Dufton, William	6.17

~ E ~

Emerson, Peter Henry	6.62, 10.18, 10.20
Emery, Alfred–see Danery, Rolf M.	6.84
Everton, Clive	1.15, 2.5, 2.7, 2.10, 2.12, 4.26, 4.29, 4.36, 5.12, 5.16, 7.42, 7.53, 7.55, 7.87, 8.13-8.15, 8.25, 7.94
'Expert, An'	7.3

~ F ~

'Forty Years' Player', A	6.51
Francis, Tony	1.13
French, Liz	4.35
Fry, Sidney H.	6.83

~ G ~

Gadsby, Paul	7.93
Gamages (Corp.)	9.0
Gardner, Philip	7.84
Gillett, Sidney	2.2, 7.32, 7.33, 7.35
Gillow & Co. (Corp.)	10.6
Gordon, Mike	3.8
Gray, George	6.73
Greig, F. L. Billington	3.1
Griffiths, Terry	1.16, 7.55, 8.29-8.30

~ H ~

Hale, Janice	7.61, 8.18-8.24
Hales, Geoff	3.14
Halter, Brian	7.54
Hardy, Frederic	6.15, 6.17
Harverson, Cecil	6.59
Haselden, John	3.13
Hattenstone, Simon	1.22
Hayes, Dean P.	7.91
Hayton, Eric	8.40
Heath, Ian	3.9
Hemming, George Wirgman	6.38
Hendry, Stephen	1.17, 4.39, 8.31-8.32
Hennessey, John	1.14, 1.20, 4.33, 7.66
Hennig, Brothers	9.28
Herbert, W. Smith	10.17
Higgins, Alex	1.7, 1.13, 1.25
Holt, Richard	5.8
Holtom, Josie	2.7
Horton, Edward	3.12, 4.29
Hotine, Frederick Martin	1.0, 6.39, 6.43, 6.44, 6.45, 6.56
Hoyle, Edmond	10.3
Hudson, Chris	6.118

~ I ~

Inman, Melbourne	6.90
International Billiards and Snooker Federation (Corp.), The	9.82
Ireland, John	3.16

~ J ~

Jackson, Charles	10.3
Jenner, David	4.40
Jones, Henry–see also 'Cavendish'	6.22, 6.23

~ K ~

Karnehm, Jack	5.10, 5.13, 7.56, 7.58
Kemp, Geoff	2.11
Kentfield, Edwin	6.7
Kingsland, Rosemary	1.19

~ L ~

Lea, Henry	10.10
Lee, Roger	7.89
Lee, Sydney	6.115
Leitch, Michael	3.6, 3.11
Levi, Riso	2.1, 5.5, 6.47, 6.49, 6.50, 6.53, 6.54, 6.58, 6.61, 6.63, 6.65, 6.71, 6.74, 6.81, 6.85, 6.91, 6.97, 6.106
Lincoln, Bob	7.6
Lindrum, Horace	5.3, 5.6, 5.11
Lindrum, Walter	6.104
Lindsay, James Ludovic–see also Crawford, the Earl of	6.31
Locock, Charles Dealtry	6.41
Long, H. Kingsley	1.4
Lowe, Ted	1.11, 3.16, 4.13

~ M ~

Macmillan, A. D.	6.100
Maloney, Jim	3.17
Mannock, J. P.	6.37, 6.46, 7.4
Mardon, Dr. Edward Russell	6.9
Marner, Daniel	4.37
Marsden, Derek	1.23
Marsden, T.	10.12
Marshall, Anne	2.7

Martin, Geoff	4.18
Meadowcroft, Jim	1.14, 4.33
Menzies, Gordon	4.36
Mingaud, Monsieur	6.5
Mitchell, J. R.	2.6
Mitchell, N. A.	4.31
Mitchell, William	1.0, 6.34, 6.45
Mond, Newman	3.2
Moore, C. Compton	7.1
Morrison, Ian	5.14, 5.15, 7.80, 8.16, 8.17, 8.35, 8.36, 8.38
Mulberry, R.	10.5
Mussabini, Scipio Africanus	1.1, 6.34, 6.46, 6.80

~ N ~

National Billiards Halls Association	7.9, 7.10
Newman, Stanley	4.5
Newman, Tom	5.2, 6.87, 6.88, 6.89

~ O ~

Oakley, H. S.	8.2
Orme, Thomas & Sons (Corp.)	6.25
O'Sullivan, Ronnie	1.22

~ P ~

Pardon, George Frederick–see also Crawley, Captain Rawdon	6.12, 6.14, 6.16, 6.19
Parrott, John	1.18
Patmore, Angela	1.7
Payne, A. G.	6.27, 6.35
Payne, Peter J.	5.17
Peall, Arthur F.	5.0, 6.96, 6.116
Perrin, Reg	7.43-7.52, 7.57, 7.60, 7.63, 7.67, 7.71, 7.73, 7.77, 7.82
Poole, Charles	4.30
Pulman, John	4.10

~ R ~

Radford, Brian	1.8, 1.10
Rafferty, Jean	7.59
Randolph, Edward Castillian–see Danery, Rolf M.	6.84
Reardon, Ray	1.9, 3.5, 3.6, 4.15, 7.66
Reece, Tom	1.4, 4.1, 6.76, 6.99

Rhys, Chris	3.11
Richler, Mordecai	2.13
Riley, E. J., Ltd. (Corp.)	7.5
Ritchie, Wallace	4.0, 6.42, 6.66, 6.68, 6.69, 10.19
Robbins, W. H.	6.34, 8.0, 8.1
Roberts, Charles	1.2, 1.3, 6.40, 6.67, 6.70, 6.75, 6.77, 6.78, 6.95, 8.5
Roberts, John (Jnr.)	6.36, 6.39, 6.43, 6.52, 6.64, 8.3, 8.4
Roberts, John (Snr.)	1.2, 6.20
Roberts, John L.	7.69
Rook, Peter	9.83
Roy, Reuben	6.11
Ruttle, W. Wilson	8.2

~ S ~

Scottish Billiards & Snooker Association (Corp.)	7.81
Scriven, B.	5.4
Shiel, Rob	7.88
Silverton, John	7.42
Smeeton, A. H.	4.27
Smith, Terry	5.15, 7.83, 7.85, 8.26-8.32, 8.33-8.34, 8.37
Smith, Willie	4.2, 6.92, 6.93, 6.113
Spencer, John	1.24, 4.12, 4.26
Squire, Sir John	7.35
'Stancliffe'	3.0
Steele-Perkins, George	6.105
Stevenson, H. W.	6.55
Stooke, Mike	7.78
Street, John	9.83

~ T ~

Taylor, Dennis	1.12, 3.10, 4.36, 8.26-8.28
Thorburn, Cliff	1.15, 4.28
Thorne, Willie	1.23
Thurston & Co. (Corp.)	2.2, 2.3, 2.4
Thurston, John	6.5
Tillotson, J.	6.6
Trelford, Donald	7.72
Turner, H.	6.10
Two Can Project, The	4.25

~ U ~

Ullyett, Roy 3.7

~ V ~

Virgo, John 3.12, 3.17

~ W ~

Watson, Jeremy	2.11
Weber, Eugene	7.87
Welch, Ian	7.95
Western, Col. Charles Maximillian	6.72
White, E.	6.3, 10.4
White, Jimmy	1.19, 4.30
White, John D. T.	7.92
White, William	6.13, 6.18
Whitehead, Eric	8.39
Whittall, Noel	7.84
Williams, Ken	4.38
Williams, Luke	7.93
Williams, Rex	4.14, 4.19, 4.24
'Winning Hazard'–pseudonym of de Vere, Albert	6.24
Women's Billiards Association (Corp.)	10.22
Word Factory, The (Corp.)	7.86
World Professional Billiards and Snooker Association (Corp.)	9.27, 9.82, 9.84
Worthington, Julian	1.16, 4.20, 4.22, 4.32, 8.6-8.12
Wright, Bessie Munro	7.36, 7.37, 7.38
Wrigley, M. H.	10.14
W, R. R.	6.30

~ Y ~

Yates, Philip	7.84
Young, Harry	6.86

~ Index Of Titles ~

~ A ~

The A.B.C. of Billiards (Dixon, S.)	6.57
The ABC of Billiards (Hardy, F.)	6.15
About Billiard Cushions	2.4
The Acts of the Game of Billiards	10.0
Advanced Billiards	6.88
Advanced Snooker	4.9
Advanced Snooker for the Average Player	4.9
Alex Through the Looking Glass	1.13
All About Billiards : How to Improve Your Game	6.96
All About Billiards and How to Pot	6.116
Armistead's Patent Billiard Angle Measurer	6.26
The Art of Practical Billiards for Amateurs	6.29
The Audacia Junior Blueprint	4.43
The Audacia Performance Plan : the Definitive Snooker Manual for Players of All Ages	4.41

~ B ~

The Bad Players Guide to Status Snooker	3.4
Bedside Snooker	3.6
The Beginner at Billiards	6.79
Behind the White Ball : my Autobiography	1.19
Benson and Hedges Book of Snooker	8.16
Benson and Hedges Snooker Year	8.26-8.32
Better Billiards and Snooker	5.12
Between Frames : Ted Lowe Talking to Frank Butler	1.11
The Billiard Annual : Fixtures, Rules of Billiards, Snooker, Bagatelle, etc. etc. : Season 1925–26	8.5
The Billiard Annual for 1902	8.0
The Billiard Annual for 1909-1910	8.1
Billiard Association Rules of Billiards, Pool, Pyramids, Snooker's Pool and Russian Pool	9.31
The Billiard Book	6.16
Billiard Hints	6.67
The Billiard Note Book	6.30
A Billiard Player in the Making	6.80
The Billiard Player's Handbook : Containing the Rules of all the Fashionable Games, Together with Some Useful Hints to Learners	10.8
Billiards (Bennett, J.)	6.23
Billiards (Broadfoot, W.)	6.33

262

Billiards (Cook, W. Snr.)	6.27
Billiards (Lindrum, W.)	6.104
Billiards (Mitchell, W. and Cooper, A. W.)	6.34
Billiards (Payne, A.G.)	6.35
Billiards (Reece, T.)	6.76
Billiards for Amateurs	6.83
The Billiards Annual and Year Book : the Official Handbook of the Billiards Association and Control Council 1927	7.8
The Billiards Association & Control Council : Constitution and Regulations	7.7
The Billiards Association and Control Council : Rules and Regulations	7.41
Billiards for the Beginner	6.114
Billiards for Beginners (Crawley, R.)	6.19
Billiards for Beginners (Roberts, J. Jnr.)	6.39
Billiards : Complete Guide to Successful Play	6.115
Billiards : with Description of a Hundred Break Illustrated with Diagrams by J. P. Mannock and Biographies and Portraits of Leading Players	6.86
Billiards Do's and Don't's	6.89
Billiards in Easy Stages	6.113
Billiard Secrets	6.42
Billiards for Everybody	6.40
Billiards for Everybody Volume II	6.75
Billiards Expounded to all Degrees of Amateur Players	6.46
Billiards : Game, 500 Up	6.9
Billiards and Games of Pool	6.84
Billiards at Home	6.78
Billiards : How to Improve Your Game	6.82
Billiards : How to Play	10.7
Billiards : How to Play and Win	6.90
Billiards : Instructions to Play the Game with Ease and Propriety	10.2
Billiards in Lighter Vein	6.85
Billiards Made Easy : With the Scientific Principles of the Side-Stroke and the Spot-Stroke Familiarly Explained	6.24
Billiards Mathematically Treated	6.38
Billiards for the Million : Volume I	6.81
Billiards for the Million : Volume II	6.91
Billiards for the Million : Volume III	6.97
Billiards in Mufti	3.1
Billiard Souvenir of the World's Champions – the Eventoscope – being topical souvenirs of current events	10.17
Billiards : the Proper Attitude in Playing the Game	10.9
Billiards Simplified (Ritchie, Wallace)	6.68
Billiards Simplified (unknown author)	6.98
Billiards Simplified : or, How to Make Breaks (Burroughes & Watts)	6.28
Billiards Simplified : or, How to Make Breaks (F. Warne)	10.13

Billiards and Snooker (Billiards Association & Control Council)	5.7
Billiards and Snooker (Karnehm, J.)	5.10
Billiards and Snooker (Morrison, I.)	5.14
Billiards and Snooker (Peall, A.)	5.0
Billiards and Snooker for Amateurs	5.6
Billiards and Snooker for Amateur Players	5.3
Billiards and Snooker Bygones	2.9
Billiards and Snooker Control Council Diary	7.76
Billiards and Snooker : a Postcard Album	7.89
The Billiards and Snooker Referees' Handbook	9.83
Billiards–Snooker Sports Annual 1947	7.37
Billiards and Snooker Strokes	5.5
Billiards and Snooker Teasers	7.11-7.31
Billiards and Snooker : a Trade History	2.6
Billiards and Snooker : Volunteer Snooker-Pool-Russian Pool-Pyramids : How To Play Well	5.4
Billiards Solitaire	6.118
Billiards : the Strokes of the Game (3 part edition)	6.49
Billiards : the Strokes of the Game (1 cloth edition)	6.53
Billiards : the Strokes of the Game Volume I	6.47
Billiards : the Strokes of the Game Volume II	6.50
Billiards : the Strokes of the Game Volume III	6.54
Billiards : its Theory and Practice	6.12
Billiards : its Theory and Practice Set Forth and Explained	6.13
Billiards through the Centuries	2.0
Billiards for all Time	2.1
Billiard Stories and Anecdotes	7.0
Billiards in Twelve Lessons	6.69
Billiards in the 20th Century	6.106
Billiards Up-To-Date	6.103
Billiard Table Games : for Tables of all Sizes	6.101
Billiard Tables, Past and Present : a Paper Read before the Liverpool Polytechnic Society, May 5, 1883	10.12
Billiard Tips	6.105
Billiard Tips : the Strokes Made in a Hundred Break	6.51
The Billiard Year-Book for 1910	8.2
Black Farce and Cue Ball Wizards : the Inside Story of the Snooker World	7.94
The Board of Green Cloth	6.59
The Book of Snooker and Billiards Quotations	7.87
The Book of Snooker Disasters and Bizarre Records	3.11
The Breaks Came My Way	1.5

~ C ~

Cannons and Big Guns	1.4
Cannons : Part II : (Volume VII of The Strokes of the Game)	6.65

Cannons (Volume VI of Billiards : the Strokes of the Game)	6.63
Catalogue of the Exhibition of Billiards Antiquities : with a History of Billiards by Sir John Squire and an Addendum on the Development of the Implements used in the Game by Sidney Gillett	7.35
Championship Snooker	7.55
Clarke's Pool Combine : Rules for a Game	10.21
Classic Snooker	4.15
Cliff Thorburn's Snooker Skills	4.28
Come to Play Snooker–see Dewch i Chwarae Snwcer	4.23
The Complete Billiard Player	6.70
The Complete Book of Snooker : incorporating Winning Snooker and Trick Shots	4.21
The Complete History of Border Snooker	7.88
Complete Snooker (Davis, J.)	4.11
Complete Snooker (Griffiths, T.)	4.22
Complete Snooker for the Amateur	4.11
Constitution and Programme	10.22
The Cruel Game : the Inside Story of Snooker	7.59
Cue for a Laugh	3.7
The CueSport Book of Professional Snooker : the Complete Record and History	8.40
Cue Tips : Hints on Billiards for 100 Uppers and Owners of Bijou Tables	6.45

~ *D* ~

Dainty Billiards : How to Play the Close-Cannon Game	6.99
Dewch i Chwarae Snwcer (Come to Play Snooker)	4.23
Double or Quits	1.23
Drop Cannons and Getting Position for Top-of-the-Table Play (Volume VIII of The Strokes of the Game)	6.71
The Duffer's Guide to Snooker	3.8

~ *E* ~

The Earlier History of Billiard Tables and Accessories as Seen From the Sales Journals of John Thurston 1818 – 1843	2.2
Eddie Charlton's Trick Shots	3.3
The Embassy Book of World Snooker	2.12
Enjoying Snooker with Ray Reardon : A Personal Guide to the Game	7.66
Everybody's Billiards Book	6.100
Eye of the Hurricane : the Alex Higgins Story	1.20

~ *F* ~

50 Years of Billiards in Grimsby	7.6
First Steps to Billiards	6.92

The Foxwold Billiard Circle : Rules and Regulations for the Various Competitions, Lists of Winners, Record Makers, Breaks and Honours, etc.	10.20
Frame By Frame Dennis Taylor : My Own Story	1.12
Frank Callan's Snooker Clinic	4.34
From the Eye of the Hurricane : My Story	1.25
Fun on the Billiard Table : Being a Collection of Amusing Tricks and Games for Amateurs, with Photographs	3.0
Fun on the Cottage Billiard Table	3.0

~ G ~

The Game Beautiful	7.3
A Game of Billiards	10.19
Game of Billiards	6.1
The Game of Billiards Clearly Explained, and the Scientific Principles of the Side Stroke	6.6
The Game of Billiards and How to Play It (1897 edition)	6.36
The Game of Billiards and How to Play It (1905 edition)	6.52
The Game of Billiards : as Practised by the Most Scientific Players	10.10
The Game of Billiards Scientifically Explained	6.7
The Game of Billiards : With a Special Treatise on Nursery Cannons	6.60
Games of Pool : Describing the Various English and American Pool Games, and Giving the Rules in Full	7.1
The Golden Rules of Snooker	3.9
That Grand and Practical Game Billiards	6.10
Greatest Moments of Snooker	7.95
Griff : the Autobiography of Terry Griffiths	1.16
A Guide to World Snooker	7.90
Guinness Book of Snooker	2.7

~ H ~

The Hamlyn Encyclopedia of Snooker	8.17
A Handbook of Billiards and Bagatelle	6.14
A Handbook of Billiards, With the Theory of the Side-Stroke, the Rules of the Games, and a Chapter on Bagatelle	6.14
Handbook and Constitution of the Women's Billiards Association	7.36
A Hand Book to the Game of Billiards	6.8
Handbook and Rules	9.81
Handbook and Rules of English Billiards and Snooker	9.80
Handbook and Rules of English Billiards · Snooker · Volunteer Snooker	9.79
Handbook and Rules of English Billiards · Snooker · Volunteer Snooker · Pool · Pyramids · Russian Pool	9.49, 9.51-9.62
Handbook and Rules of English Billiards · Snooker · Volunteer Snooker · Russian Pool	9.63-9.70

Handbook and Rules of English Billiards · Snooker · Volunteer Snooker and Snooker Plus	9.71-9.78
The Handy Book on Billiards	6.21
Hennig Bros. Book of Rules of the Games of Billiards, Pool, and Pyramids and Bagatelle	9.28
Higgins, Taylor and Me	1.14
Hints on Billiards (Buchanan, J. P.)	6.32
Hints on Billiards (Mannock, J. P.)	6.37
The History and Rules of Snooker	7.86
The History of Snooker and Billiards	2.10
Horace Lindrum's Snooker, Billiards and Pool	5.11
How to Beat Your Dad at Snooker	7.54
How to Beat Your Dad at Snooker : Including : Thoughts on Pool	7.54
How to make a Hundred Break, Billiards Made Easy	6.64
How to Play Billiards	6.87
How to Play Billiards and Pool : Showing the Laws of the Game	6.8
How I Play Snooker	4.8
How to Play Snooker (Newman, S.)	4.5
How to Play Snooker (Williams, R.)	4.19
How to Play Snooker and Other Pool Games	4.2
How to Play Snooker Pool	4.0
How to Play Snooker : a Step-by-Step Guide	4.35
How to Play and Win at Snooker	4.7
How to Pot a Ball	5.1
How to be Really Interesting	3.15
"Hurricane" Higgins' Snooker Scrapbook	1.7
The Hurricane : the Turbulent Life and Times of Alex Higgins	1.21

~ I ~

Improve Your Snooker (Davis, J.)	4.6
Improve Your Snooker (Horton, E.)	4.29
The In-off Game (Volume V of Billiards : the Strokes of the Game)	6.61

~ J ~

Jimmy White's Snooker Masterclass	4.30
John Ireland's Snooker Characters	3.16
John Roberts' Billiards Annual, 1909 : The Billiard Year Book for 1910	8.3
John Roberts' Billiards Annual, 1910 : the Billiard Year Book for 1910-11	8.4
John Virgo's Book of Snooker Trick Shots	3.17
John Virgo's Snooker Sideshow	3.12
Joyce Gardner (Women's Champion) Shows Correct Stance and Screw Loser and Cannon – Willie Smith Shows the "Postman's Knock"	6.107
Joyce Gardner (Women's Champion) and Willie Smith Cannon and Screw Loser and "Postman's Knock"	6.108
Just One Frame : Your Key to Playing Better Snooker	4.40

~ L ~

The Ladbroke Snooker International Handbook	7.53
Learn to Become a Good Billiards and Snooker Player : by Following the Instructions Given Here	5.2
The Life and Times of John Roberts	1.3

~ M ~

Masters of the Baize : Cue Legends, Bad Boys and Forgotten Men in Search of Snooker's Ultimate Prize	7.93
Master Snooker	4.31
Matchroom Snooker	4.32
Match-Winning Billiards	6.93
Miniature Billiards : and how it is Played	6.102
Minute Book of the Billiards Association 31st January, 1885 to 21st January, 1892	7.68
Mr Hoyle's Treatise on the Game of Billiards : a New Edition, Greatly Improved and Corrected, with the Assistance of Eminent Markers	10.3
Modern Billiards	6.43
Monitoring Tobacco-Sponsored Snooker on BBC TV 1985-86	7.69
Morison & Co., Billiard Table Makers, 78 George Street, Edinburgh	10.11
My Snooker Book	4.4

~ N ~

National Billiards Halls Association : Rules	7.9, 7.10
Natural Break	3.10
The New All-Round Game, New Declared All-Round Game, English cannon game [of Billiards], Rules, Directions, Instructions, Diagrams	10.14
A New Guide and Companion to the Billiard Table	6.4
News of the World Snooker Annual	8.6-8.7, 8.10-8.12
1948 Handbook and Constitution of the Women's Billiards Association	7.38
The Noble Game of Billiards (Mingaud)	6.5
The Noble Game of Billiards (Thurston & Co.)	2.3
Notes on the Game of Snooker	7.32
Notes on the Game of Snooker and why Thurston's are at Chelsea	7.33

~ O ~

The Odds of the Game of Billiards	10.1
Official Coaching Guide to the Games of English Billiards and Snooker	5.9
The Official 1990 Matchroom Snooker Special	7.80
Official W.P.B.S.A. Diary Yearbook 1987–1988	8.33
Official W.P.B.S.A. Diary Yearbook 1988-1989	8.34
Official W.P.B.S.A. Diary Yearbook 1989–1990	8.37

The 100-Break Target	6.117
On Snooker : the Game and the Characters Who Play It	2.13
Out of the Blue Into the Black : the Autobiography of John Spencer	1.24

~ P ~

The Park Drive Official Snooker and Billiards Year Book	7.42
Penalties for Foul Strokes at a Glance – Compiled from the Rules of the Billiard Association of Great Britain & Ireland	10.16
A Philosophical Essay on the Game of Billiards	6.2
Plain Talks to Billiard Players	6.94
Playing for Keeps	1.15
Play Snooker with Dennis Taylor	4.36
Play to Win : Snooker	4.33
Pocket Money : Bad-Boys, Business-Heads and Boom-time Snooker	7.70
A Poetical Essay on the Game of Billiards	10.4
Pool, Snooker and Billiards	5.11
The Possibilities of Nuku Billiards : Together with Rules for Billiards, Snooker, and Russian Pool	7.4
Pot Black	7.43-7.52
Pot Black Cue Sports Diary 1990–1991	7.85
Pot Black Diary	7.57, 7.60, 7.63, 7.67
Potting the Red Ball (Volume IV of Billiards : the Strokes of the Game)	6.58
Practical Billiards (Dawson, C.)	6.48
Practical Billiards (Dufton, W.)	6.17
A Practical Display of Billiards : Comprising the Whole Art and Science of the Game	10.5
The Practical Science of Billiards and Its "Pointer"	6.72
A Practical Treatise on the Game of Billiards	6.3
Practice Strokes at Billiards : for Tables of all Sizes	6.44
Prize Essays on "Billiards as an Amusement for all Classes, Especially in Reference to its use in Clubs, Literary Mechanics', & Other Institutes"	6.25
Pyramids and Pool Games with a Chapter on Winning Hazards	7.2

~ R ~

Ray Reardon	1.9
Ray Reardon's 50 Best Trick Shots	3.5
Red Ball Play	6.73
Remember My Name : the Authorised Biography of Stephen Hendry	1.17
The Reminiscences of a Professional Billiard Player	1.0
Rheolau Snwcer	10.23
Right On Cue : an Autobiography	1.18
"Rileys" of Accrington : Where the Billiard Tables Come From"	7.5
Roberts' Billiard Life	1.2

Roberts on Billiards	6.20
Roberts' Billiards for Amateurs	6.77
Roberts' Billiards Guide and Rules of Games	6.95
Ronnie : the Autobiography of Ronnie O'Sullivan	1.22
Rothmans Snooker Yearbook	8.18-8.24
Rules of Billiards	9.0
The Rules of Billiards	9.1-9.2
The Rules of Billiards, Pool, Pyramids and C., and C.	9.30, 9.34, 9.35
The Rules of Billiards, Pool, Pyramids, Snooker Pool, Indian Pool, Volunteer Snooker and Penalty Pool	9.36, 9.37
The Rules of the Game of Billiards, authorised by the Billiard Association of Great Britain and Ireland, Revised January 1909	9.33
The Rules of the Game of Billiards, authorised by the Billiard Association of Great Britain and Ireland, Revised and Redrafted, March 1898	9.29
The Rules of the Game of Billiards, authorised by the Billiard Association of Great Britain and Ireland, Revised and Redrafted September 1907	9.32
Rules of the Game of English Billiards	9.5-9.11
The Rules of the Game of English Billiards	9.3, 9.4
Rules of the Game of English Snooker	9.22
Rules of the Game of Snooker	9.16-9.21, 9.23, 9.24, 9.25, 9.26, 9.27
The Rules of the Game of Snooker	9.12-9.15
The Rules of the Games of English Billiards, Pool, Pyramids, Snooker, Volunteer Snooker, and Russian Pool	9.38, 9.39, 9.40, 9.41, 9.42
The Rules of the Games of English Billiards, Snooker, Volunteer Snooker, Pyramids, Pool, and Russian Pool	9.43, 9.44, 9.45, 9.46, 9.47, 9.48, 9.50
Rules of the Games of Snooker and English Billiards	9.82, 9.84
Rules and Regulations to be Observed at the Game of Billiards	10.6

~ S ~

The Science of Billiards : Explaining the Theory and Principles on which the Game is Founded	6.11
Scottish Billiards & Snooker Association : Calendar 1989/90	7.81
A Short History of Billiards and Snooker	2.8
Side and Screw : Being Notes on the Theory and Practice of the Game of Billiards	6.41
Sidney Smith : Masse Stroke and Close Cannon	6.109
Sidney Smith Shows Masse Stroke and the Close Cannon	6.110
Snooker (Arnold, P.)	7.64

Snooker (Davis, F.)	4.17
Snooker (Hale, J.)	7.61
Snooker (Lowe, T.)	4.13
Snooker (Reece, T.)	4.1
Snooker (Spencer, J.)	4.26
Snooker (Williams, K.)	4.38
Snooker (Williams, R.)	4.24
Snooker Annual	8.8-8.9
Snooker, Billiards and Pool	5.15
Snooker and Billiards : Technique ·Tactics · Training	5.16
Snooker at the Crucible	8.35
Snooker Diary	7.71, 7.73, 7.77, 7.82
Snooker : the Dictionary	3.13
Snooker Digest	7.39
Snookered	7.72
The Snooker Exercise Challenge	4.42
Snooker : the Fine Art Method	4.37
Snooker Games : Games of the Snooker Table	7.78
Snooker Guide : to Improved Play, Rule Problems, Maintenance, etc.	7.40
Snooker Guide : to Improved Play, Rule Problems, Table Upkeep, Etc.	7.34
The Snooker Handbook	7.79
Snooker : How to Become a Champion	4.14
Snooker : How to Improve Your Play	4.3
Snooker Kings	7.65
Snooker Legends	7.91
Snooker Masterclass	4.39
Snooker–the Players, the Shots, the Matches	7.83
Snooker, Pool and Billiards	7.74
The Snooker Quiz Book	7.92
Snooker : the Records	8.25
Snooker : Records · Facts and Champions	8.38
Snooker Rules OK	3.14
Snooker's Crucible : How Sheffield Became the Snooker Capital of the World	2.11
Snooker Today	7.75
Snooker Year	8.13-8.15
Some Basics of Billiards and Snooker	5.17
Souvenir of the Foxwold Billiard Circle and the Deeds of its Members to December 1st, 1908, etc.	10.18
Spencer on Snooker	4.12
Sportsviewers Guide : Snooker	7.62
The Spot-Stroke	6.22
Steve Davis Frame and Fortune : as Told to Brian Radford	1.10
Steve Davis Snooker Champion : His Own Story as Told to Brian Radford	1.8

The Story of Billiards and Snooker	2.5
Successful Snooker	4.20
Suggested Amended Billiard Rules for Amateur Players	6.62

~ T ~

Tables for Ascertaining the Factor of a Billiard Player	6.31
Tackle Snooker	4.10
Tackle Snooker This Way	4.10
Take Up Snooker	7.84
Talking Snooker	1.6
Teaching Material No. 8 : Snooker	4.25
Teach Yourself Billiards and Snooker	5.8
Ten Steps to Snooker Success	4.27
The Top-of-the-Table Game	6.55
Top of-the-Table Play, Pique and Masse Strokes, Single and Double Baulks, Safety Play, and C. (Volume IX of Billiards : the Strokes of the Game)	6.74
A Treatise on Billiards, With Instructions and Rules	6.0
Tricks on the Billiards Table	3.2
Two New Games of Billiards : New Method of Scientific Scoring	10.15

~ U ~

Understanding Billiards and Snooker	5.13
Useful Strokes for Billiard Players	6.66

~ W ~

White on Billiards : a Practical Manual, Containing the Most Recent Rules & Regulations Relating to the Game	6.18
The Whole Art of Billiards	6.56
Who's Who in Snooker	8.36
Willie Smith : Cue Grip and Bridge	6.111
Willie Smith Shows His Cue-Grip and Bridge	6.112
Winning Snooker	4.18
Winning Snooker : with Eddie Charlton	4.16
The World's Billiard Celebrities : Portrayed by Word and Camera	1.1
The World Snooker Almanac : the Top 100 Players in Photographs	8.39
World Snooker with Jack Karnehm	7.56
World Snooker with Jack Karnehm No. 2	7.58

~ REFERENCES ~

~ Books and Journals ~

Baines, Phil, *'Penguin by Design : a Cover Story 1935-2005'*, The Penguin Group, London, 2005

Chidley, John, *'Discovering Book Collecting'*, 2nd enlarged edition, Shire Publications, Princes Risborough, 1998

Clare, Norman, *'Billiards and Snooker Bygones'*, reprinted and amended edition, Shire Publications, Princes Risborough, 1996

Craven, Robert R. (Comp.), *'Billiards, Bowling, Table Tennis, Pinball, and Video Games : a Bibliographic Guide'*, Greenwood Press, Westport, Connecticut, USA, 1983

Crawley, Captain & Cook, William, *'The Billiard Book'*, new edition, Ward, Lock & Co., London, 1877

Dalby, Richard, 'In the Salerooms', *Book & Magazine Collector*, no. 290, pp.16-21, January 2008

Everton, Clive, *'The History of Snooker and Billiards'*, Partridge Press, Haywards Heath, 1986

Hayton, E. & Dee, J., *'The CueSport Book of Professional Snooker : the Complete Record and History'*, Rose Villa Publications, Lowestoft, 2004

Ledger, Bob, 'Billiards & Snooker Books', *Book & Magazine Collector*, no. 61, pp.48-54, April 1989

Matthew, H. C. G. & Harrison, Brian (Eds.), *'Oxford Dictionary of National Biography'*, Oxford University Press, Oxford, 2004

~ ibid, Vol. 23, contains brief details of F. L. Billington-Greig under the entry for his wife Greig, Teresa Mary Billington

~ ibid, Vol. 26 – contains an entry on George Wirgman Hemming

~ ibid, Vol. 33 – contains an entry on James Ludovic Lindsay, Earl of Crawford

~ ibid, Vol. 40 – contains an entry on Scipio Africanus Mussabini

~ ibid, Vol. 42 – contains an entry on George Frederick Pardon, aka Captain Rawdon Crawley

Mitchell, J. R. (Comp.), *'Billiards & Snooker : a Trade History'*, British Sports & Allied Industries Federation, UK, [1981]

Morrison, Ian, *'The Hamlyn Encyclopedia of Snooker'*, revised and updated edition, Hamlyn Publishing, Twickenham, 1987

Morrison, Ian, *'Snooker : Records · Facts and Champions'*, Guinness Publishing, Enfield, 1989

Mumby, Frank, *'Publishing and Bookselling : a History from the Earliest Times to the Present Day'*, 4th edition, Jonathan Cape, London, 1956

Pickering, David, *'Dictionary of Abbreviations'*, Cassell, London, 1996

Porter, Catherine, *'Collecting Modern Books'*, Miller's, London, 2003

Powers, Alan, *'Front Cover : Great Book Jacket & Cover Design'*, Mitchell Beazley, London, 2001

Seddon, Peter, 'Snooker Legend : Joe Davis', **Book & Magazine Collector**, no. 203, pp.59-69, February 2001

Unknown author, 'In the Salerooms', **Book & Magazine Collector**, no. 264, p.15, January 2006

Unknown author, "A to Z of Book Collecting", **Book & Magazine Collector**, no. 266, pp.22-44, March 2006

~ Web Sites Consulted ~

www.abebooks.co.uk

www.amazon.co.uk

www.bbc.co.uk/comedy/guide/articles/s/spittingimage_7775945.shtml

www.billiardsandsnookerarchive.co.uk

www.bloomsburyauctions.com

www.bl.uk (the British Library)

www.dominic-winter.co.uk

www.eaba.co.uk (English Amateur Billiards Association)

www.ebay.co.uk

www.en.wikipedia.org

www.lib.cam.ac.uk (Cambridge University Library)

www.loc.gov (Library of Congress)

www.londonmet.ac.uk/services/sas/library-services/ (London Metropolitan University Library)

www.nls.uk (National Library of Scotland)

www.llgc.org.uk (National Library of Wales)